The DELAWARE HERITAGE Cookbook

Compiled and edited by Aloah E. Hatz

A Delaware Heritage Commission book
commemorating the 200th anniversary of the United States
Constitution and Delaware's ratification as
"The First State."

THE MIDDLE ATLANTIC PRESS
Wilmington, Delaware

For the descendants of
200 years of great cooks from
"The First State"

THE DELAWARE HERITAGE COOKBOOK

A MIDDLE ATLANTIC PRESS BOOK

Copyright © 1988 The Delaware Heritage Commission
Illustrations by Allan Ruth.

A Delaware Heritage Commission book,
commemorating the ratification of the
United States Constitution by Delaware, "The First State"

First Middle Atlantic Press printing, February 1988

ISBN: 0-912608-46-3

The Middle Atlantic Press, Inc.
848 Church Street
Wilmington, Delaware

Manufactured in the United States of America

Distributed by:
National Book Network, Inc.
4720 A Boston Way
Lanham, Maryland 20706

Library of Congress Cataloging-in-Publication Data
Hatz, Aloah, E. 1922–
  The Delaware Heritage cookbook.

  Includes index.
  1. Cookery, American. 2. Cookery—Delaware.
3. Delaware—Social life and customs. I. Delaware
Heritage Commission. II. Title.
TX715.H364   1987   641.59751   87-11464
ISBN 0-912608-46-3

Table of Contents

Preface   v

Illustrations   ix
Appetizers   1
Beverages   15
Soups   19
Salads and Salad Dressings   28
Eggs and Cheese   37
Batters, Biscuits, and Breads   48
Meats   69
Poultry and Game   79
Seafood   99
Vegetables   121
Desserts   139
Pies and Pastries   152
Cookies   172
Candy   188
Cakes and Frostings   195
Butters, Pickles, and Preserves   228
Taste of Tradition   233
Measurements   300
Index   303

Consultant

Charlotte S. Johnson

Committee

Jo Domenic	Jean Santobianco
Edna Frampton	Robin Santobianco
Gayle Hatz	Jo Spence
Donna Griffith	JoAnn Swafford

Testers and Reviewers

Amy Arimoto	Judy Emmi
Dot Beard	Kay Herr
Ann Chiffons	Maggie Houser
Irene Cooley	Maxine Mann
Bernice Coulsting	Sadie Nevin
Mary Agnes Dennis	Evelyn Patterson
Frances Dennis	Joanna Prillman
Paulette Davidson	Nancy Zippe

Delaware Home Economics Association
Home Economics in Homemaking Section

Evelyn Miller, Chairlady	Becky Mitchell
Louise Clodius	Mary Newman
Holly Dianich	Ethel Schmitt
Juliette Masterson	Anita Wood

COVER

Kent A. Snell

SKETCHES

Allen G Ruth

Preface

Aloah E. Hatz proposed the idea of a special cookbook to commemorate the two hundredth anniversary of Delaware's ratification of the United States constitution. Delaware, "The First State" to ratify the Constitution, was one of only three states to ratify unanimously.

The Delaware Heritage Commission, which has been charged by the General Assembly to "plan, encourage, develop, coordinate and implement observances and activities pertaining to the achievement in Delaware of liberty and independence through a constitutional government" approved the project and encouraged Mrs. Hatz to go ahead, providing support services as needed.

Mrs. Hatz, who has been deeply involved in community activities in Claymont, has compiled three other cookbooks for local benefit. Her books *What's Cooking in Claymont*, *Claymont Sampler*, and *Claymont Potpourri* have been favorably reviewed in the Wilmington newspapers and are in wide use in the area.

Recipes were requested from leaders in the state and from groups of interested citizens. Hundreds of letters and telephone calls were made. The flow of recipes from present and former Delawareans was tremendous. Many important people shared their favorites. A number of historical receipts have been collected from former First Staters. Interested people sent in too many to use, and in order to produce a book of workable size, the committee had to pare down the number and include only one from each person.

Many volunteers assisted by testing the recipes and making suggestions for their improvement. All changes were cleared with the submitters. Mrs. Hatz wants to thank Debbie Amsden, the County Home Economist; Brock and Co., Inc.; Doris Carignan of the Delaware State Archives; Allen B. Clark, Curator of Barratt's Chapel in Kent County; Doris Hicks of the Delaware Sea Grant College of the University of Delaware; Natalie Loughran, and Shirley Bailey of the Governor's House; Kate Wheeler, Director of Tourism, Ruth Crossan, and artist Nancy Sawin. Dr. Richard A. Rooney, Jan Wrigley, Don Crawford, Helen Mechell, Jean Santobianco, and Dr. Frank J. Furgele, Superintendant of the Brandywine School District were particularly helpful.

Old receipts came from the 1834 S. Ridgely family cookbook, thanks to the Honorable Judge Henry Ridgely Horsey; and from Charles W. Atkins who shared Mrs. Charles L. Terry's receipts. State Senator Roger A. Martin shared his wealth of knowledge concerning Delaware governors.

At the time of the ratification, cookbooks were a rarity. A few had been published in England prior to 1787, and some of them were found in America. But mainly these were the work of cooks from the palaces and great houses of England who were sharing their secrets with the rich and wealthy who wished to emulate the cuisine of the nobility. Very few people could afford the ingredients required to make up the recipes.

Up through the early years of the eighteenth century, most ordinary people had the plainest of diets. The basic ingredients were cereals, in the form of bread or mush, and meat. For most purposes people did not even need a plate or knife and fork. A bowl, spoon, and fingers sufficed. Vegetables and fruits were eaten in season, but few were stored for consumption through the winter and spring. For these people a recipe book was a glimpse of another world entirely beyond their reach. Only on feast days did they enjoy the array of varied dishes described in the books.

Through the eighteenth century people with increasing frequency tried to balance their meals by introducing vegetables and fruits. Meat pies came into common use; more and more vegetables and fruits were grown and stored; and plates, knives, and forks appeared in household inventories. In the early years of the nineteenth century diets much like our own with meat, vegetable, and a starch served on a plate with knife, fork, and spoon became the standard. People varied their diets too, rather than offering the same fare day after day. By 1830 there was a much broader need for recipe books among ordinary middle-class people.

Now in our privileged times we dote on recipe books and delight in trying new dishes. A large proportion of our population can afford to experiment with new foods and enjoy the pleasures of a varied cuisine.

The Delaware Heritage Commission hopes that this book will be useful in enabling citizens of our state and elsewhere to enjoy one of the benefits of modern prosperity—a varied and pleasurable diet. Commemorating an era gone by, the book documents the past and present foodways of the state. Future First Staters looking over these recipes will have the notion of favorite foods in 1987.

Cover Illustration

The photograph of the dining room of Woodburn, the home of the Governor of Delaware, was taken by Kent A. Snell. The house was built in 1790 by Charles Hillyard and is furnished with contemporary furniture from the Spanel Estates. The silver punchbowl, purchased by the people of Delaware in 1910, was originally used on the *U. S. S. Delaware* and was crafted by William C. Codman and made by the Gorham Silver Company. It is decorated with the State Seal, the National Seal, and figures of Columbia and Liberty. The punchbowl has the capacity of 95 pints. In 1923, when the ship was decommissioned, the Navy Department returned the punchbowl to the state.

The wall cupboard contains a fine collection of Rose Medallion China and Canton-China, late 18th century (on loan from Delaware Historical Society), and four hand blown antique Syallabub glasses, late 18th century. The 19th century candlesticks over the fireplace are Brass; silver from Warzawa, Poland, and the vases are from Holland (Delft), *circa* 1895.

On the dining room table, in addition to the punchbowl and ladle, is a silver casserole and a silver cookie dish, 1865, a Wedgwood cream pitcher, late 1800s, a Wedgwood candle holder, Wedgwood candy dish, and a Wedgwood cake knife and server, 20th century, from a private collection.

Recipes for pastries and punch pictured are included in the book. Reading from left:

Chocolate fudge	Molasses pound cake
Chrusciks	Pecan nut cups
Lemon coconut chews	Sugar cookies
Snickerdoodles	Petit Fours
Peanut brittle	Pringles
Shellpot Park Punch	Seven Layer cookies

MICHAEL N. CASTLE
GOVERNOR

March, 1987

Dear Friends:

1987 is a proud year for Delawareans as we commemorate the 200th anniversary of the United States Constitution and Delaware's historic ratification as "The First State". Increasing the awareness of our heritage is one of our goals for this Bicentennial year. We also hope to provide a record of the present for the benefit of future generations.

This cookbook, sponsored by the Delaware Heritage Commission, represents a valuable part of our current culture and our culinary heritage. Delawareans have always eaten well and all who enjoy good food can certainly appreciate our dining heritage – built on the diversity of agricultural products found within the boundaries of our state and the seafood delicacies abundant in our waterways.

As Delaware celebrates her preeminent position as "The First State" to ratify the United States Constitution, I invite you to join with us in sampling a "taste" of Delaware.

Sincerely,

Michael N. Castle
Governor

LEGISLATIVE HALL
DOVER.   19901
302/736-4101

CARVEL STATE OFFICE BLDG.
WILMINGTON.   19801
302/571-3210

ILLUSTRATIONS

	Page
Barratt's Chapel, Kent County	1
Delaware State House, Dover	15
John Dickinson Mansion, Kent County	22
Stone Tavern, Little Creek	28
Old Court House, Sussex County	37
Gormley's Store, Millcreek	44
Hale-Byrnes House, Stanton	46
Kalmar Nyckel, Wilmington	57
Woodburn, Dover	69
Lombardy Hall, Wilmington	79
The Skipjack	81
Columbus Inn, Wilmington	84
Mermaid Tavern, Hockessin	94
Wilmington Club, Wilmington	97
Cannon House Kitchen	100
Block House (Robinson House Summer Kitchen)	107
The Corner Cupboard Inn, Rehoboth Beach	113
Eden Hill Farm, Dover	121
The Practical Farmer Inn, Claymont	126
Octagonal Schoolhouse, Dover	140
Read House, New Castle	156
Ridgely House, Dover	170
"The Buck" Tavern	195
Friends Meeting House, Wilmington	228
Parson Thorne Mansion, Milford	247
Old "Brick Hotel House," Georgetown	260
Belmont Hall, Smyrna	261

APPETIZERS

DELAWARE SPECIALS

Yield: 40 pieces

1 cup grated sharp cheese
¼ cup mayonnaise (not salad
  dressing)
⅛ cup green onion, chopped fine

3 ¼-ounce can pitted black
  olives, chopped fine
5 English muffins

Mix together first four ingredients and spread on 5 English muffins, which have been split and quartered. Bake at 350° until cheese melts.

The mixture can be made 24 hours ahead. The muffins can be prepared 1 or 2 hours ahead. Spread mixture on muffins, put them on cookie tray and wrap in foil. Remove foil; bake as usual.

Sadie Nevin, Claymont, Del.

BARRETT'S CHAPEL
Kent County, Delaware

1

BITTERBALLEN Hot and Spicy

Yield: Approximately 36 savory balls

3 tablespoons butter
5 tablespoons flour
1 cup chicken broth
½ pound cold cooked veal,
  shredded
1 tablespoon finely chopped
  parsley

½ teaspoon salt
A dash of freshly ground black
  pepper
1 teaspoon Worcestershire sauce
2 egg whites
½ cup fine dry bread crumbs
Vegetable oil

Form a roux by melting the butter, rubbing in the flour to make a paste, then adding the broth. Cook on low heat until thickened. Add the cooked veal, parsley, salt, pepper, and Worcestershire sauce, and mix well. Form this mixture into 1-inch balls. Beat egg whites until foamy. Dip balls into egg whites, then coat with bread crumbs.

Pour 1 to 1½ inches oil in 12-inch skillet; heat to 370°. Drop balls into hot oil; fry until golden brown; remove from skillet; drain.

Serve with prepared mustard (Dijon type is good).

Traditionally in Holland when the hour between five and six arrives and the day's work is over, it is time for a glass of Dutch gin or "genever," called a "borrel." A snack such as bitterballen must always accompany a "borrel." These crispy, golden-brown balls are made with chopped meat, dipped in mustard sauce. Bitterballen are served so hot that foreign guests are warned not to pop them right into their mouths.

With the compliments of the Royal Netherlands Embassy

BROCCOLI FONDUE

Yield: approximately 3 cups

1 package frozen chopped
  broccoli
½ cup almonds
1 bunch scallions with tops
¼ pound butter
1 small can sliced mushrooms,
  drained

8 ounces processed cheese
10 ¾-ounce can cream of
  mushroom soup
Dash of pepper
1 teaspoon Worcestershire sauce
¼ teaspoon hot pepper sauce (I
  use 3 drops)

Cook broccoli according to package directions, then drain. While broccoli is cooking, toast almonds in 375° oven until lightly browned, then crumble. Chop scallions finely. In a fondue pot, melt butter and sauté scallions for 10 minutes until translucent, not brown. Add broccoli, almonds, and rest of ingredients, mix and heat until cheese is melted and mixture is bubbling.

Serve out of the fondue pot with French or dark bread chunks or crackers. Can also be served with toast triangles.

The fondue can be prepared, then frozen.

Karla Crossan, Townsend, Del.

PIZZA FONDUE

2-pound can stewed tomatoes
8-ounce package sharp cheese,
  shredded
½ teaspoon oregano

Sausage, cooked, and/or pepperoni, optional
2 loaves of Italian bread

Combine tomatoes, cheese, and oregano in saucepan. Heat over a medium-low heat until all the cheese has melted and mixture is hot. Pour into fondue pot. Dip in chunks of stale or toasted Italian bread. The sausage and the pepperoni may also be dipped.

Carol Comegys, Newport, Del.

PARTY CANAPES

Yield: 48 canapes

6 ¾-ounce can chunk ham or
  1 cup cooked, ground ham
2 tablespoons mayonnaise
2 tablespoons piccalilli or
  sweet relish

Salt
8 slices bread (white, rye,
  whole wheat)
Prepared mustard

Mix ham, mayonnaise, relish, and salt. Chill. Trim crusts from bread. With rolling pin, lightly flatten bread slices. Spread with mustard. Spread ham mixture evenly on bread slices. Roll up jelly roll fashion. With sharp knife, slice each roll into 6 circles. Chill or serve immediately.

Aileen Clifford, Claymont, Del.

BLUE CHEESE LAGOON

Yield: 1 quart

2 eggs
1½ teaspoons salt
½ teaspoon dry mustard
¼ teaspoon white pepper
2 cups light, tasteless salad oil

½ cup milk
Juice of one lemon
1 tablespoon vinegar
1 teaspoon onion juice
1 cup Blue cheese

Beat eggs with salt, mustard, and pepper in a blender on high. When thick, add salad oil very slowly, beating continuously and thinning with milk as needed. Slowly add lemon juice, vinegar, and onion juice. Stir in crumbled cheese. Store in refrigerator.

Can be used chilled as a dip for appetizers or at room temperature as a salad dressing.

Clarence Champlin, Wilmington, Del.

PARTY CHEESE BALL

Yield: 2 large balls

2 8-ounce packages cream
  cheese
¼ cup mayonnaise
⅓ cup grated Parmesan cheese
2-½-ounce package sliced dried
  beef, chopped

2 tablespoons chopped onion
1 teaspoon horseradish
Chopped nuts

Combine all ingredients. Shape into ball. Roll in nuts. Chill.

Nancy Carey, Claymont, Del.

DELAWARE CHICKEN WINGS

Yield: 15 or 20 chicken wings

1 large package chicken wings
1 teaspoon salt
½ cup soy sauce
½ cup spiced peach syrup
4 tablespoons sugar
½ teaspoon monosodium
  glutamate

2 tablespoons lemon juice
10 drops hot pepper sauce
2 cloves garlic, minced
1 tablespoon brown sugar

Put wings in roasting pan and sprinkle with salt. Mix next 7 ingredients together and brush generously on wings. Roast in 250° oven 1½ hours until wings are golden brown and tender. Turn and sprinkle with brown sugar. Roast 20 more minutes.

Barbara Blackney, High Point, N.C. formerly of Claymont, Del.

CRAB APPETIZERS

Yield: 24 wedges

1 stick margarine
1 small jar Old English cheese
  spread
1-½ teaspoons mayonnaise

½ teaspoon garlic salt
6-½-ounce can crabmeat
6 English muffins, split

Combine margarine, cheese, mayonnaise, garlic salt, and crabmeat. Spread on 6 English muffins. Recipe may be frozen at this point. Bake 10 to 15 minutes at 425°. Cut each muffin into wedges.

Jean Jones, Springfield, Pa.

HOT CRAB APPETIZER

Serves 4 to 6

8-ounce package cream cheese
1 tablespoon milk
1 cup crabmeat
2 tablespoons chopped onion

½ teaspoon horseradish
¼ teaspoon salt
Dash of pepper

Blend cream cheese with milk. Add remainder of ingredients, blending well. Spoon into shallow, 6-inch deep baking dish and bake at 375° for 15 minutes. Serve with party rye or crackers.

A favorite of Newark's Mayor Bill Redd.

Anne H. Redd, Newark, Del.

CRAB DIP

Serves 8 to 12

2 8-ounce packages cream
   cheese, softened
2 6-½-ounce can crab meat
1 medium onion, minced

1 tablespoon horseradish sauce
1 tablespoon Worcestershire
   sauce
Dash pepper

Combine all ingredients and pour into buttered 1½-quart casserole. Bake at 375° for 15 minutes. (In a microwave, bake 10 minutes at 40 and 3 minutes at high.)

You can use a food processor for the crab and onion to speed things along.

Bruce Bartoe, a friend of Delaware

DILL DIP

Yield: approximately 2 cups

1 cup sour cream
1 cup light salad dressing
2 tablespoons dill weed

2 tablespoons dried onion flakes
1 tablespoon seasoned salt
3 tablespoons dried parsley flakes

Combine all ingredients. Serve with raw vegetables.

Carolyn Burlew, Wilmington, Del.

HOT DOGS IN BOURBON

Yield: approximately 50 pieces

1 pound hot dogs
1 cup catsup

1 cup brown sugar
½ cup bourbon

Cut each hot dog into 5 pieces. Place in chafing dish with mixture of catsup, sugar, and bourbon. Simmer for two hours.

Serve from chafing dish using toothpicks or small forks.

Madeline Arnold Dunn, Laurel, Del.

HAM DIP

Yield: approximately 1½ cups

½ cup mayonnaise
8 ounces cream cheese
2½ ounces deviled ham
2 tablespoons pimento

½ teaspoon onion juice
¼ teaspoon Worcestershire sauce
Dash salt and pepper

Add mayonnaise gradually to cheese. Blend until smooth. Add remaining ingredients. Mix well. Serve with chips.

Lorraine Carver, Wilmington, Del.

PINK HERRING

Yield: 1½ quarts

1 4-to 6-ounce jar herring
   tidbits, draining optional
1 pint sour cream

1 can (16 ounces) whole-berry
   cranberry sauce
1 or 2 large red onions, sliced

Mix all ingredients and refrigerate overnight to blend flavors. Serve with crackers, party rye, or pumpernickel as an hors d'oeuvre.

If this is too sweet for your taste, add more sour cream and/or more herring. (I do!)

Alene Groll, Wilmington, Del.

JOHN'S LIVER PATÉ

Serves 10 to 12

1 pound chicken livers
2 tablespoons butter
¼ cup thinly sliced onion
2 hard-boiled eggs, riced

¼ tablespoon sugar
2 tablespoons sherry
Salt and pepper to taste
Heavy cream (optional)

Chop livers and sauté in butter. Add sliced onions and cook until onions are soft and liver cooked through. Remove from heat and put through a food mill into a mixer bowl. Add eggs, sugar, sherry, salt, and pepper, and beat until thoroughly mixed. If too thick, add heavy cream until the consistency of thick batter. Place mixture into a serving mold and refrigerate until chilled. Serve with plain crackers. Saltines are still best.

Mayor John Hughes, Rehoboth Beach, Del.

MARINATED MUSHROOMS

Serves 4 to 6

1 pound mushrooms
1 package dry Italian salad
   dressing
Oregano to taste

1 tablespoon chopped parsley
1 clove crushed garlic
Salt and pepper

Wash mushrooms quickly. Steam them for 10 minutes. In meantime, mix salad dressing according to package directions, then add the other spices. After mushrooms are steamed, add while hot to dressing mixture and place all in a jar and shake—or in dish or bowl and stir well. Eat at once or will keep in refrigerator indefinitely.

"Oh, so good!"

Dorothy Sherwood

NEW CASTLE COUNTY STUFFED FRESH MUSHROOMS

Serves 10

*1 pound large Delaware
  mushrooms
1 quart water
1 teaspoon salt
1 tablespoon lemon juice
3 to 4 chopped green onions,
  tops and all*

*¼ cup butter
¾ cup beef bouillon
¼ pound Delaware crabmeat
1 cup seasoned bread crumbs*

Wash and core mushrooms, reserving stems. Bring water, salt, and lemon juice to boil; add mushroom caps. Boil for 2 minutes. Drain. Dice mushroom stems. Sauté onions and mushroom stems in butter until tender. Add bouillon, crabmeat, and bread crumbs. Fill mushroom caps with mixture, place in shallow baking pan, and bake at 350° for 15 to 20 minutes.

Top them off with local crabmeat—"Quite a treat!"
Delaware ranks Fourth in the United States in the production of mushrooms.

Delaware Department of Agriculture

Delaware Agriculture
Product

PARTY MUSHROOMS

Serves 6 to 8

*1½ pounds mushrooms
½ to ¾ cups chicken broth*

*5 tablespoons butter
Salt to taste*

Wash, peel, and stem mushrooms. Place all ingredients in a frying pan, and cook, covered, for about 5 minutes. Remove cover and cook until broth evaporates.

Serve with meal or as an appetizer.

Chris Price, Townsend, Del.

SALMON PARTY SPREAD

Yield: approximately 2 cups

8-ounce package cream cheese
15½-ounce salmon, cleaned and
  deboned
1 tablespoon lemon juice
1 teaspoon horseradish
¼ teaspoon liquid smoke
  (available in gourmet section
  of supermarkets)

2 tablespoons grated onion and
  juice
6 sprigs of parsley, chopped fine
¼ cup pecans, chopped

Cream the cheese and add remaining ingredients. Shape in a mound. When serving, use a nice serving board or dish. Garnish with 6 to 8 sprigs freshly chopped (fine) parsley and ¼ cup chopped pecans.

Serve with crackers.

Margaret A. Brown, Claymont, Del.

SAUSAGE BALLS

Yield: 48

1 pound fresh sausage, hot or
  mild according to preference
2 cups grated or shredded
  Cheddar cheese

3 cups packaged biscuit mix
2 tablespoons water

Remove casing from sausage and crumble. Mix all ingredients together. Roll mixture into small bite-sized balls. Place on cookie sheet. Bake at 400° for 10 minutes.

Karla Pfirrmann, Wallace, N.C., formerly of Claymont, Del.

HOT SHRIMP DIP

Yield: About 1 cup

8 ounces cream cheese
6-ounce can shrimp
1 tablespoon milk

1 teaspoon Worcestershire sauce
1 teaspoon horseradish
1 teaspoon minced onion

Mix all ingredients together with electric mixer. Put into ovenproof dish. Bake uncovered at 350° for 20 minutes. Best served with firm crackers.

Fred Wrigley

SHRIMP LOG

Yield: 2 loaves

2 4-¼-ounce cans shrimp
   (rinsed, drained, and shredded)
8-ounce bar sharp cheddar
   cheese, grated

6 to 8 scallions, finely chopped
1 cup mayonnaise
Dash of garlic salt

Mix all ingredients well and shape into 2 loaves. Serve with crackers or party rye. Keeps in refrigerator 2 weeks.

Loreta J. Workman, Georgetown, Del.

TEX-MEX DIP

Serves 16 to 20

3 medium-size, very ripe
  avocados
2 tablespoons lemon juice
½ teaspoon salt
¼ teaspoon pepper
1 cup sour cream
½ cup mayonnaise
1 ¼-ounce package taco
  seasoning mix
2 cans (10-½ ounces each) plain
  or jalapeño flavored bean dip

1 large bunch green onions with
  tops, chopped (about 1 cup)
3 medium tomatoes, seeded and
  coarsely chopped
2 cans (3-½ ounces each) pitted
  ripe olives, drained and
  coarsely chopped
8 ounces shredded sharp cheddar
  cheese
Large round tortilla chips

Peel, pit, and mash avocados (food processor is great for this) with lemon juice, salt, and pepper. Combine sour cream, mayonnaise, and taco seasoning in a separate bowl.

To assemble: Spread bean dip on a large (at least 16-inch) round, shallow serving platter; top with the avocado mixture; layer with the sour cream taco mixture. Sprinkle with onions, tomatoes, and olives. Cover with shredded cheese. Serve slightly chilled with round tortilla chips.

I like to bring the top two layers in an inch each to accent the different colors.

Marsha Walters, Wilmington, Del.

ZUCCHINI APPETIZERS

Yield: About 4 dozen

3 cups thinly sliced, unpared
　zucchini (about 4 small ones)
1 cup packaged biscuit mix
½ cup finely chopped onion
½ cup grated Parmesan cheese
1 to 2 tablespoons snipped
　parsley
½ teaspoon salt

½ teaspoon seasoned salt
½ teaspoon dried marjoram or
　oregano
Dash of pepper
1 garlic clove, finely chopped
½ cup vegetable oil
4 eggs, slightly beaten
Mushrooms (optional)

Mix all ingredients together in bowl. Bake in greased oblong 9 by 13 by 2-inches pan at 350° until golden brown (about 50 minutes). Cut into pieces about 1 by 2 inches.

Betty Merchant, Claymont, Del.

APPETIZER COMBINATIONS

CHEESE	FRUIT	BREAD AND CRACKERS
American	apples, melon, pears	onion wafers
Bleu	pears, peaches	poppyseed crackers
Cheddar	apples, berries, melon slices	whole wheat
Edam	apples, orange sections, pineapple chunks	black bread
Gouda	raspberries, orange sections	toast points with butter
Muenster	grapes, tangerine sections	corn bread
Provalone	bananas, apples, grapes	warm Italian bread
Swiss	tangerine and orange sections	toast points with butter

BEVERAGES

The State House
Dover, Delaware

BRIDE'S PUNCH

Serves 24

2 cups orange juice
1 cup pineapple juice
1 cup grenadine syrup
6-ounce can frozen (pink)
   lemonade, undiluted

½ cup orange liqueur
2-liter bottle 7 Up or 2 bottles
   champagne

Mix juices together as a base for the punch and chill. At serving
time, pour juice base, orange liqueur, and fizzy into punch
bowl. Serve in punch cups.

Nancy Zippe, Wilmington, Del.

DAIQUIRI PUNCH

Serves 40

1 quart lemon juice
5 12-ounce bottles lime juice
2 quarts orange juice
2 cups superfine sugar

2 quarts club soda, chilled
1 quart light rum, chilled
Cracked ice

Mix fruit juices with sugar until thoroughly blended. Refrigerate for 2 hours. Stir in soda and light rum. Pour over cracked ice in glasses. Serve immediately.

Mary J. Smith, Georgetown, Del.

STRAWBERRY DAIQUIRI

Serves 6 to 8

4 ounces limeade
½ shot Triple Sec
3 shots rum

Handful frozen strawberries
2 cups chopped ice

Blend all ingredients together. Pour into chilled glasses and serve.

Nancy Bloom, Dover, Del.

CLARK'S EGGNOG

Serves 12 to 15

12 eggs, separated
1¾ cups sugar

3 quarts milk
Nutmeg

Mix 12 egg yolks and sugar together. Beat until well creamed. Add milk and fold in the stiffly beaten egg whites. Add nutmeg to taste.

If you like a thinner eggnog, use 4 quarts of milk.
This is a delicious family drink for the holidays.

Daniel E. Clark, Jr., Greenwood, Del.

CLAYMONT HIGH SCHOOL FRUIT PUNCH

Yield: 9 quarts

4 6-ounce cans frozen orange
juice
2 6-ounce cans frozen lemon
juice

46-ounce can pineapple juice
2 32-ounce bottles ginger ale

Add required amount of water to orange juice cans. Mix remainder of ingredients, stir, and add ice.

During the 1950s, the Claymont High School Student Council served this punch at dances they sponsored.

Helen Griffiths, Bryn Mawr, Pa.

LEMONADE

Yield: 1 gallon

Juice of 10 lemons
Juice of 2 limes

3 cups sugar, adjust to taste
Water to make one gallon

Squeeze juice from lemons and limes into a large jug or bottle. Add sugar. Add enough water to make one gallon. Float thin slices of 1 lemon and 1 lime when served. Age at least one day.

I like this on hand during the summer. 'Tis a great change from iced tea and very refreshing.

Lois Snoddy, Clemson, S. C.

RASPBERRY CORDIAL

Serves 48 (1 ounce servings)

1 quart fresh raspberries   1 quart whiskey
1 pound sugar

Put berries and sugar in bottom of a wide mouth jar. Add whiskey. Cover loosely and let stand until sugar is dissolved—about 3 or 4 months.

Note: I usually test this about the third month. If the berries aren't sweet enough, the mixture will need more sugar.

Lorraine Minnich, Wilmington, Del.

WASSAIL

Serves 20

1 cup sugar   2 cups orange juice
4 cinnamon sticks   6 cups claret
1 lemon, sliced   ½ cup lemon juice
2 cups pineapple juice   1 cup dry sherry

Boil sugar, cinnamon sticks, and 3 lemon slices in ½ cup water for 5 minutes, strain. Heat but do not boil the remaining ingredients. Add the sugar syrup, garnish with remaining lemon slices, and serve hot.

Wassailing is an ancient English custom. The master of the house drank the health of those present. Each, in turn, passed the bowl along, repeating the Saxon phrase *wass hael*, "be well."

Claymont Potpourri cookbook

SOUPS

A Salute to American Cooking
On the Eastern Shore the best people prided themselves on the delicacy of the soups that went into their fine bone china soup plates. A gentleman was often judged by how silently he could eat soup.

HOSPITALITY BOUILLON

Serves 10

1 pound beef
1 beef knuckle
1 cup chopped carrot
½ cup chopped onion
½ cup chopped turnip

½ cup snipped parsley
2 teaspoons salt
⅛ teaspoon cayenne
12 cups water

In large kettle combine all ingredients with water. Cover and simmer for 2 hours. Strain the broth. Season to taste. Serve hot.

Served by the charming, hospitable Dolley Madison. Excellent for arriving or departing guests, especially if the weather is cold or dreary.

Jane Inman, Claymont, Del.

BLUE SATIN CHEESE SOUP

Serves 4 to 6

4 tablespoons butter
¼ cup each finely minced green
  onion, green pepper, and
  celery
½ cup flour
1 14-ounce can chicken broth
4 ounces blue cheese, crumbled

1 cup light cream
1 cup milk
2 ounces dry sherry
Freshly ground pepper
Sour cream
Minced chive
Croutons

Melt butter in heavy saucepan, add vegetables, and sauté very slowly until vegetables are soft but not brown. Add flour and cook over low heat a few minutes until flour is cooked but not brown. Warm chicken broth and add to vegetables, stirring to prevent lumps. Simmer 2 minutes. Add crumbled blue cheese and stir until smooth. Add cream and milk and heat to serving temperature (do not boil). Add sherry, freshly ground pepper to taste, and serve garnished with sour cream, chives, or croutons. "Mmm-good!"

This recipe for cheese soup has received many such comments. It was served at a governor's conference in Des Moines, featured in *Colonial Homes* magazine, and now I would like to share it with you.

Pat Mumford, Santa Maria, Cal., formerly of Claymont, Del.

CORN CHOWDER

Serves 4 to 6

2 tablespoons diced salt pork
½ cup diced onion
2 cups cubed raw potatoes
1 cup boiling water
1½ teaspoons salt
½ teaspoon pepper

3 ears of fresh corn, uncooked,
   cut from cob or a 10-ounce
   package of frozen sweet
   corn
3 cups milk or half and half

Fry salt pork in a skillet until crisp. Add onions to salt pork, sauté 5 minutes over low heat. Add potatoes, water, salt, and pepper, and cook gently, covered, 15 minutes or until potatoes are tender. Add corn and cook gently, covered, 5 minutes or until done. Add milk, mix well, heat thoroughly, but do not boil.

Just plain good.

Surely that taken from Nature, mixed with Talent, and served to our Palate is a most amazing thing.

Tom Johnson, Pendleton, S. C., formerly of Claymont, Del.

CRAB SOUP

Serves 4 to 6

2 tablespoons butter
1½ cups flour
2½ cups milk
1 teaspoon salt
¼ teaspoon black pepper

⅛ teaspoon red pepper
1 pound crabmeat
1 cup cream
2 hard-boiled eggs
½ cup sherry or white wine

Melt butter. Stir in flour. Add milk, salt, and peppers. Heat *slowly* until mixture thickens. Add crabmeat and cream. Press eggs through a sieve; add to soup. Slowly add sherry. Serve at once.

Rich, but delicious.

Mrs. James Edwards, Wilmington, Del.

BOON DOCKS RED CRAB SOUP

Serves 15 to 20

4 quarts water
1 quart diced carrots
1 quart chopped onions
3/4 quart celery chopped
1/4 pound butter

1/8 cup Old Bay seasoning
1/8 cup Worcestershire sauce
1 1/2 quarts diced potatoes
1 quart crushed tomatoes
2 pounds crabmeat

Bring water to boil. Add carrots, onions, celery, butter, and seasonings and cook 30 minutes. Add potatoes and cook 20 more minutes. Add tomatoes and simmer 10 minutes. Add crabmeat and remove from heat. Store leftover soup in refrigerator and reheat individual portions in microwave, as needed.

The Boon Docks is a hunter's retreat for rest and refreshment during duck, deer, and geese hunting seasons.

Patricia H. Keeler, Smyrna, Del., Boon Docks Restaurant

ITALIAN CHICKEN SOUP
(Wedding Soup)

1 4 to 5-pound stewing
  chicken
Water
3 stalks celery
1 onion, halved
Salt and pepper to taste
8-ounce can tomato sauce
3 pounds endive greens

1 pound hamburger
Fresh bread crumbs
1 cup grated Italian cheese
2 tablespoons parsley
Salt and pepper
1 clove of garlic, chopped
2 eggs

Place chicken in a large pot and cover with water. Heat. When water comes to a boil, skim film from top. Add celery, onion, salt and pepper, and tomato sauce. Let boil approximately 2½ hours until chicken is cooked.

While chicken is cooking, boil endive greens in another pot for about 10 minutes. Drain *well*. When soup has cooked, remove enough broth into another pot to cover meatballs.

Form miniature meatballs by adding last 7 ingredients. Cook ½ hour in reserved broth. Add well-drained endive to meatballs and enough liquid from cooked chicken to make a good pot of soup. Cook another 20 minutes. Serve with warm Italian bread.

Sliced chicken, garnished with parsley, makes a nice accompaniment to the soup. A meal in itself.

Connie Massarelli, Indian Field, Del.

JO'S GUMBO

Serves 4 to 6

6 chicken wings
4 to 6 tablespoons vegetable oil
4 large onions, chopped fine
6 tablespoons sifted flour
Chicken stock
3 or 4 cloves of garlic, minced
2 heaping tablespoons dried
    parsley
1 cup cooked ham, diced
1 large can tomatoes
1 large can tomato paste

3 large bay leaves
3 sprigs thyme
1 teaspoon red pepper sauce
Salt and pepper
1 dozen or more raw, cleaned
    shrimp
1 dozen fresh oysters, including
    liquor
1 can crabmeat
½ teaspoon filé powder

Stew the chicken wings and reserve the stock. Put vegetable oil in iron skillet; add onions and cook until they are light yellow. Remove the onions to a soup pot.

Add the flour to the oil in the skillet. Cook until flour browns. Add enough water to the chicken stock to make 4 cups. Slowly add 2 cups of the stock to the flour, stirring; then add the garlic and parsley. Add the rest of the stock, the chicken wings, ham, tomatoes, tomato paste, bay leaves, thyme, red pepper sauce, salt and pepper to taste. Adjust seasonings.

Simmer over low heat for 45 minutes, stirring often. Add the shrimp, oysters and oyster liquor, and the crabmeat. Cook 15 minutes more, allowing soup to come to a boil. Remove from heat. Add the filé powder immediately. Stir in well. Filé powder will thicken the soup slightly and give it the characteristic gumbo taste. Serve over rice.

This can be made with just chicken, ham, or with some of all three kinds of seafood. Just increase total amount to compensate for whatever is omitted.

A specialty in the Spence household, gumbo is an exciting seafood dish that has held its popularity over the last 200 years.

Jo Spence, Bethel, Del.

KIELBASA SOUP

Serves 4

1½ pounds fresh kielbasa
Water
2 pounds sauerkraut
1 medium onion, diced

¼ cup butter
10-¼ ounce green pea soup
Salt and pepper to taste

Place kielbasa in 4-quart pot and add enough water to cover. Bring to boil, skim fat from top of water, prick kielbasa, and simmer for 30 minutes. Rinse, drain, and squeeze excess water from sauerkraut. Add to kielbasa and simmer for 45 minutes. In a frying pan, sauté onions in butter until golden brown. Stir diced onions and butter into sauerkraut and kielbasa. Let simmer for about 5 minutes. Add soup to kielbasa mixture. Simmer for a few minutes.

Serve with chunk of rye bread and enjoy! Delicious flavor.

A family favorite of young and old.

Mary Czukiewski, Wilmington, Del.

INGE'S POTATO SOUP

Serves 4 to 6

3 large onions
3 large carrots
3 large celery stalks and leaves
3 large garlic cloves
Water
Salt and pepper
Parsley flakes
Onion salt

Garlic salt
10 large potatoes
½ pound butter
½ pint light cream
1 or more quarts milk
2 cups chicken or beef stock
Paprika

Place onions, carrots, celery, and garlic cloves in a pot. Cover with water. Add salt, pepper, parsley flakes, and onion and garlic salts to taste. Cook until vegetables are soft. Puree vegetables with the cooking liquid in a blender or food processor.

While vegetables are cooking, peel and cook the potatoes. When potatoes are soft, mash them with the butter, cream, milk, and stock. Add vegetable puree to the potatoes, adding more milk if necessary; soup should be fairly thick. Garnish with paprika.

To reheat, warm very slowly to prevent soup burning; or reheat in a microwave oven on medium setting.

Note: Added touch of flavor: I keep a carton in my freezer in which I collect leftover vegetable and meat juices saved from meals during the week. This makes a nutritious addition to soups, stews, or gravy. It's a "waste-not, want-not" technique I learned from a farm friend when I had a big family to cook for.

Inge R. Parks, Wilmington, Del.

HOMEMADE VEGETABLE SOUP

Serves 8 to 10

Ham bone
1 quart tomatoes
20-ounces frozen mixed vegetables
4 medium onions, chopped

6 large celery sticks, chopped
Handful of alphabet macaroni
6 potatoes, chopped
2 quarts water

Put everything in a pressure cooker. Cook for 20 minutes after control starts to jiggle.

Sharon Litano, Dover, Del.

ICED ZUCCHINI SOUP

Yield: 5 to 6 cups

1 pound zucchini, cubed
   (approximately 3 medium)
1 medium onion, coarsely
   chopped
2 scallions, coarsely chopped
   (including green tops)
1 stalk celery, coarsely chopped
5 sprigs parsley

2 sprigs fresh basil or 1 teaspoon
   dried basil
3 cups chicken broth
Salt and pepper to taste
1 cup light cream
2 egg yolks
Fresh parsley

Combine all but last 3 ingredients in a 3- to 4-quart pan and bring to boil. Reduce heat to medium and simmer uncovered 40 to 50 minutes. Pour half of cooked mixture into blender, cover, and puree. Transfer to large bowl. Repeat with remaining mixture.

Beat cream and egg yolks together until well blended. Add to puree and mix well. Cover and refrigerate to chill. Stir well before serving and garnish with fresh parsley. Keep chilled. Delicious and different.

Mrs. H. K. Graves, Bethel, Del.

SALADS & SALAD DRESSINGS

Stone Tavern, Little Creek

APRICOT SALAD

Serves 8 to 12

2 3-ounce packages apricot
   gelatin dessert
2 cups boiling water
1 cup miniature marshmallows

12-ounce can crushed pineapple
2 cups cottage cheese
2 cups frozen whipped topping

Dissolve gelatin in boiling water, stir well. Add marshmallows and pineapple; mix well. Refrigerate until gelatin has the consistency of egg whites. Add cottage cheese and thawed whipped topping; mix well. Pour into a 9 by 13 by 1½-inch pan or large mold. Best made a day or so beforehand.

Ann Chiffons, Claymont, Del.

SWEDISH BEET, APPLE, AND HERRING SALAD

Yield: About 5 cups, enough for a buffet of 10 to 14 people

½ cup boiled new potato, peeled and diced (about 1 medium potato)
1½ to 2 cups apples, peeled, cored, and diced
1 cup pickled beets, diced
¼ cup minced dill pickle
1 small jar herring tidbits, drained and chopped
2 hard cooked eggs, shelled and sliced

2 tablespoons butter or margarine
1 tablespoon flour
½ cup heavy cream
½ cup water
2 tablespoons white vinegar
1 tablespoon sugar
1 tablespoon prepared horseradish
1 small onion, peeled and minced
Salt and pepper

To make the dressing: In a small saucepan, melt butter over low heat. Stir in flour and then gradually add the cream and water. When smooth, add the vinegar, sugar, horseradish, and onion. Bring to a simmer and cook 5 minutes, stirring constantly. Add salt and pepper to taste. Remove pan from heat and let cool completely.

Combine the potato, apple, beets, pickles, and herring. Add dressing and mix gently. Put into oiled 5-cup mold or bowl; cover and chill. Turn mold out onto platter or form into a mound on a serving plate and garnish with sliced eggs.

An interesting and delicious addition to a buffet table. I serve this at the Christmas Smorgasbord and at my Swedish Midsummer's Festival in June. Sometimes I omit the herring, but it isn't really Swedish without it!

Ruth Crossan, Newark, Del.

PURPLE CABBAGE SALAD WITH SWEET AND SOUR DRESSING

Serves 6 to 8

1½ cups sugar
2 teaspoons dry mustard
2 teaspoons salt
⅔ cup cider vinegar
3 teaspoons onion juice

2 cups vegetable oil
3 tablespoons poppy seeds
1 head purple cabbage, shredded
1 grapefruit
1 avocado

Make the dressing by combining the sugar, mustard, salt, vinegar, and onion juice in a bowl. With an electric mixer, gradually beat in the oil, almost a drop at a time. When the oil is all incorporated, stir in the poppy seeds.

Just before serving, peel and section the grapefruit; peel and slice the avocado. Place the shredded cabbage in a salad bowl. Alternate grapefruit and avocado slices around the bowl. Pour dressing over cabbage. Note: this dressing will keep in the refrigerator for a week to ten days.

Elaine T. Dickerson, Milford, Del.

CHICKEN SALAD

Serves 8

3 cups diced cooked chicken
2 cups sliced celery
2 tablespoons diced pimento
1 cup heavy cream
½ cup sour cream
1 tablespoon lemon juice
2 to 3 teaspoons chopped candied
   ginger

¼ cup slivered almonds, toasted
Salt and pepper to taste
8 slices pineapple
16-ounce can jellied cranberry
   sauce (cut in 9 slices)
8 large lettuce leaves

Toss together chicken, celery, and pimento. In a separate bowl, combine cream and sour cream; whip until soft peaks form. Fold in lemon juice and ginger. Mix with chicken. Fold in almonds, salt, and pepper. Chill.

In lettuce cups, layer 1 slice pineapple, a slice of cranberry jelly, then top with chicken salad. Cut remaining cranberry slices in wedges for garnish.

Freda Donovan, Wilmington, Del.

HOT CHICKEN SALAD

Serves 4

2 cups diced white chicken
   meat
¾ cup diced celery
½ cup toasted slivered almonds
¼ teaspoon salt
2 teaspoons Accent
1 cup mayonnaise (salad
   dressing is too rich)

2 teaspoons grated onion
2 tablespoons lemon juice
½ cup Cheddar cheese (sharp,
   not extra sharp)
1 cup crushed potato chips

Mix first 8 ingredients; put in uncovered shallow baking dish. Mix cheese and chips together and sprinkle on casserole. Bake at 450° for 10 minutes.

Super!

Helen Irons, Claymont, Del.

CUCUMBERS IN SOUR CREAM

Serves 6 to 8

2 medium cucumbers
Salted water
1 cup sour cream
2 tablespoons finely minced
    onion

2 tablespoons cider vinegar
½ teaspoon salt
½ teaspoon ground dill seed
Dash of pepper
Dash paprika

Peel and slice cucumbers; the thinner, the better. Soak in salted water for 30 minutes. Drain well and chill. Mix sour cream, onion, vinegar, salt, dill, and pepper just before serving. Add cucumbers and garnish with paprika. Good served with ham.

Ginny Steiner, Wilmington, Del.

WYLMA'S FROZEN FRUIT SALAD

Serves 4 to 6

¼ cup sugar
¼ cup white vinegar
2 eggs, slightly beaten
2 tablespoons butter
½ pint heavy cream, whipped
20-ounce can pineapple tidbits,
    drained

2 cups colored miniature
    marshmallows
1 pound can white cherries,
    drained and pitted

In a saucepan mix first three ingredients and cook just until thickened, stirring. Add butter to warm mixture. Stir and cool. Fold in the whipped cream.

Add the cooked and cooled dressing to the fruit. Mix well and freeze. Serve frozen.

Wylma Mumford, Council Bluffs, Iowa

FROZEN FRUIT SALAD

Serves 6 to 8

1 cup mayonnaise
1 cup whipped cream
3-ounce package cream cheese
3 tablespoons sugar

1 cup canned fruit cocktail
6-ounce bottle maraschino
   cherries

Cream together mayonnaise, whipped cream, and cream cheese. Fold in sugar, fruit, and cherries. Put in ice cube tray and freeze. Cut in cubes or serving-size pieces for salad over lettuce.

Favorite salad for Christmas time.

Virginia S. Townsend, Wilmington, Del.

HOT LETTUCE

1 tablespoon peanut oil
Sprinkling of salt and pepper
Small clove of garlic
½ head iceberg lettuce (use
   outside wilted leaves)

1 tablespoon oyster sauce
   (thinned with sherry or
   water)

Heat oil in wok or large soup pan, adding salt, pepper, and garlic. Stir quickly and remove garlic (don't allow garlic to brown). Add lettuce. Cook for about 2 minutes, turning lettuce leaves frequently. Add oyster sauce, stir, and cover. Cook one minute more. Serve at once. The lettuce should retain its fresh greenness and crispness.

Margarete R. Cosgrove, Laurel, Del.

PINK SALAD

Serves 4 to 6

16-ounce carton cottage cheese
  (fairly smooth type)
9-ounce container frozen whipped
  topping
3-ounce package gelatin dessert
  (cherry, strawberry, or
  raspberry)

15¼-ounce can crushed
  pineapple, drained
11-ounce can mandarin oranges,
  drained

Mix all ingredients together and refrigerate until firm.

To change color, use other flavor gelatin dessert. Goes well with chicken divan.

Dorothy Whitford, Monterey, Cal.

UNDER-THE-SEA SALAD

Serves 6

16-ounce can pear halves
3-ounce package lime gelatin
  dessert
¼ teaspoon salt (optional)

1 cup boiling water
1 tablespoon lemon juice
2 3-ounce packages cream cheese
⅛ teaspoon cinnamon (optional)

Drain pears, reserving ¾ cup of the syrup. Dice pears and set aside. Dissolve gelatin and salt in boiling water. Add reserved syrup and lemon juice. Pour 1¼ cups into an 8 by 4-inch loaf pan or 4-cup mold. Chill until set but not firm, about 1 hour. Meanwhile, soften cheese until creamy. Very slowly blend in remaining half cup of gelatin, beating until smooth. Add cinnamon and pears and spoon into pan. Chill until firm, about 4 hours. Unmold. Garnish with crisp salad greens, mayonnaise, and additional pears, if desired.

Compliments of General Foods Corporation, White Plains, N.J.

CHEF'S DRESSING

Yield: 1 cup (Approximate cal/serv.: 1 tablespoon = 40)

⅓ cup tomato juice
⅓ cup vegetable oil
¼ cup cider vinegar
¼ teaspoon pepper

½ teaspoon oregano
½ teaspoon mustard
¼ teaspoon soy sauce

Combine all ingredients and shake well.

Variation: for scallion or chive dressing; add 2 tablespoons of finely chopped scallions or chives.

American Heart Association of Delaware, serving Delaware since 1949

HOMEMADE COLE SLAW DRESSING

Yield: approximately ¾ cup

½ cup mayonnaise
2 tablespoons vinegar (I use
  wine vinegar)
1 tablespoon grated onion

¼ teaspoon celery seed
2 tablespoons sugar
½ teaspoon salt
⅛ teaspoon pepper

Mix all together and refrigerate.

Dorothy Beard, Wilmington, Del.

COLE SLAW DRESSING

Yield: approximately ¾ cup

½ cup mayonnaise
2 tablespoons cider vinegar
1 tablespoon sugar
1 teaspoon horseradish

1 teaspoon prepared mustard
2 tablespoons evaporated milk,
    undiluted

Mix all ingredients together.

Most popular with students and parents over three decades of teaching home economics.

Evelyn C. Miller, Wilmington, Del.

FRENCH DRESSING

Yield: approximately 1 cup

2 cloves garlic, bruised and
    minced
1 teaspoon black pepper

1 teaspoon salt
¾ cup vegetable oil
¼ cup cider vinegar

Mix first three ingredients in a bottle or jar. Then add oil and vinegar. Shake.

Estella Guigon

GERMAN DRESSING

Yield: ¾ cup

½ cup light cream
2 tablespoons white wine
    vinegar

2 tablespoons sugar
⅛ teaspoon Worcestershire sauce

Mix together.

Ruth Clark, Furstenfeldbruck, Germany, formerly of Milford, Del.

EGGS & CHEESE

BRUNCH BAKE

Serves 8 to 10

16 slices white bread, buttered
5 to 8 ounces dried beef
4 cups grated sharp cheese

8 eggs, beaten
1 quart milk

Place 8 slices of bread in oblong, 9-by 13-inch casserole, buttered side down. Cover with half of the dried beef and cheese. Layer remaining bread, dried beef and cheese. Beat eggs, and stir together with milk. Pour over bread mixture. Chill overnight. Next morning, bake 1 hour at 300°. Let stand a few minutes, then serve.

A great combination of foods that happens to taste terrific!

Donna Griffith, Wilmington, Del.

DELAWARE FARMERS' BREAKFAST

Serves 6 to 8

6 slices bacon, cut in 2-inch
    pieces
1 small green pepper, chopped
2 tablespoons onion, chopped
3 large potatoes, cooked, peeled
    and cubed

½ cup sharp Cheddar cheese,
    shredded
6 eggs
Salt and pepper

Fry bacon until crisp. Drain, reserving 3 tablespoons drippings. Add pepper, onion, and potatoes to drippings; cook about 5 minutes, until browned.

Sprinkle cheese over potatoes and stir until melted. In a separate bowl, beat eggs; pour over potato mixture. Cook over low heat, stir gently. Season with salt and pepper. Sprinkle bacon over top and serve.

This delightful dish can also be made in a greased casserole. Bake approximately 45 minutes.

Charlotte Givens, Bethel, Del.

EGG CASSEROLE

Serves 10

¼ cup flour
¼ cup butter, melted
2½ cups milk
¼ teaspoon thyme
¼ teaspoon marjoram

1 pound Cheddar cheese, grated
2 dozen hard-boiled eggs, sliced
1 pound bacon, fried and
    crumbled
½ cup snipped parsley

In saucepan, stir flour into melted butter and gradually stir in milk. Add thyme, marjoram, and cheese. Cook, stirring constantly until cheese melts. In a large casserole, layer sliced eggs, crumbled bacon, and parsley with the cooked sauce. Bake at 350° for 30 minutes.

Cleo Dalson, San Antonio, Tex.

GRANNIE'S CASSEROLE

Serves 6

6 *eggs, hard-boiled*	2 *tablespoons liver puree*
½ *tablespoon mushrooms, boiled*	*Salt and pepper*
and chopped	*White sauce*
½ *ounce butter*	2 *ounces ham, chopped*
Parsley, chopped	4 *ounces cheese, grated*

Halve eggs. Remove yolks, blend together with mushrooms, butter, parsley, and liver puree; season with salt and pepper to taste. Pipe back into halved white of egg. Place in a dish and warm in low oven. Make a mild cheese sauce, pour over eggs and top with chopped ham and grated cheese. Brown under grill. Serve hot.

Countess De La Warr, London, England

The State of Delaware was named for Sir Thomas West, Lord De La Warr (1577-1618), who was governor and captain general of Virginia from 1610 until his death in 1618. At that time Virginia was the name given to all English lands between the Spanish holdings to the south and French claims to the north.

In August, 1610, Captain Samuel Argall, sailing the *Pennace Discovery*, on his way from Jamestown to Bermuda, came to the entrance of a large bay and named this point of land Cape La Warr for his governor. Subsequently, the English used this name for both the bay and the river, and later for the land along the western shores.

In 1613, the Dutch explorer Cornelius Jacobsen Mey renamed Cape La Warr for himself, thus today it is called Cape May.

The De La Warr estate in England is referred to as well in A. E. Milne's well-known *Winnie the Pooh*.

PASTINA AND EGGS

Serves 2 to 4

1 cup Ronzoni Acini Pepe 44
    macaroni
2 or 3 eggs

Salt and pepper
Grated cheese

Cook macaroni. Drain, leave a little water in the pot. Put pot with macaroni and water back on burner on low heat. Beat eggs and add to macaroni. Stir. Add salt and pepper and cheese to taste. Stir, scrambling eggs. Serve warm.

This dish can be used as a main dish also, since it is Italian, or as a side dish. Great as a fast dish before a shopping spree!!

Paulette Davidson, Claymont, Del.

POACHED EGGS
à la FLORENTINE

Serves 6

2 pounds fresh spinach or 2
    10-ounce packages frozen leaf
    spinach
5 tablespoons sweet butter
12 eggs
Salt and freshly ground pepper
    to taste

¼ teaspoon nutmeg
2 cups heated Mornay sauce
1 cup grated Swiss Gruyere or
    Jarlsberg cheese (if you are
    serving a meat dish, such as
    sausage, omit cheese as it
    makes the dish too rich).

Sauté spinach in butter until tender. If using frozen spinach, cook, drain very well, and add butter. Poach eggs lightly and place on bed of spinach in oblong dish. Season to taste.

Top eggs with Mornay Sauce and cheese. Sprinkle with nutmeg. Bake uncovered at 300° for 20 minutes or until hot. Broil lightly to brown top slightly.

MORNAY SAUCE

Yield: 3 cups

2 cups Bechamel sauce (below)
¾ to 1 cup canned chicken
   consomme

¾ cup grated Gruyere or
   Jarlsberg cheese
White pepper to taste
Salt

Prepare Bechamel Sauce. Add consomme and cheese. Stir until cheese is melted and well-blended. Freeze one cup—Great on broccoli.

BECHEMEL SAUCE

4 tablespoons sweet butter
4 tablespoons flour
2 cups light cream

½ teaspoon salt
White pepper to taste

Make a roux of the butter and flour. Cook at least 3 minutes. Slowly add cream, salt, and pepper, stirring to make a smooth sauce.

Enjoy! A grand combination of flavors

Beverly Raspanto, Malvern, Pa.

QUICHE INTERNATIONAL

Serves 6 to 8

9-inch baked pie shell
½ cup chopped cooked chicken or
   turkey or 1 5-ounce can
   boned chicken
½ cup grated Parmesan cheese
6 eggs

10¾-ounce can condensed
   cream of celery soup,
   undiluted
½ cup half and half or milk
½ teaspoon salt

Preheat oven to 375°. Sprinkle chicken and cheese into pie shell. Beat together remaining ingredients until well blended. Pour over chicken and cheese. Bake until a knife inserted near center comes out clean, 30 to 40 minutes. Let stand 5 minutes before serving.

To bake pie shell, line unbaked pie shell with 12-inch square of aluminum foil. Fill with rice or dried beans or peas. Cover rim of shell with edges of foil. Bake in preheated 450° oven until lightly browned at edges, 10 to 15 minutes. Lift out foil and rice. Cool on wire rack.

The can of soup adds richness and flavor to this easy, elegant quiche. Substitute chopped cooked ham for the chicken, if you wish.

Compliments of the American Egg Board, Park Ridge, Ill.

DELAWARE SCRAMBLED EGGS

Serves 4 to 6

10¾-ounce can condensed
  chicken or cheese soup
8 eggs
1 tablespoon chopped parsley

1 tablespoon chopped chives
½ cup chopped cooked chicken
  (optional)
3 tablespoons butter

Stir soup in bowl until smooth; add eggs one at a time, blending well. Stir in parsley, chives, and chicken. Melt butter in 10-inch frying pan; pour in soup mixture. Cook over low heat. As mixture begins to set, cook as for omelet, lifting cooked portions to enable uncooked portions to flow to bottom. When eggs are completely set, serve.

This is quite a special omelet, equally good for a luncheon or supper.

Tina Cannon, Harrisonburg, Va., formerly of Claymont, Del.

CHEESE

GORMLEY'S STORE SAWIN
FOUNDED 1896

CHEESE PUFFLE 'N' BROCCOLI

Serves 4

4 slices white bread
10-ounce package frozen chopped
　broccoli
2 tablespoons margarine
1 cup Swiss cheese, slivered
½ teaspoon salt

Dash of hot pepper sauce
2 teaspoons instant minced onion
3 eggs
1 cup instant skim milk powder
1½ cups hot water

Preheat oven to 375°. Grease a 9-inch square pan. Cut slices of bread into triangles and line pan. Cook broccoli in boiling water and drain well. Combine broccoli with margarine, cheese, salt, hot pepper sauce, and minced onion. Spoon over bread. In a medium bowl beat eggs; then add milk powder and hot water. Mix and pour over broccoli. Bake 20 to 25 minutes until puffed and set.

Bette Hines, Northfield, N. J.

MACARONI AND CHEESE

Serves 4

1 cup milk
1 tablespoon flour
1 to 2 tablespoons margarine
1 teaspoon onion, minced
Salt and pepper to taste
1 teaspoon dry mustard
  (optional)

2 cups elbow macaroni, cooked
  and drained (1 cup raw)
1 cup Cheddar cheese or
  Velveeta cheese, shredded

Measure milk into pan and blend in flour until no lumps remain. Add margarine, onion, and other seasonings, and cook until sauce thickens. Stir in macaroni and cheese. Bake in greased 1-quart casserole, uncovered, at 400° for 15 minutes or until slightly browned and bubbly. May be frozen and baked later.

Soft, moist, and nourishing.

National Cancer Institute, Delaware Division

CRUNCHY CRUST MACARONI

Serves 6 to 8

2 cups macaroni, uncooked
1 stick butter
¼ cup flour
¼ cup milk

8 ounces shredded Cheddar cheese
½ teaspoon dry mustard
1 teaspoon Worcestershire sauce
12 Ritz crackers

Cook macaroni, drain, and set aside. Make a white sauce by melting ½ stick of butter in a saucepan; stir flour into the milk, then add to melted butter. Cook sauce over low to medium heat, stirring until sauce is smooth and thick. Add shredded cheese, stirring until cheese is melted. Stir in mustard and Worcestershire sauce. Combine with cooked macaroni.

Prepare the crunchy crust by melting the remaining stick of butter. Crumble Ritz crackers into melted butter. Stir. Sprinkle over top of macaroni. Bake at 350° for 35 minutes.

Ethel Schmitt, Wilmington, Del.

HALE-BYRNES HOUSE

SWISS PIE AND CRAB SAUCE

Yield: 2 9-inch pies

2 9-inch pie shells
8 eggs, separated
3 cups evaporated milk

1 teaspoon salt
¼ teaspoon nutmeg
12 ounces shredded Swiss cheese

Bake shells in 450° oven. Remove. Reduce oven temperature to 350°. Beat egg yolks slightly. Add evaporated milk, salt, and nutmeg. Beat egg whites until stiff; fold egg yolk mixture into whites. Carefully fold in cheese. Pour into partially cooked pie shells. Bake at 350° for 40 to 45 minutes or until inserted knife comes out clean. Let stand 5 minutes before serving.

Crab Sauce

2 tablespoons butter or
  margarine
4 teaspoons flour
⅛ teaspoon salt

2 cups evaporated milk
2 packages Snow Crab (or ½
  pound crabmeat, well-
  drained)

In a saucepan, melt butter; blend in flour. Add salt and evaporated milk. Cook, stirring until thickened. Add crabmeat. Stir thoroughly. Serve poured over Swiss pie.

Janet Kledt, Claymont, Del.

BATTERS, BISCUITS, AND BREADS

DUMPLINGS

1 cup flour
½ teaspoon baking powder
1 tablespoon solid vegetable
    shortening

½ teaspoon salt
Water

In a bowl mix flour, baking powder, and salt. Cut in shortening. Add water until dumplings begin to get sticky. Roll until *very thin* (that's the secret). Drop in boiling water in which peas, lima beans, chicken, etc., have been cooked and cook about 5 minutes.

Delaware State Senator Roger Martin, Newark, Del.

CHOCOLATE PANCAKES

Yield: 18 to 24

1½ cups flour
1 teaspoon baking soda
¼ cup sugar
½ teaspoon salt
¼ cup cocoa

2 eggs
1 cup milk
¼ cup butter, melted
½ cup milk-chocolate chips

Sift first 5 ingredients together. Beat eggs lightly; add milk. Add to flour mixture. Mix well. Add melted butter and chocolate chips.

Grease griddle and when hot, spoon on 2 tablespoons of pancake batter for each pancake.

A good friend served any time of day, but they shine at breakfast.

Famous pancakes of the cooking classes, 1974-1978, in Old Green Street Elementary School, Claymont, Del.

RICOTTA LATKES

1 pound ricotta	2 tablespoons butter, melted
4 eggs	1 tablespoon sugar
6 tablespoons flour	1 teaspoon vanilla

Put all ingredients in a blender container. Process until very smooth (like thick cream). Heat a greased griddle over medium heat. Make pancakes using 1½ to 2 tablespoons of batter. When a few bubbles form on pancake surface, turn once and cook briefly.

Serve with applesauce, sour cream, yogurt, jam, or fresh fruit.

Ida Rowe, Bethel, Del.

DUTCH CREAM WAFFLES

Yield: approximately 8 waffles

1 cup sifted flour	3 eggs, separated
4 teaspoons baking powder	1 cup heavy cream
¼ teaspoon salt	

Sift dry ingredients. Beat egg yolks vigorously. Add cream and continue beating hard. Stir in flour combination, and beat until smooth. Beat eggs until stiff peaks form; fold egg whites into batter. Refrigerate batter 30 minutes. Bake in preheated waffle iron until delicately browned. Serve with butter and warm honey or maple syrup.

The Dutch introduced waffles to America. It was their custom to give a new bride a waffle iron with her initials and the date of her wedding carved into it.

Olive Van Riper Cormog, *The Claymont Sampler*

BISCUITS AND MUFFINS

SPICED APPLE MUFFINS

Yield: 12 to 14 muffins

2 cups flour (sifted before
  measuring)
½ cup sugar
4 teaspoons baking powder
½ teaspoon salt
1 teaspoon cinnamon

4 tablespoons butter, melted
1 cup milk
1 egg, beaten
1 cup finely chopped raw apple
2 tablespoons sugar

Sift together flour, sugar, baking powder, salt, and ½ teaspoon cinnamon. Combine melted butter, milk, and egg. Mix thoroughly and add to dry ingredients. Fold in apples and drop in well-greased muffin tins.

Mix together the 2 tablespoons sugar and the remaining ½ teaspoon cinnamon and sprinkle on the muffins. Bake at 400° for 15 to 20 minutes.

My all-time favorite.

Mildred McCormick, Wilmington, Del.

BISCUITS

Yield: 12 to 15 biscuits

3 cups all-purpose flour
2 tablespoons sugar
1 tablespoon plus 1½ teaspoons
    baking powder
¾ teaspoon cream of tartar

Dash of salt
¾ cup solid vegetable shortening
1 egg, beaten
¾ cup buttermilk

Preheat oven to 450°. Mix first five ingredients; cut in shortening until mixture resembles coarse meal. Combine egg and buttermilk; add to flour mixture.

Turn out onto lightly floured board; knead 8 to 10 times; roll dough to 1-inch thickness. Cut with 2½-inch biscuit cutter. Place on ungreased baking sheet and bake for 15 minutes or until golden brown.

This is a biscuit that IS a biscuit.

Don Prillman, Claymont, Del.

BLUEBERRY MUFFINS

Yield: 18 to 24

½ cup butter, softened
1½ cups sugar
2 eggs
3 cups flour
5 teaspoons baking powder

Pinch salt
½ cup milk
1 pint blueberries, washed and
    drained

Cream butter and sugar; add the eggs. Mix flour, baking powder, and salt in another bowl. Alternate adding flour and milk to butter-sugar mixture. Fold in berries and put in greased muffin tins. Bake 30 to 35 minutes at 350°.

This is a very easy and good family recipe from the seventh generation granddaughter of Richard Bassett, Delaware's fourteenth governor (1799-1801) and signer of Delaware's Ratification.

Jane Bayard Curley, New York, N. Y.

BLUEBERRY OATMEAL MUFFINS

Yield: 18 muffins

1 cup plus 2 tablespoons quick
  cooking rolled oats
1 cup buttermilk
1 tablespoon vanilla
1 cup unbleached all purpose
  flour
1 tablespoon baking powder
1 teaspoon salt
1 teaspoon cinnamon
½ teaspoon baking soda

½ teaspoon freshly grated
  nutmeg
¼ cup walnuts, finely chopped
  (optional)
1 egg
¾ cup firmly packed light brown
  sugar
¼ cup unsalted butter
1⅓ cups blueberries

Generously butter 18 large muffin cups. Position rack in center
of oven and preheat to 400°. Blend oats, buttermilk, and vanilla
in medium bowl and set aside. Combine flour, baking powder,
salt, cinnamon, baking soda, nutmeg, and walnuts, and mix
well. Set aside.

Combine egg and brown sugar in large bowl; blend 1 minute
with electric beaters. Add butter and beat 1 minute longer. Add
buttermilk mixture and beat 2 minutes. Add dry ingredients,
and blend just until flour is incorporated, do not overmix. Fold
in berries.

Fill each muffin cup half full. Bake until muffins are lightly
browned, about 15 to 20 minutes. Turn out onto rack and let
cool.

Ryan's Berry Farm, Frankford, Del.

CHEESE BISCUITS

Yield: 75 to 100

1 glass Old English cheese	*1 cup flour*
1 stick butter	*Dash cayenne*

Preheat oven to 425°. Have all ingredients at room temperature. Cream cheese and butter. Add flour and cayenne, and mix thoroughly. Put in refrigerator to chill approximately half an hour. Remove and roll into marble-sized balls. A pecan half may be pressed into top, if desired. Bake in oven about 10 minutes. Dough may be frozen in balls and baked later.

Mrs. William W. Pleasants, Bethel, Del.

CINNAMON MONKEY BALLS

Serves 10 to 12

3 packages refrigerated butter- *milk biscuits*	*3 tablespoons cinnamon* *½ cup butter*
1 cup sugar	*¾ cup brown sugar*

Cut 30 biscuits into quarters. In a bag mix sugar and cinnamon, drop in biscuit pieces, shake until well coated and all sugar-cinnamon mixture is gone. Layer biscuit pieces in a greased tube pan.

Melt butter and brown sugar and pour over biscuits. Bake at 350° for 30 minutes. Cool for 20 minutes in inverted pan. This allows butter and sugar mixture to drop to bottom of pan.

Michele F. Samluk, Wilmington, Del.

COCONUT MUFFINS

Yield: one dozen

1¾ cups flour
⅓ cup sugar
2½ teaspoons baking powder
½ cup fresh or dried shredded
  coconut

1 beaten egg
¾ cup milk
⅓ cup tasteless salad oil
1 teaspoon coconut flavoring

Preheat oven to 400°. Stir flour, sugar, and baking powder together. Lightly mix in the coconut. Make a well in the center. Mix the egg, milk, oil, and flavoring together and add to the dry ingredients. Stir lightly, until just moist. Fill muffin pans ⅔ full. Bake for 20 to 25 minutes.

I use these often for gifts and put them in fabric-lined baskets. They are usually a hit and so very easy to make.

Adapted from *Better Homes and Gardens Best-Ever Muffins.*

Mary S. Hinkle, Dover, Del.

HONEY GRAHAM MUFFINS

Yield: 12 muffins

1 cup whole wheat flour
¾ cup white flour
1 tablespoon baking powder
1 tablespoon brown sugar
1 teaspoon salt

¾ cup milk
¼ cup honey
3 tablespoons tasteless salad oil
1 egg
½ cup dates

Preheat oven to 400°. Mix first 5 ingredients together. Add milk, honey, oil, egg, and dates. Bake for 15 to 20 minutes.

Kim Rogers Burdick, Wilmington, Del.

FRENCH ORANGE PUFFS

Yield: 18 muffin-sized puffs or 24 mini-sized puffs

2 cups biscuit mix	Grated rind of 1 orange
¾ cup milk	⅓ cup butter, melted
1 egg	½ cup sugar
2 tablespoons sugar	1 teaspoon cinnamon

Preheat oven to 400°. Combine first 4 ingredients. Beat vigorously for 30 seconds. Batter will be slightly bubbly. Blend in orange rind.

Grease bottom of small muffin cups or mini cups. Fill two thirds full. Bake for 10 or 15 minutes. Immediately roll baked puffs in melted butter, then in a mixture of sugar and cinnamon.

A hot and tasty basket of mini puffs with your morning beverage will bring a smile that won't come off.

Aloah E. Hatz, Claymont, Del.

SWEET POTATO NUT MUFFINS

Yield: 22 muffins

2 cups flour, sifted	1 cup sugar
2 teaspoons baking powder	½ cup milk
½ teaspoon baking soda	2 eggs
1 teaspoon salt	5 tablespoons butter, melted
1½ teaspoon cinnamon	1 cup pecans, chopped
1 cup mashed cooked sweet potatoes	

Preheat oven to 350°. Sift together first 5 ingredients. Combine cooled sweet potatoes, sugar, milk, and eggs in mixing bowl. Add dry ingredients and melted butter; mix until blended. Stir in pecans. Pour into muffin cups and bake for 25 to 30 minutes, or until toothpick inserted comes out clean. Serve with plenty of melted butter.

So satisfying for supper or luncheon.

Etta Appleton

BREADS

APPLE CINNAMON BREAD

Yield: 4 to 5 baby loaves

1 package dry yeast	2 eggs
¼ cup water	½ teaspoon cardamom
¾ cup milk	5 to 5½ cups flour
¼ cup margarine	3 apples, peeled, cored, and
¼ cup sugar	sliced
1 teaspoon salt	

Preheat oven to 350°. Grease and flour 4 or 5 baby loaf pans (5 ¾- by 3¼- by 2-inch). Dissolve yeast in warm water. Scald milk and stir in margarine, sugar, and salt. Let milk mixture cool to lukewarm; stir in yeast. Add eggs and cardamom. Beat in 1½ cups flour.

Cover and let rise in warm place for 40 minutes or until double in bulk. Stir in enough flour to make a workable dough (3½ to 4 cups). Knead in ½ cup more flour. Cover and chill for 30 minutes. Divide dough among prepared pans. Press sliced apples into top of loaves. Prepare topping.

Topping

¼ cup margarine	¼ cup brown sugar
1 tablespoon cinnamon	½ cup sliced almonds
1 tablespoon sugar	

Melt margarine and stir in cinnamon, sugars, and almonds. Drizzle topping over loaves. Bake for 30 minutes or until apples are tender. Let cool for 10 minutes in pans before removing.

Kate Bednarski, Wilmington, Del.

KALMAR NYCKEL

BEER BREAD

Yield: 1 loaf

3 cups self-rising flour   1 can beer
3 tablespoons sugar

Preheat over to 350°. Mix all ingredients, pour into greased loaf pan. Bake for 45 to 55 minutes.

Ethel Wells, Wilmington, Del.

PHILADELPHIA CINNAMON BUNS

Yield: approximately 24

¼ cup warm water
1 package active dry yeast
butter
syrup (golden cane, molasses, or
  honey)
¼ cup pecan pieces (optional)
1 teaspoon salt
¾ cup plus 1 tablespoon sugar
1¼ cups of milk

5 cups sifted flour
½ cup of shortening (½ of it
  lard, if you wish)
2 eggs
softened butter
brown sugar
cinnamon
raisins
syrup

Preheat oven to 350°. Put warm water in a cup and sprinkle the yeast over it.

Butter 3 9-inch round pans (or square or oblong ones). Pour in about ¼ inch of syrup, molasses, or honey. Sprinkle with pecan pieces.

In a saucepan, add the salt and 1 tablespoon of sugar to the milk; heat just until tiny bubbles form around the edges. Cool. When milk is lukewarm, stir in yeast and then gradually beat in 2 cups of the flour. Beat well, cover, and set it aside to get bubbly.

Meanwhile, beat shortening, ¾ cup sugar, and eggs until very fluffy and light. When yeast mixture is bubbly, beat in the shortening mixture, a tablespoon at a time. After this is thoroughly blended, gradually add the remaining 3 cups of flour. Do not beat hard, just mix in well. The dough will be quite sticky. Cover and let stand in a draft-free spot until dough doubles in bulk.

Turn one-third of the dough out onto a floured counter or board. Roll it out into a neat rectangle about ¼-inch thick. Spread dough generously with the softened butter. Sprinkle thickly with brown sugar, cinnamon, and as many raisins as you like.

Drizzle syrup over dough. Beginning at the long end of the rectangle, roll it up like a jelly roll. (If you leave a narrow margin of dough bare, it will be easier to roll.)

With a sharp knife, cut the roll into ¾-inch-wide pieces. Place them side by side, just barely touching one another, in the prepared pans. Repeat process with the remaining dough.

Cover pans and let buns rise until double in bulk. Then bake in oven about 35 to 40 minutes, or until tops are beautifully browned. Turn out of pans as soon as taken from oven.

"Sticky-topped morsels of delight."

Mrs. Robert McKeown

CINNAMON TWISTS

Yield: approximately 2 dozen

1 cup sour cream	3 cups sifted flour
3 tablespoons sugar	2 tablespoons softened butter or
⅛ teaspoon baking soda	margarine
1 teaspoon salt	⅓ cup brown sugar
1 package yeast	1 teaspoon cinnamon
1 large egg	1 cup confectioner's sugar
2 tablespoons soft shortening	orange juice

Preheat oven to 375°. Heat the sour cream to lukewarm. Stir in sugar, soda, and salt. Add yeast and stir until dissolved. Add egg, shortening, and flour. Roll out to oblong 24 by 26 inches. Spread with soft butter. Mix brown sugar and cinnamon. Add cinnamon mixture on half of oblong. Fold over, cut into 1-inch strips. Twist strips and place on greased cookie sheet. *Let stand for 1 hour.* Bake for 12 to 15 minutes. Gradually stir orange juice into confectioner's sugar until mixture is consistency of icing. Spread over twists.

Jeanne Meding, Sunrise, Fla., formerly of New Castle, Del.

MOM MOM MITCHELL'S CORNBREAD

Yield: 1 loaf

1 cup water
2 cups milk
1½ cups white cornmeal
1 stick margarine

1 cup sugar
½ teaspoon salt
2 beaten eggs

Preheat oven to 400°. Heat water and milk together over low heat. Add cornmeal, cooking over low heat until thick. Then add last four ingredients, mixing well. Pour into greased 8- by 8-inch pan or 8- by 11-inch pan, preferably glass. Bake for 35 to 45 minutes or until golden brown.

This makes a moist cornbread.

Lynne Baynard, Dover, Del.

DOUGHNUT BALLS

Yield: 25 doughnuts

⅓ cup sugar
½ cup milk
1 egg
2 tablespoons shortening
1½ cups flour

½ teaspoon salt
1 teaspoon baking powder
½ teaspoon nutmeg
Vegetable oil
Confectioner's sugar (optional)

Mix sugar, milk, and egg. Melt shortening and add to mixture. Sift together flour, salt, baking powder, and nutmeg and add to mixture. Combine both by stirring until smooth. Heat oil to 365° to 375°. Drop dough by teaspoonfuls into hot oil, and cook for 3 to 4 minutes. Roll in confectioner's sugar, if you desire.

Bea Collins, Milton, Del.

EGGLESS, SNOWFLAKE DOUGHNUTS

Yield: approximately 3 dozen

1 cup hot mashed potatoes	1½ cups sugar
2 tablespoons butter	4 cups flour
1½ cups milk	4 teaspoons baking powder

Mix butter into potatoes. Add sugar and milk. Beat well; add flour and baking powder a little at a time. Roll ½-inch thick. Cut and fry in hot fat until golden brown. Drain in colander and while hot dip in any of the following:
1. mixture of 2 teaspoons cinnamon and 4 tablespoons sugar
2. confectioner's sugar
3. confectioner's sugar plus orange juice
4. chocolate
5. confectioner's sugar and then press in dish of coconut
6. fry whole, fill with jelly
7. confectioner's sugar plus milk (make runny) glaze

Lois Lesher, Delaware State Representative, 1973-1976

ITALIAN CHEESE BREAD

Yield: 1 loaf

¼ pound Swiss cheese
¼ pound sharp Cheddar cheese
4½ cups all-purpose flour
2 teaspoons sugar
¼ teaspoon salt
2 packages yeast

1 cup warm water
1 cup margarine
6 eggs, beaten
½ cup grated Parmesan cheese
Dash of pepper (optional)

Preheat oven to 350°. Cut Swiss and Cheddar cheese into ¼-inch cubes; set aside. Sift flour with sugar and salt. Dissolve yeast in warm water. Cream margarine and stir in beaten eggs and yeast. Gradually add flour mixture. Beat with an electric mixer until satiny. (You may need a dough hook.) Stir in cheese cubes, Parmesan cheese, and pepper.

Cover and let rise until double in size. Stir down and let rise again. Then transfer to greased 10½-inch tube pan. Let rise again until double. (The 3 risings usually take at least 3 hours, depending on the temperature of your kitchen.) Bake for 40 minutes. Let cool 20 minutes before removing from pan. Dough may be frozen and will keep a week to 10 days well-wrapped at room temperature.

This recipe is adapted from one my grandmother always made for Easter morning. It was often eaten with Italian salami for breakfast.

Jean A. Buchanan, Wilmington, Del.

SHAKER CIDER BREAD

Yield: 2 loaves

1 cup butter or margarine
3 cups sugar
4 eggs
6 cups sifted flour
1 teaspoon baking soda
½ teaspoon salt

5 teaspoons nutmeg, freshly
  grated (can use 2 teaspoons
  ground nutmeg, but fresh is
  best)
1 cup apple cider or apple juice

Preheat oven to 350°. Cream butter, add sugar gradually and beat thoroughly. Add eggs and beat again until sugar is almost dissolved, 15 to 20 minutes. Mix all dry ingredients together. Add these alternately with apple cider to batter mixture. Bake in two 9½- by 5½-inch greased and floured loaf pans for 1 hour or more until tested done.

Slice thin and spread with cream cheese, if desired. Cider bread can also be baked in a 10-inch tube pan.

Mrs. Frances Clark, Greenwood, Del.

EASY FRENCH BREAD

Yield: 2 loaves

1 package yeast
1½ cups warm water
1 tablespoon sugar
1½ teaspoons salt

1 tablespoon solid vegetable
  shortening
4 cups white flour

Preheat oven to 375°. Dissolve the yeast in ½ cup of warm water. Combine sugar, salt, shortening, and 1 cup of water. Add flour and mix well. Mix thoroughly every 10 minutes for an hour with a wooden spoon. Make 2 balls. Dump out to rest 10 minutes. Roll each ball into a rectangle. Roll up from long end. Grease cookie sheet. Sprinkle dough with cornmeal. Score top of dough. Let rise 1½ hours. Bake for 35 to 45 minutes.

That's right, no kneading. Can substitute 2 cups whole wheat flour and 2 cups white flour for a different taste.

Connie Cox, Newark, Del.

LEMON BREAD

Yield: 1 loaf

¾ cup sugar
½ cup margarine
2 eggs
2 cups unsifted flour
2 teaspoons baking powder
½ teaspoon salt

⅔ cup water
1 tablespoon grated lemon rind
4 tablespoons lemon juice
½ cup chopped walnuts or
    pecans
¼ cup light corn syrup

Preheat oven to 350°. In large bowl of electric mixer, beat sugar and margarine until well blended and fluffy. Beat in eggs. Stir in flour, baking powder, and salt until well mixed. Add water, lemon rind, and 2 tablespoons lemon juice, stir in nuts, turn batter into 9- by 5- by 3-inch pan.

Bake for 50 minutes. Stir together corn syrup and remaining lemon juice. Take loaf pan out of oven. Pour syrup mixture over loaf, then return loaf to oven, baking 5 minutes more until tester comes out clean. Cool 10 minutes before removing from pan. Let stand at room temperature overnight (slices better).

Cecelia Carney, Dover, Del.

LEMON PECAN BREAD

Yield: 1 loaf

¾ cup butter
1½ cups sugar
3 eggs
2¼ cups flour
¼ teaspoon baking soda
¼ teaspoon salt

¾ cup buttermilk
¾ cup chopped pecans
1 teaspoon grated lemon rind
½ cup sugar
juice of 1 lemon

Preheat oven to 350°. Cream butter, gradually add sugar and eggs, one at a time, beating after each addition. Combine flour, baking soda, and salt; add to creamed mixture alternately with buttermilk. Stir in pecans and lemon rind.

Pour batter into greased 9- by 5- by 3-inch loaf pan. Bake for 1 hour and 15 to 20 minutes. Remove from oven. Mix together ½ cup sugar and lemon juice and pour over bread while it is still hot to glaze it.

Betty Fulmer, Wilmington, Del.

MINCEMEAT BREAD

Yield: 1 loaf

2 cups sifted flour
4 teaspoons baking powder
1 teaspoon salt
1 egg, beaten
½ cup milk

½ cup brown sugar
3 tablespoons melted shortening
   or oil
1 cup prepared moist mincemeat

Combine dry ingredients in one bowl and wet ingredients in another. Pour the wet mixture into the dry mixture and mix.

Turn into a greased loaf pan and bake in a preheated 350° oven for 1 hour. Cool on rack for 10 minutes, then turn out of pan and complete cooling on rack.

Rich and delicious. Anyone who likes the taste of mincemeat will also enjoy mincement bread.

Kitty Forester, Wilmington, Del.

PUMPKIN BREAD

Yield: 2 loaves

1¾ cups flour
1½ cups sugar
½ teaspoon salt
¾ teaspoon each cinnamon,
   nutmeg, cloves
¾ teaspoon baking powder
1 teaspoon baking soda

2 eggs
¼ cup vegetable oil
½ cup water
1 cup canned pumpkin
½ cup raisins
½ cup chopped walnuts

Preheat oven to 350°. Sift together flour, sugar, salt, spices, baking powder, and baking soda. Beat eggs in separate bowl and set aside. Mix oil, water, and pumpkin together, add eggs and pour into dry ingredients, mixing well. Add raisins and chopped walnuts.

Pour into 2 1-pound coffee cans, filling half full, or 6 to 8 soup cans, filling half full. Bake for 1½ hours.

Elaine T. Bradley, Felton, Del.

IRISH SCONE

Yield: 1 loaf

3 cups all-purpose flour
¾ cup granulated sugar
2 teaspoons baking powder
1 teaspoon salt

1⅓ cups milk
1 egg, slightly beaten
1½ sticks of margarine, melted
1 or 2 cups raisins

Preheat oven to 325°. Mix dry ingredients together. Very slowly stir in milk, egg, and cooled margarine. Fold in raisins. Pour batter into 5- by 9- by 2-inch loaf pan and bake for 1 hour.

Joan D. Waters, Claymont, Del.

YEAST ROLLS

Yield: 3 to 4 dozen

1 cup sugar
1 cup solid vegetable shortening
1 teaspoon salt
1 cup mashed potatoes

1 cup scalding milk
1 yeast cake
½ cup lukewarm water
2 eggs, slightly beaten

Mix together sugar, shortening, salt, mashed potatoes, and milk. Let cool until lukewarm. Dissolve yeast in water. Stir well and add to potato mixture. Add eggs and enough flour to make a stiff dough. Let rise for 3 hours. Knead down dough. Shape into clover leaf rolls or individual large rolls. Put rolls into well greased muffin tins to rise for 2 to 3 hours until doubled in size. Preheat oven to 350°. Bake rolls for 25 to 30 minutes.

Linda Hudson, Millville, Del.

BLUEBERRY ZUCCHINI BREAD

Yield: 2 loaves

3 eggs
1 cup vegetable oil
2 cups sugar
2 cups grated zucchini,
   including skin
3 teaspoons vanilla
3 cups sifted flour
1 teaspoon salt

1 teaspoon baking soda
3 teaspoons cinnamon
Dash of nutmeg
1 teaspoon baking powder
½ cup chopped walnuts
1 cup fresh blueberries, washed
   and stemmed

Preheat oven to 325°. Beat eggs until light and foamy. Add oil and sugar, grated zucchini, and vanilla. Mix well. Sift together flour, salt, soda, spices, and baking powder. Add to liquid mixture and mix well. Add nuts and blueberries.

Pour into two 9- by 5- by 2-inch *well-greased* loaf pans. Bake for 1 hour or until done. Cool at least 20 minutes before removing from pans.

Freezes very well and remains moist.

Libby Hancock, Wilmington, Del.

MEATS

WOODBURN CIRCA 1790
the GOVERNOR'S MANSION

CITY CHICKEN

Veal
Pork, lean
2 cups breadcrumbs
1 egg

Oil
Chicken bouillon
Water

Allow about ½ pound each of veal and pork per person. Pre-heat oven to 350°. Cut veal and pork into 1-inch cubes. Dip cubes in breadcrumbs, then beaten egg, then breadcrumbs. Secure breadcrumbs by gently squeezing in hand. Deep fry until golden brown. On wood or metal skewers, alternate cubes of the two meats. Place in roaster. Bake for 2 to 3 hours or until tender. While baking, baste with a mixture of chicken bouillon and water.

Carol Rooney, Wilmington, Del.

PORK CHOP CASSEROLE

Serves 6

6 pork chops, medium thick	*2 carrots, sliced*
1 egg, beaten	*2 medium onions, sliced*
Bread crumbs	*10¾-ounce can cream of*
4 to 5 white potatoes, sliced	*mushroom soup*

Preheat oven to 350°. Dip pork chops in beaten egg and coat with bread crumbs. Fry until lightly brown. Place in bottom of greased baking dish. Cover with layer of raw potatoes. Boil the sliced carrots in just enough water to cover until slightly soft.

Fry onions in same pan pork chops were fried in and when soft, add carrots to this. Pour mixture over pork chops and potatoes, cover, and bake about 1 hour.

Add just enough water to cream of mushroom soup to make a smooth mixture, pour over pork chops, cover, and cook ½ hour more. Serve this dish with a green salad, popovers, and a fruit dessert.

Why not treat the family?

Jean Santobianco, Claymont, Del.

BARBEQUED BABY SPARERIBS

Serves 4 to 6

5 pounds baby spareribs   Curry powder
Salt and pepper to taste   Barbecue sauce (below)

Preheat oven to 400°. Prepare spareribs by removing excess fat
and cutting ribs into as many pieces as desired. Place flesh side
up on a rack in a shallow roasting pan. Sprinkle with salt and
pepper and very lightly with curry powder.

Cook spareribs for 1 hour, brushing with warm barbecue sauce
every 10 minutes.

BARBECUE SAUCE

Yields: 2½ cups

1 cup finely chopped onion   1 teaspoon dry mustard
1 clove garlic, minced   1 tablespoon lemon juice
¼ cup butter, melted   ½ cup vinegar
1 cup catsup   2 teaspoons Worcestershire sauce
½ cup dry sherry   ⅓ cup water
1 tablespoon light brown sugar

In a deep saucepan sauté onions and garlic in melted butter for
3 to 4 minutes. Add remaining ingredients and bring to a boil.
Lower heat and simmer, uncovered, for 1 hour, stirring frequently to prevent scorching.

A favorite served at the Governor's Mansion, Dover, Del.

PORK CHOPS IN SOUR CREAM AND MADEIRA

Serves 4

4 loin pork chops   *⅓ cup sour cream*
3 tablespoons Madeira   *Salt and pepper*

Pan broil 4 pork chops. When tender and a nice brown on both sides, remove them from pan. Remove excess fat from the pan. Add Madeira and sour cream, stirring well into the gravy. Return chops to the pan and cook for 10 minutes, frequently basting the chops.

Rose Haley, Wilmington, Del.
From *A Jug of Wine*, Morrison Wood

HAM DELIGHT

Serves 6 to 8

8-ounce package spaghetti   *10¾ ounce can tomato soup*
2 medium slices cured ham   *Parmesan cheese, finely grated,*
2 medium onions, chopped fine   *to taste*
1 pound fresh mushrooms, sliced   *Salt*

Cut ham in small pieces, removing fat. Melt some ham fat in a skillet. Brown ham over low heat. Remove ham from skillet. Brown onions in ham drippings until translucent and golden; then add the ham, mushrooms, tomato soup, and salt to taste. Cover and simmer 40 minutes. Cook spaghetti in salted water and drain. Serve mixture over cooked spaghetti. Sprinkle Parmesan cheese over each serving.

Pearl Austin, Bethel, Del.

SCHINKENFLECKERL

Serves 6

4 cups uncooked broad noodles   1 pound ham, chopped
1 heaping tablespoon butter   Salt to taste
2 eggs, separated   1 tablespoon fine bread crumbs
2 tablespoons sour cream

Boil 2 quarts salted water. Break noodles into squares. Cook noodles according to package directions until almost tender. Drain noodles and rinse in cold water, drain, cool.

In mixing bowl, cream butter, egg yolks, and sour cream. Add chopped ham, cooked noodles, salt to taste; carefully fold in stiffly beaten egg whites.

Grease 8-inch square baking casserole, sprinkle with bread crumbs over pan. Tilt pan to make sure crumbs line the inside surface, and turn pan upside down and knock out excess crumbs. Fill with noodle mixture. Bake at 350° until top is golden and slightly crusted.

Serve with vegetables or salad.

This is a typical Austrian specialty, so popular that it was used as the theme of a song by the famous Viennese composer, Herman Leopoldi. He sang: "Why does the meat play hide-and-seek with the fleckerl."

Charlotte Shedd, Wilmington, Del.

BEEF WITH BAMBOO SHOOTS AND PEPPERS

Serves 4 to 6

2 tablespoons soy sauce
2 tablespoons dry sherry
  (optional)
1 tablespoon cornstarch
½ teaspoon sugar
1 pound beef (round or flank)
2 tablespoons vegetable oil
1 clove garlic, halved
1 medium green pepper, cut into
  ½-inch strips

1 medium red pepper
2 scallions, cut into ½-inch
  slices
8-ounce can bamboo shoots,
  sliced
½ cup beef broth
1 cup long grain rice
10¾-ounce can beef consomme
10¾-ounce can beef broth
1 tablespoon butter

Combine in oblong casserole the first 4 ingredients. Cut the beef into thin strips and marinate in above mixture for 20 to 30 minutes. In a wok or skillet, heat oil, brown the garlic, then discard garlic. Stir-fry the peppers in the oil 2 to 3 minutes. Push peppers aside; stir-fry the scallions and bamboo shoots, push aside after 1 to 2 minutes. Drain beef. Stir-fry the beef 3 to 4 minutes, then mix beef with vegetables in wok. Add the beef broth and heat until sauce boils.

Mix rice, consomme, broth, and butter in casserole and bake at 350° for 1 hour.

Jean Johnson, Seneca, S. C.

BEEF BURGUNDY

Serves 6 to 8

2 pounds beef round, cubed
2 tablespoons flour
1 stick butter
1 tablespoon vegetable oil
2 4-ounce cans mushroom caps
1-pound can small onions
2 10-ounce cans beef broth
10¾-ounce can water

8-ounce can tomato sauce
2 cups dry red wine
¼ teaspoon dry thyme
½ teaspoon dry parsley
½ teaspoon black pepper
Salt to taste
1 pound wide noodles, cooked
    and drained

Coat beef cubes with flour. Heat butter and oil in Dutch oven. Add beef cubes. Cook and turn over medium high heat until well-browned. Drain mushrooms and onions; add to meat and cook until browned. To mixture in pan, add beef broth, water, tomato sauce, wine, thyme, parsley, pepper and salt. Stir well, bring to a boil, cover and simmer for 1½ to 2 hours, stirring occasionally to prevent sticking. (Add a little water if sauce becomes too thick.)

Serve over cooked wide noodles.

Judy Emmi, Claymont, Del.

BEEF AND CABBAGE CASSEROLE

Serves 6

2 tablespoons butter or
    vegetable oil
½ cup chopped onion
1 pound ground beef

Salt and pepper
6 cups cabbage, coarsely chopped
10¾-ounce can tomato rice
    soup

Preheat oven to 350°. In oil or butter, sauté onion, ground beef, and salt and pepper. Using a 2 or 2½ quart baking dish, spread 3 cups of cabbage and cover with meat mixture. Top with 3 more cups of cabbage. Pour the soup over the above mixture and bake uncovered for 1 hour.

Bess Boggs, Delaware's First Lady 1953-1960.

EASY BRISKET

Serves 8 to 10

6-8 pound brisket
2 envelopes dried onion soup
   mix
¼ cup red wine

½ pound fresh mushrooms or
   4-ounce can of mushrooms,
   drained

Preheat oven to 375°. Remove all fat from brisket. Empty one package onion soup mix on sheet of aluminum foil (large enough to cover brisket), and lay meat on top. Cover meat with other package of onion mix, wine and mushrooms. Seal in foil. Place in oven in pan and cook for 3½ to 4½ hours.

Judith Arenson, Wilmington, Del.

SAUCY ITALIAN STYLE POT ROAST

Serves 6 to 8

1 pound small macaroni shells,
   cooked
3 to 5 pound pot roast
2 tablespoons lard or drippings
2¼ cups water

½ teaspoon salt
2 28-ounce cans tomato puree
1 envelope spaghetti sauce mix
½ cup stuffed olives, sliced
2 tablespoons flour

Cook macaroni shells according to package directions. Brown pot roast in drippings. Remove; drain well. Add 1 cup of water and the salt. Cover and simmer for 1½ hours. Add puree, spaghetti sauce mix, olives, and 1 cup water. Simmer another 1½ hours until tender.

Remove meat to a heated platter. Add the cooked macaroni to sauce. Simmer for 10 minutes.

To thicken sauce, make a paste by shaking together the flour and ¼ cup water; add to sauce in pan. Slice pot roast, place on a meat platter, and serve macaroni with sauce around the meat.

Rita Keenan, Wilmington, Del.

SAVORY CHUCK STEAK

Serves 6 to 8

3½ pounds chuck steak (sliced 1-inch thick)
2 tablespoons flour
½ teaspoon salt
⅛ teaspoon pepper

2 tablespoons vegetable oil
1 envelope onion soup mix
1 cup cold water
1 cup chili sauce

With a sharp knife, remove fat from meat and slice meat into ¼-inch slices. In a large bowl toss meat with flour, salt, and pepper.

In a large skillet, in hot oil, brown steak strips. Add onion soup mix, water, and chili sauce. Simmer covered 25 minutes or until meat is tender. Serve steak over hot noodles.

Irene Volmi, Newark, Del.

KEN'S FLANK STEAK ROLL UPS

Serves 6

2½ to 3 pounds of flank steak
2 slices bacon, cut into ½-inch pieces
2 dill pickles, sliced lengthwise
½ teaspoon salt
Dash pepper

¼ cup flour
2 tablespoons vegetable oil
½ cup water
¼ cup catsup
1 teaspoon Worcestershire sauce

Cut steak into 8 rectangular pieces. Lay pieces of bacon and a slice of pickle on each. Roll up and fasten with a toothpick. Add salt and pepper to the flour; roll meat in mixture, and brown in hot fat.

Place in 1½ quart casserole. Combine water, catsup, and Worcestershire sauce. Pour over meat. Cover and bake at 350° until done (about 2 hours).

Pickle will disappear and flavor the meat. Absolutely delicious!

Beth Langston, Stanton, Del.

ROUND STEAK STUFFED WITH VEGETABLES

Serves 4

1½ to 2 pounds round steak
  (pounded flat)
Salt and pepper to taste
2 tablespoons olive oil
2 garlic cloves, crushed
2 carrots, grated
1 onion, chopped

1 to 2 stalks celery and/or ½ cup
  zucchini, sliced
1 cup mozzarella cheese or Swiss
  cheese
2 cups tomato or spaghetti sauce
Parmesan cheese

Pound steak flat. Rub in salt, pepper, olive oil, and garlic. Arrange the vegetables and cheeses down the center of the meat and roll up meat like a jelly roll, tie in several places.

Heat a large frying pan and add some olive oil, brown the roll quickly on both sides. Place the roll in a baking dish, add the tomato or spaghetti sauce; cover. Bake at 350° for 1 hour.

Serve with an apricot salad and sour cream biscuits.

Rebecca C. Spence, Palm City, Fla., formerly of Bethel, Del.

BARBECUE SAUCE FOR MEAT

Yield: approximately 3 cups

¼ cup butter
2 onions, chopped
3 garlic cloves, crushed
24-ounce bottle of catsup
2 tablespoons vinegar

2 tablespoons celery seed,
  ground
1 tablespoon white sugar
½ ounce chili powder
2 tablespoons lemon juice

Melt butter and sauté onion and garlic until lightly browned. Add remaining ingredients except lemon juice and simmer for a few minutes. Strain and cool. Add lemon juice.

Use to baste ribs, beef, etc.

Jack Bretz, Omaha, Neb.

POULTRY AND GAME

LOMBARDY HALL

APRICOT CHICKEN

Serves 6

8-ounce jar apricot preserves
8-ounce bottle Wishbone Russian
  dressing

1 envelope onion soup mix
1 chicken, cut up, or breasts and
  thighs

Mix ingredients together and pour over chicken. Bake at 350° for approximately 1½ hours, basting often.

Serve with corn bread or sour cream biscuits.

Ethelene Krauss, Claymont, Del.

BARBECUE CHICKEN

Serves 4 to 5

½ cup cooking oil
1 cup vinegar
2 tablespoons salt
1½ teaspoons poultry seasoning

¼ teaspoon white pepper
1 egg
5 chicken halves

Beat oil, vinegar, salt, seasonings, and egg together. You can marinate the chicken in this for 3 or 4 hours before cooking, or just brush on chicken, then grill it.

Served with popovers or Johnny cake, it makes a delicious meal.

Mary Pilgrim, Belleville, Wis.

BARBEQUE CHICKEN CASSEROLE

1 3-4 pound frying chicken
1 teaspoon salt
2 teaspoons cider vinegar
2 teaspoons butter
2 teaspoons Worcestershire sauce
4 teaspoons water

2 teaspoons lemon juice
1 teaspoon prepared mustard
½ teaspoon red pepper
1 teaspoon paprika
1 teaspoon chili powder
2 teaspoons catsup

Sprinkle chicken pieces with salt. Combine next 10 ingredients making a sauce, and dip chicken pieces into sauce. Place chicken into a well greased casserole pouring any remaining sauce over chicken. Bake at 500° for 15 minutes. Reduce heat to 350° and bake approximately 1¼ hours.

Louise Keim, Claymont, Del.

THE SKIPJACK

CHICKEN à la KING

Serves 4

6- or 8-ounce can sliced
   mushrooms, drained, keep
   liquid
½ cup diced green pepper
½ cup butter or margarine
½ cup flour
1 teaspoon salt
¼ teaspoon pepper

2 cups light cream
1¾ cup chicken broth (17-ounce
   can)
2 cups cubed chicken or turkey
4-ounce jar pimento, chopped
   (optional)
1 small can peas, drained
   (optional)

In large skillet, cook mushrooms and pepper in butter for 5 minutes, stirring. Over low heat, blend in flour, salt, and pepper. Cook until bubbly. Remove from heat. Stir in cream, broth, and ¼ cup mushroom liquid. Return to heat, bring to boil, stirring, and boil 1 minute. Reduce heat, stir in chicken, pimento, and peas. Heat through. (About another ¼ to ½ cup chicken broth and/or mushroom liquid can be added, if needed to thin.)

Serve in hot toast cups, heated pastry shells, or over toast. Leftovers can be frozen and reheated.

Add this to your laurels as a hostess.

Charlotte Johnson, Pendleton, S.C., formerly of Claymont, Del.

CHICKEN à la LILLIAN

Serves 4

8 pieces of chicken, of your
   choice
Salt and pepper
6 or 7 cups water
Wide noodles or rice for 4
   servings
1 medium green pepper, chopped
   fine
1 medium onion, chopped fine
1½ cups mushrooms, sliced or
   button mushrooms
2 bay leaves

Salt and pepper
3 tablespoons flour
½ cup water
2 teaspoons lemon juice
¾ cup mayonnaise
¾ cup cooked peas, drained
   (canned or frozen)
1 cup Cheddar cheese, finely
   grated
Bread crumbs
Dots of butter

Season chicken pieces with salt and pepper and boil in 6 or 7 cups water until tender. Remove chicken and set aside. Save broth.

Cook enough wide noodles or rice according to package direction for 4 servings (I prefer noodles), drain, and set aside.

Sauté green pepper, onion, and mushrooms until soft and lightly browned. Add to 2½ cups reserved chicken broth, bay leaves, salt, and pepper to taste and let boil slowly 8 or 10 minutes.

Mix flour and water together. Add lemon juice and mayonnaise; stir thoroughly to make gravy.

Grease a 9- by 13- by 2-inch baking dish. Add noodles or rice. Place chicken on noodles and cover with gravy mixture, stirring lightly to let gravy down into noodles or rice. Add peas. Sprinkle cheese over top, then bread crumbs and dots of butter. Bake until bubbly and brown on top, about 40 to 50 minutes.

This recipe is being shared with us by the great granddaughter of Governor James Ponder, Delaware's forty-fourth governor, 1871-1875.

Lillian Ponder Hunter, Wilmington, Del.

CHICKEN BREASTS WITH HAM

Serves 6

3 whole chicken breasts, split, skinned, and boned (about 1½ pounds)
1 envelope seasoned coating for chicken, any flavor
¼ pound mushrooms, thinly sliced
3 tablespoons butter or margarine

½ cup dry white wine or chicken broth
¼ cup light cream or half and half
6 slices boiled ham
6 slices (thin) Swiss cheese

Coat chicken with seasoned coating mix as directed on package. Arrange in a single layer in ungreased baking dish. Bake at 400° for about 20 minutes. Meanwhile, sauté mushrooms in butter until tender and slightly browned. Stir in wine and cream. Pour over chicken in baking dish. Top each chicken breast with a slice of ham, then a slice of cheese. Bake 5 minutes longer or until cheese just begins to melt.

Becky Mitchell, Newark, Del.

CHICKEN CASSEROLE

Serves 8 to 10

4 chicken breasts
Water
10¾-ounce can mushroom soup
8 ounces sour cream

6 ounces croutons
¼ pound butter
1 cup chicken stock

Cover chicken with water. Boil 4 breasts of chicken until done; cool, then cube and place in oblong casserole.

Preheat oven to 350°. Mix mushroom soup and sour cream. Pour over chicken. Add croutons. Melt butter and mix with chicken stock; drip over croutons. Bake for 1 hour.

Chicken is a cook's best friend.

Frances M. Dennis, Wilmington, Del.

COLUMBUS INN

ORIGINALLY SCHMALZ
BAKERY,
THEN A
TOLL HOUSE
INN.

SAWIN   1885

CURRIED CHICKEN

Serves 4 or more

1½ pounds chicken, boned
3 large potatoes (or 4 medium
 size)
2 tablespoons vegetable oil
1 medium onion, chopped
2 teaspoons curry powder
 (Indonesian preferred)

2 teaspoons soy sauce
1 tablespoon white cooking wine
½ teaspoon salt
1 cup water
1 teaspoon sugar or to taste

Cut chicken into 2-inch cubes, and set aside (half-frozen meat is easier to work with). Boil and skin potatoes. Mash coarsely so some lumps remain. Brown chicken in vegetable oil over high flame. Add potatoes, onion, curry powder, soy sauce, wine, salt, and water. Stir and cook over medium heat in large deep saucepan or wok. Add sugar (about 1 heaping teaspoon). Cook for 15 minutes. Mixture should be thick like a stew. Serve over steamed rice.

A favorite of Lt. Governor S.B. Woo.

Katy Woo, Newark, Del.

CHICKEN DIVAN

Serves 6 to 8

2 10-ounce packages frozen
  broccoli
3 to 4 chicken breasts
10¾-ounce can cream of
  mushroom soup
½ cup mayonnaise

½ to ¾ teaspoon lemon juice
½ teaspoon curry powder
Salt and pepper to taste
Ritz crackers
Butter
Cheddar cheese, grated

Cook broccoli for 3 minutes, drain well. Boil chicken breasts until tender, take from bone and cut into chunks. Place broccoli in bottom of 2-quart baking dish and top with chunked chicken. Make sauce of remaining ingredients and pour over above.

Crush 1 stack Ritz crackers. Melt butter; pour over crackers. Pour evenly over casserole. Sprinkle cheese over all. Bake at 375° for 35 minutes, covered; 10 minutes additional, uncovered.

A pink salad is a good accompaniment.

Commander Dennis Whitford, Monterey, Cal., formerly of Claymont, Del.

CHICKEN ELEGANT

Serves 6

4 chicken breasts or 3 breasts
   and 6 thighs
Water
½ teaspoon pepper
3 bay leaves
½ teaspoon rosemary
1 onion
2 stalks celery

10¾-ounce can of cream of
   mushroom soup
1 pint sour cream
¼ pound butter
8-ounce package herb stuffing
   mix
1 cup chicken broth plus 3
   tablespoons, reserved

Boil chicken in enough water to cover with pepper, bay leaf, rosemary, onion, and celery for 45 minutes to an hour. Cool and bone chicken. Save broth. Mix mushroom soup, sour cream, and 3 tablespoons chicken broth. Mix with chicken, and put chicken mixture in 9- by 13-inch glass baking dish. Melt butter and pour over stuffing mix; add one cup reserved chicken broth.

Put stuffing mix over chicken. Cover dish with foil. Bake at 350° for 20 minutes. Uncover and bake 15 minutes longer.

Mrs. Marvin Searles, Bethel, Del.

EDWIN & MAUD
UNDER SAIL

FIFTEEN MINUTE CHICKEN

Serves 6

2 chicken breasts
¼ cup flour
¼ cup butter
Salt and pepper to taste (white
   pepper, if you have it)
1 tablespoon crushed fresh
   rosemary

3 tablespoons raspberry vinegar
   or lemon or orange juice,
   Madeira, sherry, white, or red
   wine
1 tablespoon finely chopped fresh
   parsley

Skin, bone, and cut chicken into finger-size pieces about 3 inches long. Roll chicken pieces, a few at a time, in flour. Pat off excess. In a large skillet, melt butter until it sizzles. Add chicken and toss or stir over high heat 3 to 5 minutes or until chicken is no longer pink. Stir in salt, pepper, and rosemary. Add the vinegar, or one of the alternative ingredients, to deglaze the pan. Sprinkle the parsley on top.

This is especially good served over brown rice.

Governor Michael N. Castle, 1985-   , Dover, Del.

MEEMAW'S CHICKEN

Serves 12

2 cups sour cream
¼ cup lemon juice
4 teaspoons Worcestershire
  Sauce
4 teaspoons celery salt
2 teaspoons paprika
1 teaspoon garlic salt

½ teaspoon pepper
6 whole boned chicken breasts,
  split
1¾ cups bread crumbs (more if
  necessary)
½ cup butter
½ cup vegetable oil

Combine first 7 ingredients in large bowl. Add chicken and marinate overnight. The next day, roll chicken in bread crumbs (may take more). Place in shallow buttered pan. Refrigerate overnight.

Melt the butter and stir in oil. Pour half of butter-oil mixture over chicken. Bake at 350° for 45 minutes. Turn chicken and add rest of butter-oil mixture, bake 15 to 30 minutes longer or until chicken is tender.

Marjorie Whitaker, New Castle, Del.

CHICKEN AND OYSTER POT PIE CHESAPEAKE

Serves 1

Pastry dough
1 mushroom, sliced vertically
5 pieces of sliced carrot
1 tablespoon green peas
3 ounces white meat of chicken,
  cooked

2 ounces (3) shucked oysters,
  raw
¾ cup Velouté sauce

Line a ramekin with pie pastry and bake for approximately 25 minutes or until lightly browned.

Cook the vegetables. Cut the chicken into bite-size pieces and sauté until cooked. Place in the ramekin. Add the cooked vegetables and oysters. Pour hot Velouté sauce over all; bake at 425° for 10 minutes or until completely heated.

Note: When making these in quantity, put ramekins in large shallow pan. Fill pan until water comes three quarters up the sides of the ramekins, then bake.

Velouté Sauce
Yield: approximately one gallon

10 ounces butter
10 ounces bread flour
1 gallon clam or oyster broth,
  hot (or chicken stock)

Salt and pepper to taste

In a saucepan, melt the butter; stir in the flour to make a roux. Cook over low heat for 5 to 6 minutes; do not brown. Slowly whip in stock until sauce is thickened and smooth. Adjust seasoning. Continue to cook sauce for 30 minutes. Strain and use immediately or freeze.

Note: Do not cut down quantities to make less sauce.

The New Castle Inn Restaurant, New Castle, Del.

CHICKEN PARISIANNE

Serves 3 or 4

4-ounce package dried beef
3 or 4 chicken breasts, split and
  boned

10¾-ounce can cream of
  mushroom soup
1 cup sour cream

Line lasagna pan with dried beef. Place chicken on top. Combine soup and sour cream and pour over chicken. Bake, uncovered at 325° for 1½ hours. Serve over hot rice.

Easy to prepare. Add a green salad and hot rolls.

Joanna Prillman, Claymont, Del.

POLISH BAKED CHICKEN
(*Kurczie Smietanne*)

Serves 6

4 tablespoons butter
2 large onions, sliced thin
6 chicken breasts, split, boned
¼ teaspoon salt
¼ teaspoon pepper

¼ teaspoon garlic salt
¼ teaspoon paprika
1 pint sour cream
3 tablespoons flour

Melt butter in oblong baking dish. Add onion, chicken, salt, and pepper. Season with garlic salt and paprika. Bake at 350° for 45 minutes. Combine sour cream with flour, pouring some hot juice in from the chicken. Mix well. Pour over cooked chicken and bake an additional 10 minutes.

Delicious served with buttered noodles or rice.

Agnes J. Scott, Wilmington, Del.

SESAME CHICKEN WITH CRAB

Serves 6

½ pound crabmeat
2 eggs, beaten
½ cup mayonnaise
3 breasts of chicken, split and boned
2 cups fresh bread crumbs

½ teaspoon Old Bay seasoning
Salt and pepper
Sesame seeds
1 egg, beaten
Flour
Butter

Combine crabmeat, eggs, and mayonnaise. Place crab mixture on back of chicken breasts; tuck chicken and skin into a roll and refrigerate until firm. Roll chicken in crumbs combined with Old Bay seasoning, salt, and pepper. Dip in egg and flour and sauté chicken in butter until done. Sprinkle sesame seeds on top. Serve with a gravy made with mushrooms and Madeira wine.

Chef Jean Scott, Waterworks Cafe, Wilmington, Del.

'76 CHICKEN STICKS

Serves 6

12 chicken drumsticks—legs without thighs
½ cup flour, divided
1 egg, beaten
1 tablespoon sherry
1 teaspoon MSG

1 teaspoon salt
½ teaspoon ground ginger
¼ teaspoon pepper
½ cup pecans, finely chopped
¼ cup sesame seeds
½ cup corn oil

Dust chicken with 2 tablespoons flour. Mix egg and wine. Dip chicken in mixture. Mix together next 6 ingredients and remaining flour. Coat chicken with this mixture. Brown the chicken pieces in oil. Cook over medium heat until fork tender.

Second prize winner in the 1976 Delmarva Chicken Cooking Contest.

Ernestine Edwards, Lewes, Del.

SWEET n' SMOKY CHICKEN

Serves 4

1 Perdue chicken, cut into
  serving pieces
1 large onion, sliced
½ teaspoon hickory-smoked salt
⅛ teaspoon pepper

¼ cup catsup
¼ cup maple syrup
2 tablespoons cider vinegar
1 tablespoon prepared mustard

Preheat oven to 350°. Remove giblets and leave fat; rinse chicken, pat dry. Place onion slices in bottom of 8- by 12-inch baking pan. Place chicken in single layer, skin side up, on top of onion. Sprinkle with hickory salt and pepper. In a small bowl, combine remaining ingredients; pour over chicken. Bake, uncovered, about 1 hour or until juice runs clear when meat is pierced with a fork.

Courtesy of Frank Perdue, Salisbury, Md.

CHICKEN OR TURKEY CASSEROLE

Serves 6

3½ to 4 cups of chicken meat,
  cooked and chopped
8 ounces Velveeta cheese slices,
  coarsely shredded
10¾-ounce can cream of chicken
  soup

1 cup chicken broth
¼ cup melted margarine
8-ounce package herb stuffing
  mix

In a 9- by 13-inch baking dish or 2½-quart casserole, make one layer of chicken. Top with a layer of cheese, more chicken, and a final layer of cheese. Mix cream of chicken soup and chicken broth together to make a gravy. Pour over chicken and cheese.

Melt margarine and mix in stuffing mix. Put this on top of casserole. Cover dish with foil. Bake at 350° for 20 minutes. Remove foil and continue to bake for 15 minutes more.

Doris Helmick, Claymont, Del.

DOVES

Serves 4

Black pepper   Butter
Curry   4 doves

Make a mixture of equal parts black pepper and curry. Melt butter. Arrange the doves in a casserole, breast-side down, brush melted butter on the inside of the doves, then sprinkle with pepper-curry mixture. Turn doves over and repeat on the breast side. Turn doves again and bake at 325° for about 15 minutes; turn doves over and bake until they begin to look crispy. Put doves very briefly under the broiler to crisp the skins. Doves should be cooked until juice runs clear.

I usually serve them with Chicken Rice-A-Roni, but wild rice is much better.

The men shoot the doves during the hunting season in the fall, then bring them home and clean them. They are frozen until we get enough for a meal. Then I clean them again after they have been thawed and pick off any remaining feathers.

Judith Roberts, Lewes, Del.

MERMAID TAVERN

SAWIN

PICKLED DUCK WITH MUSTARD SAUCE

Serves 10

2 ducks, 4½ to 5 pounds each
⅔ cups water
1⅓ cups salt plus 1½ tablespoons
2 cups sugar
2 large bunches parsley

2 bay leaves
Pepper to taste
2 cups chicken stock
Kale and gooseberries for garnish

Marinate ducks overnight in mixture of water, salt, and sugar. Before cooking, drain and wash. Fill cavities with parsley and bay leaves. Season with pepper. Place in large roasting pan and roast at 450° for 15 minutes. Add stock to depth of ¼ inch; lift ducks so stock can run underneath. Continue cooking 30 to 35 minutes, adding stock, if necessary. Cool 15 minutes.

Slice breasts and thighs thinly so that there are a total of 20 slices. Reserve remaining duck for other uses. To reheat, wrap stacked slices of duck in foil and place in warm oven for 20 minutes. Serve with mustard sauce and red cabbage and garnish with kale and gooseberries.

MUSTARD SAUCE

Yield: approximately ⅓ cup

2 egg yolks
⅔ teaspoon red wine vinegar
⅔ teaspoon mushroom (or plain)
   soy sauce
3 teaspoons sugar

2 teaspoons Dijon mustard
1 tablespoon plus 1 teaspoon
   vegetable oil
2 teaspoons port or Madeira
2 teaspoons cognac

Place first 5 ingredients in a blender. Run blender 20 seconds, then add oil slowly until mixture thickens. Remove from blender. Fold in port or Madeira and cognac. Serve with duck.

Graciously submitted by the wife of the Swedish Ambassador, Countess Ulla Wachtmeister, Washington, D. C.

PHEASANT SUPREME WITH SAUCE POIVADE

Serves 4

2 12- to 14-ounce pheasants
   (wild or farm raised)
Salt
Pepper
Butter
2 cups white wine
1 cup water
1 carrot
1 stalk celery
1 small onion
10¾-ounce can chicken broth

1 cup currant jelly
1 cup sweet Marsala
1 tablespoon cornstarch
3 tablespoons water
Salt
Freshly ground black pepper
4 shallots
½ pound mushrooms
¼ loaf thin sliced white bread
1 teaspoon dried basil
1 tablespoon dried tarragon

Cut the legs, thighs, wings, and backbone from the pheasant, but do not split the breast. Rub pheasant parts well with salt, pepper, and a little butter. Store in refrigerator until ready to roast.

Preheat oven to 450°. Cut as much meat as possible from the legs and thighs. Reserve the bones. Put 1 cup of the white wine and 1 cup of water in a pot. Add dark meat; simmer until tender, about 20 to 30 minutes. Meanwhile, chop the bones in half. Chop the carrot, celery, and onion. Put bones in roasting pan; scatter chopped vegetables around them. Roast the bones until brown.

When dark meat is tender, remove from liquid (reserve liquid) and let meat cool. Add browned bones and vegetables to liquid and simmer on the top of the stove for approximately 45 minutes. You should have about 2 cups of stock. If necessary, add 1 can of chicken broth or 1 cup of water flavored with 1 chicken bouillon cube. Strain stock and set aside.

In another saucepan, melt the currant jelly with the Marsala. Add the stock and bring to a boil. Dissolve cornstarch in water and stir into sauce to thicken it. Season this sauce with the freshly ground pepper and salt. Dice shallots and mushrooms. Cook in the remaining cup of white wine until tender.

Cut the bread into small cubes. Melt the butter and sauté the bread cubes until golden brown. Dice the cooked dark meat. Add to mushrooms and shallots. Stir in croutons. Season with basil, tarragon, salt, and pepper. Recipe may be prepared up until this point. Refrigerate for a few hours.

Place pheasant breasts in a roasting pan and cook in a 450° oven for about 15 minutes (for medium rare pheasant). Do not overcook or meat will be too dry. Remove from oven; let sit for 15 minutes. Cut meat from bones and slice. Reheat shallot-mushroom dressing and sauce if necessary. On each serving plate, layer breast meat, dressing, then top with sauce.

Original recipe of Karl Haring, executive chef, Wilmington Club, 1954-1979, submitted by Executive Chef Ed Hennessy and Sous Chef Tom Howell.

WILMINGTON CLUB
CIRCA 1850

PHEASANT IN CREAM

Serves 6

2 pheasants, quartered
2 10¾-ounce cans cream of
  chicken soup
1 cup white wine
2½ tablespoons Worcestershire
  sauce

1½ teaspoons salt
⅔ cup chopped onion
½ teaspoon minced garlic
2 6-ounce cans mushroom
  crowns
Paprika

Arrange pheasants in baking pan. Mix other ingredients, except paprika, and pour over the birds. Sprinkle paprika over the top and bake at 350° for 1½ hours. Baste often during cooking and sprinkle more paprika after the last basting. If pheasants are large, bake about 2 hours.

This is excellent served with wild rice, and chicken may be substituted for the pheasants.

A favorite of Delaware's seventy-second governor, Sherman W. Tribbitt, 1973-1977, submitted by Jeanne W. Tribbitt

SEAFOOD

CRAB IMPERIAL

Serves 6

4 tablespoons butter or
   margarine
4 tablespoons flour
2 cups milk
1 teaspoon salt
⅛ teaspoon pepper
½ teaspoon celery salt
Dash cayenne (red pepper)

1 egg yolk, beaten
2 tablespoons sherry
1 cup soft bread crumbs
1 pound crab flakes
1 teaspoon minced parsley
1 teaspoon minced onion
¼ cup buttered crumbs
Paprika

Melt butter or margarine; add flour and blend. Gradually add milk and seasonings and cook over low heat, stirring constantly until thickened. Gradually add egg yolk and cook 2 minutes more. Remove from heat; add sherry, soft bread crumbs, crabmeat, parsley, and onion. Gently mix and pour into well greased casserole. Top with buttered crumbs. Sprinkle with paprika. Bake in hot oven (400°) for 20 to 25 minutes.

You will be proud to serve this dish.

Elbert N. Carvel, Delaware's sixty-fifth and sixty-ninth governor, 1949-1953, 1961-1965

IMPERIAL CRAB CAKES

Serves 4 to 6

2½ tablespoons margarine
4 tablespoons flour
1 cup milk
1 pound crabmeat
3 slices bacon, fried and
  crumbled (reserve fat)
¼ cup green pepper, chopped
1 egg, beaten

1 tablespoon mayonnaise
1 tablespoon prepared mustard
1 tablespoon Worcestershire
  sauce
1 teaspoon salt
⅛ teaspoon pepper
Bread crumbs

Melt margarine, add flour, and stir until bubbly. Gradually add milk; stir until thickened. To the white sauce, add crabmeat, bacon, green pepper, egg, mayonnaise, mustard, Worcestershire sauce, salt, and pepper. Shape into cakes and coat with bread crumbs. Refrigerate crab cakes one hour before cooking. When ready to cook, heat reserved bacon fat and fry crab cakes until golden brown.

Carolyn Thoroughgood, Newark, Del.

SAMBO'S CRAB CAKES

Serves 4 to 6

1 pound crabmeat	*1 tablespoon horseradish*
3 tablespoons self-rising flour	*2 teaspoons prepared mustard*
1 egg	*1 tablespoon Old Bay seasoning*

Mix ingredients well. Form into cakes and deep fry at 350° until golden brown.

Gaining in popularity since the opening in 1953, Sambo's is well-known for its Delaware blue crab dishes.

Elva Murray
Sambo's Tavern, Leipsic, Del.

SAVORY CRAB MEAT DINNER

Serves 2 to 4

2 slices white bread
¼ cup milk
1½ cups crabmeat
¼ cup plus 2 tablespoons melted
    butter
¼ teaspoon herb seasoning
Dash of cayenne
Dash of paprika

Dash of pepper
2½ pound chicken, split in half
2 tablespoons soft butter
½ teaspoon salt
¼ cup sherry
2 tablespoons catsup
¼ teaspoon garlic salt

Cut bread into cubes; add milk to bread and toss until all milk is absorbed. Blend crabmeat and 2 tablespoons melted butter with the seasonings. Add crabmeat to the bread and milk mixture and toss lightly.

Preheat oven to 350°. Rub 2 halves of chicken with 2 table-spoons soft butter, sprinkle with salt and paprika. Place chicken halves, skin side up in baking pan. Bake 35 minutes. Combine ¼ cup melted butter, sherry, catsup, and garlic salt. Spoon 1 to 2 tablespoons of butter mixture on each chicken half; cook until tender. Turn chicken over; fill breast cavities with crabmeat mixture. Bake 30 to 35 minutes longer, basting with butter sauce.

This delicious dish was a 1968 winner in the Crisfield, Maryland, Annual Crab Cooking Contest.

Corinthia Blizzard, Seaford, Del.

SIMPLE CRAB QUICHE

Yield: 1 9-inch quiche, serves 6 to 8

Pastry for 9-inch quiche
6-ounce can lump crabmeat or
  fresh crabmeat
4 ounces shredded Swiss or
  mozzarella cheese
⅓ cup minced onions
1 tablespoon minced fresh
  parsley

4 eggs, beaten
2 cups half and half
½ teaspoon salt
⅛ teaspoon red pepper or 3 to 4
  drops red pepper sauce
Parsley sprigs (optional)

Preheat oven to 425°. Line a 9-inch quiche dish or deep dish pie plate with pastry. Trim excess around edges. Prick bottom and sides of pastry with a fork. Bake for 5 minutes. Cool.

Sprinkle crabmeat, cheese, onions, and parsley evenly into pastry shell. Combine next 4 ingredients, stirring well; pour over crabmeat mixture. Bake at 325° for 35 to 40 minutes or until set. Garnish with parsley sprigs, if desired.

Emma H. Craft, Dover, Del.

POOR MAN'S LOBSTER

Serves 4

¼ cup cider vinegar
2 cups water
1 teaspoon salt
1 teaspoon seafood seasoning

1 teaspoon celery seeds
1 pound frozen haddock
Melted butter

Bring first 5 ingredients to a boil in a skillet. Add frozen haddock and cook 10 minutes on each side. May have to cook a little longer if haddock is not completely cooked. Drain, serve with melted butter.

Looking for an inexpensive dinner? This is the way to go.

Arlene Martin, Claymont, Del.

PILOT BOAT BREAKFAST

Serves 3

6 large potatoes
6 skinned cod fillets (use fresh
    cod if possible, but any lean
    fish such as striped bass or
    weakfish can be substituted)

6 hard-cooked eggs
1 pound broiled bacon
2 onions, diced
Salt and pepper
Melted butter

Peel potatoes and boil until done, about 20 minutes. Bake or steam fish until done (about 10 minutes). Dice potatoes and cover with cooked fish. Crumble bacon and chop eggs. Sprinkle bacon pieces and chopped eggs on fish. Add raw onions to taste and pour melted butter over all. Add salt and pepper to taste. An easy, quick, nutritious meal.

Years ago this was a meal prepared for the Delaware Bay pilots before they took command of a vessel heading up Delaware Bay. It can be breakfast, lunch, or dinner—any way it is truly an excellent, hearty, rich meal.

University of Delaware, Delaware Sea Grant College Program

DAD CARPER'S BROILED SPANISH MACKEREL

Serves 4

3 to 5 pounds mackerel
¼ pound of butter

½ cup French dressing
Salt and pepper

Wipe slices of mackerel dry. In a baking pan, melt butter; stir in French dressing. Add mackerel. Broil, turning frequently until brown.

"A delicious quick seafood dish!"

Jean Carper, Seminole, Fla. (mother of U. S. Congressman Tom Carper)

BAKED ROCK FISH

Serves 4

3 to 5 pounds rock fish
Salt and pepper to taste
Paprika
Juice of 1 lemon
1½ cups bread crumbs

2 teaspoons chopped onion
½ cup celery
2 tablespoons parsley
2 tablespoons butter

Clean and remove backbone from fish, leaving pocket. Season with salt, pepper, and paprika. Pour lemon juice over fish.

Mix bread crumbs, onion, celery, parsley, and butter together. Fill fish with dressing and sew together. Bake at 350° 1 hour or longer.

Charles Wesley Atkins, chef to Delaware's seventieth governor, Charles L. Terry, 1965-1969

BAKED SHAD

Serves 4

4 to 5 pounds shad
3 tablespoons butter, melted

3 tablespoons cider vinegar
Salt and lemon pepper

Rub cleaned shad inside and out with melted butter and vinegar. Sprinkle with salt and lemon pepper. The shad roe may be placed in the cavity, if desired. Wrap and seal shad in foil. Bake in a covered pan at 275° for 6 to 8 hours. The bones will disintegrate as the fish bakes.

University of Delaware Sea Grant Marine Advisory Service

ELEVEN FISH ROASTED ON A PLANK

Eleven fish was the name the Dutch settlers gave shad because it arrived on the eleventh of March. The first shad was presented to the governor. As it became more common it became known as the "poor man's fish." The rich ate it on the sly. Adams, our second president, was a shad man. The Dutch cooked their shad on a birch plank over the coals of a wood fire.

SWEET AND SOUR SHARK

Serves 4

1½ pounds shark
½ cup flour
6 tablespoons vegetable oil
1 teaspoon salt
Pepper
1 large green pepper, cut into
   ¼-inch rings
1 large carrot, sliced thinly
2 celery stalks, sliced
1 scallion, sliced

20-ounce can sliced pineapple
Water
½ to 1 cup sugar
2 tablespoons cornstarch
¾ cup cider vinegar
1 tablespoon soy sauce
¼ teaspoon ginger
1 chicken or vegetable bouillon
   cube

Preheat oven to 350°. Wash shark, cut in 1-inch by 2-inch pieces, and pat dry with paper towels. Dredge shark in flour. Heat oil in large skillet. Add shark, a few pieces at a time, and cook quickly on all sides. Remove to shallow roasting pan and sprinkle with salt and pepper. Layer sliced vegetables on shark.

Drain the pineapple by pouring juice into 2-cup measure. Add water to make 1¼ cups. Put pineapple slices on vegetables. In a medium saucepan, combine sugar, cornstarch, pineapple juice, vinegar, soy sauce, ginger, and bouillon cube. Bring to boil, stirring constantly; boil 2 minutes. Pour over shark, vegetables, and pineapple. Bake, uncovered, 30 minutes. Serve with fluffy rice.

Doris Hicks, University of Delaware Marine Grant Department

BLOCK HOUSE
at Robinson House
CLAYMONT, DE

MOLDED TUNA

Serves 12

3 6½-ounce cans tuna
4 hard-boiled eggs, chopped
1 cup celery, chopped

2 envelopes unflavored gelatin
½ cup cold water
3 cups mayonnaise

Combine first three ingredients. Sprinkle gelatin in cold water in a small cup. Put cup in boiling water so gelatin dissolves. Stir gelatin in mayonnaise. Add tuna mixture. Blend well. Pour in 13- by 9-inch or 9- by 5- by 3-inch oblong pan. Chill.

Serve on lettuce cups with fresh peas and hot rolls.

Kathy Edwards, Laurel, Del.

POLYNESIAN TUNA BAKE

Serves 4 to 6

⅔ *cup chopped green pepper*
10¾-*ounce can tomato soup*
2 *tablespoons brown sugar*
1 *tablespoon onion, minced*
1 *teaspoon lemon rind, grated*
3 *tablespoons lemon juice*
2 *teaspoons soy sauce*
2 6½-*ounce cans tuna, drained,*
   flaked

1 *cup flour*
1½ *teaspoons baking powder*
¼ *teaspoon salt*
½ *cup milk*
2 *tablespoons oil*
1 *teaspoon sesame seed*

Mix together first 8 ingredients in a saucepan. Simmer covered for 10 to 15 minutes. Pour into 2 quart casserole.

Preheat oven to 375°. Make biscuits by combining flour, baking powder, and salt. Add milk and oil. Stir until well mixed. Drop biscuits by teaspoonfuls on hot tuna mixture. Sprinkle with sesame seed. Bake for 25 to 30 minutes, or until brown.

This dish was a favorite of the late Harvey Stahl, Claymont's first school superintendent.

Miriam Stahl, Claymont, Del.

OYSTERS WITH SCALLOPED CORN

Serves 6

2 cups canned corn, creamed
  or whole kernels
2 eggs, beaten
2 tablespoons butter
2 tablespoons flour
½ cup cream

1 teaspoon salt
8-ounce can oysters and
  liquor
6 or 8 soda crackers, slightly
  broken

Preheat oven to 350°. Mix all ingredients and pour into a well-oiled 2-quart casserole. Sprinkle with more cracker crumbs. Bake in oven until inserted knife comes out clean. Casserole may be set in a pan of water in oven to bake like a custard.

A great company dish.

Thelma Good, Malvern, Pa., formerly of Claymont, Del.

OYSTER FRITTERS

Yield: 18

1½ pints stewing oysters, or 2
  8-ounce cans
⅔ cup flour
1 egg
½ teaspoon salt

3 dashes pepper
2 tablespoons cream
1⅓ teaspoons baking powder
1 rounded tablespoon shortening

Drain liquor from oysters, stir in half of flour gradually. Add unbeaten egg, salt, and pepper. Stir in remaining flour. Add cream. Add baking powder. Stir all ingredients slowly until batter and oysters are creamy and blended. In an iron skillet melt shortening. Fry oyster batter by tablespoonfuls. Brown nicely on both sides.

Mrs. Emma C. Donovan, Odessa, Del.

PAELLA
Filled with Fruits of the Sea
Serves 12

1 cup olive oil
1 pound ham, cut in ½-inch cubes
6 sausages (Chorizos or hot Italian) thinly sliced, casing removed
2 3-pound frying chickens, cut up or 6 to 8 drumsticks, 6 to 8 thighs, and 2 whole deboned frying chicken breasts
1 teaspoon poultry seasoning
Salt and pepper
3 cloves garlic, chopped fine
1 large Bermuda onion, chopped
1 large green pepper, chopped
2 celery stalks, chopped

4 cups uncooked rice
2 packages Bijol or saffron (½ teaspoon, ground)
2 cups canned tomatoes
1 teaspoon salt
2 4-ounce cans pimentos, drained and chopped
4 cups chicken broth
Juice of one lemon
2 pounds raw shrimp, shelled
6 lobster tails (6 ounces each), cut in half (optional)
10-ounce package frozen peas
2 dozen well-scrubbed small clams (or use canned clams)
6 oysters in shells (optional)

In olive oil, brown ham and sausages; remove ham and sausages, drain. Layer meat in an 8-quart casserole or a large roasting pan. Sprinkle chicken with poultry seasoning, salt, and pepper. Brown chicken in hot olive oil; place chicken, except drumsticks, on ham and sausage.

Preheat oven to 350°. Cook garlic, onion, green pepper, and celery in pan drippings; stir in rice, saffron, tomatoes, salt, and pimento; pour into casserole. Combine broth and lemon juice; pour over casserole. Bury drumsticks vertically in rice leaving bone ends sticking up. Put paper frills over bone ends. Bake uncovered in oven for 15 minutes. Add shrimp and lobster (removed from shell). Bake about an hour or until rice is tender, stirring now and then. A little more broth may be added if rice appears dry. Add peas, stirring lightly to blend. Push clams into rice, mouth side up. While paella is baking, clean oysters by soaking in salted water for 10 minutes, drain and repeat twice. Add oysters on top of paella. Cover and bake 15 minutes or until clam shells pop open.

Serve with a mixed salad, Galleta (Spanish water crackers), and Brillante Rosada (pink Spanish wine). For dessert serve flan (egg custard with a burnt almond topping).

Quite a challenge and expensive if using lobster, but you will never regret it.

C. R. (Grampop) Adamson

SEAFOOD PUFF

Serves 6

10 ounces frozen shrimp
3 eggs, separated
1 tablespoon all-purpose flour
Pinch of ground nutmeg
1 cup mayonnaise
1 tablespoon butter or margarine, softened

¼ teaspoon salt
¼ teaspoon pepper
¼ cup plus 1 tablespoon grated Parmesan cheese

Cook seafood according to package directions; drain well. Beat egg yolks; add flour, mixing well. Stir in nutmeg, mayonnaise, butter, salt, pepper, and Parmesan. Add seafood, mixing lightly.

Beat egg whites at room temperature until stiff but not dry; gently fold into seafood mixture. Pour into a lightly buttered 9-inch-square baking dish. Bake at 350° for 30 minutes. Cut into squares to serve.

Delicious with lobster and crabmeat. Especially good with crabmeat, and we are so close to the crabmeat capital of the world!

Caroline Detjen, Wilmington, Del.

SCALLOPS

Serves 6

1 pound scallops
¼ cup all-purpose flour
2 tablespoons butter or
   margarine
2 tablespoons olive oil

1 tomato, coarsely diced
1 tablespoon parsley flakes
1 tablespoon lemon juice
¼ teaspoon garlic powder

Cut scallops in half, dust with flour, sauté in oil until golden brown. Add tomato, parsley, lemon, and garlic. Cook until tomato is heated and scallops are tender. Serve with lemon wedge.

The house which has become the Corner Cupboard Inn was built in 1926 by James Hall Anderson, a former lieutenant governor of Delaware. It became an inn some time around 1934 and has continued as such to the present day.

The Corner Cupboard Inn, Rehoboth Beach, Del.

SHRIMP AND CRABMEAT CASSEROLE

Serves 12

2 9¾-ounce cans frozen
   shrimp soup
2 tablespoons mayonnaise
1 teaspoon Worcestershire sauce
1 large green pepper, diced
1 stalk celery, diced
1 medium onion, diced

1 cup potato chips, crumbled
10-ounce package frozen crabmeat,
   drained and cleaned
1 pound shrimp, cooked
8- to 10-ounce can chop suey
   vegetables, drained

Preheat oven to 375°. Thaw soup and mix with mayonnaise and Worcestershire sauce. Add pepper, celery, and onion. Mix together ½ cup crumbled potato chips and crabmeat. To this mixture add cooked shrimp and Chinese vegetables. Combine all thoroughly and pour into 9- by 13-inch baking dish. Top with remaining ½ cup crumbled potato chips. Bake for 45 minutes.

Serve over rice or Chinese noodles.

"A succulent combination of crab and shrimp."

Marilou Clifford

SHRIMP CREOLE

Serves 4

⅔ cup vegetable oil
½ cup flour
1¾ cups thinly sliced scallions
⅓ cup chopped celery
1 cup chopped onion
½ cup chopped green pepper
4 teaspoons finely minced garlic
3 tablespoons finely minced fresh
  parsley
1-pound can tomatoes, drained
8-ounce can tomato sauce
1 tablespoon minced chives
4 tablespoons dry red wine
4 whole bay leaves, crushed

6 whole allspice or 2 teaspoons
  crushed allspice
2 whole cloves
2 teaspoons salt
¾ teaspoon black pepper
½ teaspoon cayenne pepper
¼ teaspoon chili powder
¼ teaspoon mace
¼ teaspoon dried basil
½ teaspoon dried thyme
4 teaspoons lemon juice
2 cups water
2 pounds whole fresh shrimp,
  peeled and deveined

In a heavy 6 to 8 quart pot, heat the oil, gradually add the flour, stirring constantly. Cook over low heat, stirring constantly until a medium brown roux is formed. Remove from heat and add the fresh vegetables and parsley. Mix well with the roux, return to low heat and cook, stirring constantly. When the vegetables begin to brown, mix in tomatoes and tomato sauce. Add the remaining ingredients, except the shrimp, and mix well. When the mixture begins to boil, reduce heat and simmer for 45 minutes. Add the shrimp, bring to boil again, cover, reduce heat, and simmer for 20 minutes. Allow to stand, covered, at room temperature about 10 minutes before serving.

Hint: it is best to get all the ingredients measured and chopped prior to beginning cooking. Receipe can be easily doubled.

A delightful, different dish.

Capt. William Dalson, U.S.A.F., San Antonio, Tex., formerly of Claymont, Del.

MRS. RUSSELL W. PETERSON'S "SEAFORD" SHRIMP

Serves 4

4 cups cooked shrimp, fresh
  (about 2 pounds)
4 tablespoons lemon juice
1 teaspoon salt
1 teaspoon paprika
1 teaspoon dry mustard
½ cup butter

4 tablespoons flour
¼ teaspoon white pepper
2 cups half and half or light
  cream
1 tablespoon sherry
1½ cups coarse buttered bread
  crumbs

Preheat oven to 350°. Mix shrimp, lemon juice, salt, paprika, and mustard. Let stand, covered, in refrigerator several hours to blend flavors. Melt butter. Remove from heat, blend in flour, salt, and pepper. Gradually stir in cream, mixing until smooth and well blended. Add sherry. Cook over low heat, stirring constantly until thickened and smooth. Add shrimp, pour into buttered 9- by 13-inch casserole. Cover with bread crumbs. Bake for 30 to 35 minutes, or until top is golden brown and sauce bubbles.

Because this is so rich, I like to serve it over melba toast rather than rice.

Lillian T. Peterson, Delaware's First Lady, 1973–1977

SESAME SHRIMP AND ASPARAGUS

Serves 6

1½ pounds asparagus
2 small onions
1½ pounds shrimp
1 tablespoon sesame seeds

⅓ cup vegetable oil
4 teaspoons soy sauce
1¼ teaspoons salt

Diagonally cut asparagus into 2-inch pieces. Slice onions; shell and devein shrimp. In 10- to 12-inch skillet (or wok), toast sesame seeds over medium heat until golden, stirring and shaking pan occasionally. Remove seeds and set aside. Heat oil in same pan to medium high heat. Cook asparagus, onions, and shrimp until shrimp are pink and vegetables are tender crisp; about 5 minutes. Stir in sesame seeds, soy sauce, and salt until just mixed.

This delicious recipe was given to me by Kathy Deckard.

Mary Fifer Fennemore, Wyoming, Del.

CRABMEAT DRESSING

Serves 4 to 5

6½-ounce can crabmeat
2 eggs, beaten
2 tablespoons melted butter
½ small onion, diced
¼ medium green pepper, diced
½ cup diced celery

¼ cup chopped parsley
¾ cup fine corn bread crumbs
1 slice white bread, crumbled
½ teaspoon Worcestershire sauce
¼ teaspoon dry mustard
Salt and pepper

Mix all ingredients and put in shallow baking pan. Bake at 400° about 25 minutes. Cut in squares and serve.

Can also be stuffed in fish, which can be baked or fried.

Ruth Harris, Georgetown, Del.

PAN-FRIED TROUT WRAPPED IN BACON

Serves 4

4 *whole trout (about ½ pound*
   each) cleaned and washed
Salt
Freshly ground black pepper
Milk
Flour
2 tablespoons olive oil

¼ cup butter
8 slices thick-sliced bacon
4 lemon wedges
½ cup softened butter
4 tablespoons parsley, finely
   chopped
Lemon juice

Dry trout thoroughly both inside and out. Season generously with salt and pepper. Dip trout in milk. Shake off excess, then coat with flour, patting it on gently so it sticks to the skin.

Melt 1 tablespoon of the oil and 2 tablespoons of butter in each of two skillets. When hot and sizzling, place two trout in each pan. Cook over moderate heat for 8 to 10 minutes, turning trout carefully with a spatula after 4 minutes.

Transfer trout to baking sheet. Remove skins and cover fish with strips of bacon, cut to fit. Broil until bacon is browned and heated through.

Make parsley butter by combining butter with parsley, blending well. Season generously with lemon juice, salt, and pepper. Chill until firm.

Garnish cooked fish with lemon wedges and serve with parsley butter.

Helen Weeks, Northfield, N.J.

WARREN'S STATION CRABCAKES

Serves about 40

10 pounds fresh crabmeat
5 cups mayonnaise
1 cup mustard
2 tablespoons pepper
1 tablespoon spicy seafood
    seasoning
3 ounces Worcestershire sauce

1 tablespoon MSG
20 slices stale bread
20 eggs
1 pound butter, melted
Oil
Dry bread crumbs

Cube bread. Mix all ingredients together, except crabmeat and bread, in extra large bowl. Add crabmeat and bread cubes with dry bread crumbs and form into patties. Fry in hot grease until dark brown or bake in oven at 350° for 15 minutes.

A favorite of those who dine at Warren's Station.

Jeff Mumford, Fenwick Island, Del.

SEAFOOD SAUCES

COCKTAIL SAUCE

¼ tablespoon seafood seasoning
1 tablespoon lemon juice
½ tablespoon salt
½ cup catsup
¼ cup chili sauce

Mix well and serve with any seafood.

Great to top crab and shrimp.

TARTARE SAUCE

1 cup mayonnaise
1 tablespoon minced pickles
1 tablespoon minced parsley
1 tablespoon minced onion
1 tablespoon minced capers

Mix ingredients thoroughly and serve cold.

George W. Taylor, Sun City, Cal., formerly Sussex County, Del.

VEGETABLES

EDEN HILL
FARM - DOVER

EASY ASPARAGUS CASSEROLE

Serves 6 to 8

8½-ounce can green asparagus
8½-ounce can of peas
4 hard-boiled eggs, sliced
½ cup slivered blanched almonds

10¾-ounce can cream of
 mushroom soup
¼ cup milk
12 cheese crackers, crushed

Put first 4 ingredients in 2-quart casserole in layers. Heat soup and milk and pour over ingredients in casserole. Put crushed crackers on top. Bake at 300° for about 1 hour.

Asparagus, originally called sparrow grass, was first brought to America from Holland in 1786.

Vera Davis, Delaware State senator, 1948-1952

HONEY BAKED BEANS

Serves 6 to 8

2 cups navy beans
¼ pound salt pork
½ cup honey
1 teaspoon salt

1 teaspoon dry mustard
1 teaspoon ginger
1 tablespoon finely chopped
  onion

Soak washed navy beans in water overnight. Cover with fresh water and simmer until tender. Save this water. Cut salt pork in half, placing half of pork in bottom of bean pot. Add beans, cover with water drained from beans, and add the remaining ingredients. Stir. Add remaining salt pork to top of beans. Cover and bake 6 hours. Uncover bean pot during last hour. Add more water if needed.

My husband raised bees for a hobby and we usually cooked with honey for that reason.

Martha Wooster Rogers, Greene, N. Y.

JIM'S BAKED BEANS

Serves 6 to 10

½ cup dark brown sugar,
   packed
Catsup
1 teaspoon crazy or seasoned salt
½ medium onion, chopped fine
1 to 2 teaspoons yellow prepared
   mustard

15¾-ounce can kidney beans
15¾-ounce can pork and beans
   or vegetarian beans
16-ounce can pinto beans or
   15-ounce can navy beans
Bacon

Mix together brown sugar and catsup to make a thick puree. Stir in salt, onion, and mustard. Let stand 5 to 10 minutes.

Drain the canned beans, wash and redrain them. Note total weight and adjust sauce measurements accordingly. Stir in sauce. Either put in a Crockpot and cook for 8 hours on Slow, or place in a casserole and bake at 300° for 8 hours, adding water occasionally to keep beans moist.

In a skillet, brown enough bacon strips to cover the top of the casserole; bacon should be light brown, but not crisp. Drain bacon. One half hour before beans are cooked, place browned bacon on top of beans and finish cooking.

Jim Johnson, Seneca, S. C., formerly of Claymont, Del.

CUBAN BLACK BEANS
(Frijoles Negros)

Serves 6

1 pound black beans
1 large onion
1 large green pepper
4 bay leaves
½ cup olive oil

1 teaspoon garlic powder
2 teaspoons oregano
2 teaspoons cumin
2 to 3 tablespoons catsup
Dash of salt

Soak beans overnight. Drain. Cook beans until soft. Drain. Saute onion, green pepper, and bay leaves in oil. Add garlic powder, oregano, cumin, catsup, and salt. Remove bay leaves. Pour mixture over black beans. Stir and serve.

Note: soak up black bean spills right away. The liquid stains—especially if it spills on Formica.

Vary quantities according to number of guests to be served. Be generous, all will be eaten.

JoAnn Swafford, Wilmington, Del.

RED CABBAGE

Serves 10

2 medium heads red cabbage
5 to 6 tablespoons butter
3 tablespoons plus 2 teaspoons
  black currant preserves,
  pureed

4 tablespoons red wine

Slice five center slices from each cabbage, ¼- to ½ inch thick. Sauté in hot butter about 3 minutes, until barely soft, so cabbage slices keep their shape. Stir in preserves and wine to glaze cabbage.

A Swedish accompaniment to Pickled Duck with Mustard Sauce.

Countess Ulla Wachmeister, Washington, D. C.

SKILLET CABBAGE

Serves 4

4 cups shredded cabbage
1 green pepper, cut in strips
2 cups diced celery
2 large onions, thinly sliced
2 tomatoes, chopped

¼ cup bacon fat
2 teaspoons sugar
1 teaspoon seasoned salt
Pepper to taste

Combine all ingredients in skillet. Cover. Cook 15 minutes over medium heat (or longer).

Serve for lunch with rye bread. A family favorite for years.

Linda Alford, Barbourville, Ky.

UKRANIAN NOODLES AND CABBAGE

Serves 4

2 cups cooked egg noodles
1 tablespoon melted butter
¼ cup grated Cheddar cheese
¼ teaspoon salt
2 cups shredded cabbage

½ small onion, chopped
2 tablespoons butter
Salt and pepper
¼ cup buttered bread crumbs

Combine the cooked noodles with the butter, cheese, and salt. Cook cabbage briefly with onion in the butter until wilted but crisp. Season to taste with salt and pepper. Arrange the noodles and cabbage in alternate layers in a baking dish. Top with buttered bread crumbs. Bake at 350° for 30 to 35 minutes.

Sophie Szotkiewicz, Wilmington, Del.

HOLIDAY BAKED CORN

Serves 4

1 cup dried sweet corn   *1 teaspoon salt*
3 cups cold milk   *2 tablespoons sugar*
2 tablespoons butter, melted   *2 eggs, well beaten*

Grind dried corn in blender or food chopper. Add remaining ingredients thoroughly. Bake in buttered casserole at 375° for 50 minutes.

Mary Cartwright

THE PRACTICAL FARMER INN... CLAYMONT

BLACK-EYED PEAS FOR NEW YEAR'S DAY

Serves 4

1-pound package black-eyed
  peas
¼ pound salt pork (trim off
  rind)
1 onion, cut up or chopped

2 small potatoes, diced
½ stick margarine or 4
  tablespoons solid vegetable
  shortening

Put 5 or 6 slices salt pork in pan and wash it. Put it in a pan and cook.

Place the peas in a pot and wash them. Cover with cold water. Bring to a boil and cook for 10 minutes, turn the fire off and let stand with the lid on for about 30 minutes. Drain. Add the peas to the fat meat and add onion. Cook at least 1 hour or until done.

Add potatoes (and spoon dumplings, if desired). If stock isn't rich enough, add ½ stick of margarine or vegetable shortening.

Variation: You can add shoepeg white corn to mixture the last 10 minutes of cooking or substitute the fat meat with ham. This recipe is good served with good ole Delaware biscuits made from scratch, or Sussex County corn bread!

It is a tradition in Sussex County that if you eat black-eyed peas on New Year's Day, you'll have good luck all year. Black-eyed peas are served on almost every table in the area in some way at this time of the year.

Elizabeth P. Ruff, Blades, Del.

RICE PILAF

Serves 6

1 green pepper, diced
1 onion, diced
½ pound butter
1 cup rice (regular)

Dash oregano
2 cups water
4 chicken bouillon cubes

Sauté pepper and onion in butter. Add rice and brown slightly. Add oregano, water, and chicken bouillon cubes. Cover. Steam for 20 minutes until rice is cooked.

Kathleen DiBonventura, Claymont, Del.

POTATOES DELMONICO

Serves 4 to 6

¼ pound butter
3 tablespoons flour
2 teaspoons salt
¼ teaspoon pepper
1½ cups hot milk
¾ cup grated cheese (your
   selection)

4 hard-cooked eggs, sliced
4 cups potatoes, cooked, cooled,
   and sliced ¼-inch thick
Dash paprika

Melt butter, add flour and mix. Add seasonings and hot milk, a little at a time. Cook until smooth and thick; then simmer about 15 minutes. Blend ½ cup cheese into sauce. Add egg slices and potatoes. Pour into medium size, well-greased 9- by 13- by 2-inch oblong pan. Spread evenly. Sprinkle top lightly with additional ¼ cup cheese and a dash of paprika. Bake at 400° about 30 minutes. Then place under broiler until top is brown.

Serve with meat, fowl, or seafood. This is very good and substantial for a light luncheon or supper dish with a salad.

Peggy Roppolo, Chicago, Ill.

HASH BROWN POTATO CASSEROLE

Serves 8 to 10

32-ounce package frozen hash
  brown or shoestring potatoes
½ cup melted butter or
  margarine
10¾-ounce can undiluted cream
  of chicken soup
12 ounces American cheese,
  grated

8-ounce container sour cream
1 onion, chopped
2 cups crushed cornflakes
½ cup melted butter or
  margarine

Preheat oven to 350°. Place frozen potatoes in 9- by 13-inch baking dish and allow to thaw. Mix together ½ cup melted butter, soup, cheese, sour cream, and onion, and spread over potatoes. Top with crushed cornflakes and drizzle with ½ cup melted butter or margarine. Bake uncovered for 40 to 45 minutes.

So nice for a covered dish luncheon.

Mildred Furgele, Lakeville, Pa.

OVEN FRIED POTATOES

Serves 8

½ cup vegetable oil
2 tablespoons grated Parmesan
  cheese
1 teaspoon salt
½ teaspoon garlic powder
½ teaspoon paprika

¼ teaspoon coarsely ground
  black pepper
8 large unpeeled potatoes, cut
  into 8 wedges (Idaho or
  Russet)

Combine oil, cheese, salt, and seasonings. Coat a cookie sheet with small amount of this mixture. Arrange potatoes, skin side down, on cookie sheet. Brush with remainder of mixture. Bake at 375° for 45 minutes, basting occasionally.

Leftovers are great for breakfast.

Mary Jane Richter, Dover, Del.

GLORIFIED SWEET POTATOES

Serves 14 to 16

4 cups mashed sweet potatoes
  (canned or cooked fresh)
1 cup sugar
⅓ cup milk
¾ cup butter, melted
4 eggs, well beaten

½ cup whiskey or 1 teaspoon
  vanilla
½ teaspoon salt
½ teaspoon cinnamon
½ teaspoon nutmeg
Marshmallows

Place sweet potatoes in mixer bowl. Add sugar, milk, butter, and eggs. Mix, then add remaining ingredients and blend well. Spoon mixture into well-greased 2-quart casserole and bake at 300° for 30 minutes. Cover top of casserole with marshmallows, continue baking until marshmallows are browned and partially melted. Recipe may be prepared a day ahead and refrigerated until baking.

Ruth Grandel, Claymont, Del.

PEACH SWEET POTATO PUFFS

Serves 8

2 cups cooked or canned sweet
  potatoes, mashed
1 teaspoon lemon juice
2 tablespoons brown sugar
¼ teaspoon salt

2 tablespoons butter
2 tablespoons orange marmalade
  (optional)
Dash of ground cloves
8 canned peach halves

Mix together sweet potatoes, lemon juice, sugar, salt, butter, marmalade, and cloves. Whip until fluffy. Arrange peaches flat side up in greased 10- by 6- by 2-inch pan. Fill peaches with sweet potato mixture. Dot with additional butter. Bake in preheated 400° oven for 20 minutes.

Great served as a separate dish as an accompaniement to roasts, ham, or turkey. Sometimes I arrange the filled peaches around the platter the meat is served on.

Donna Campbell, Newark, Del.

SPANAKOPATA
(Spinach Pie)

Serves 12

2 (10 ounce) packages fresh
  spinach
½ pound feta cheese,
  crumbled
½ pound cottage cheese

6 eggs, beaten
¾ pound butter, melted
Salt and white pepper
¾ pound phyllo sheets

Clean spinach and place in large bowl. Add feta cheese, cottage cheese, eggs and seasonings, and mix thoroughly. Grease a 9- by 13-inch pan. Brush each of eight phyllo sheets with melted butter and place into the pan. Spread spinach mixture evenly and cover with eight more individually buttered phyllo sheets. Cover with brown paper. Bake at 350° for one hour until golden brown. Cut into diamond shapes and squares and serve hot. May be cut small for appetizer or larger for entree.

Mrs. Maurice Cannon, Bethel, Del.

CREAMED SPINACH

Serves 12

5 ounces salt pork, finely
  chopped
4 tablespoons bacon drippings
8 tablespoons onion, chopped

5 pounds frozen spinach chopped
Salt and pepper
½ cup light cream
2 teaspoons cornstarch

In a frying pan sauté salt pork until browned. In another pan sauté onions in bacon drippings. Cook and drain spinach. Add onions and salt pork. Heat cream over low heat. Sprinkle with cornstarch; stir until sauce thickens. Pour sauce over spinach.

Note: 2 bunches fresh spinach equal approximately 2 packages (12 ounces each) of frozen spinach.

Dinner Bell Inn, Dover, Del.

SPINACH PIE

Yield: 1 pie

10-ounce box frozen spinach, chopped
1 or 2 tablespoons butter or margarine
Salt and pepper

8 ounces American cheese (mild or sharp), grated
Pie crust to cover
1 egg, beaten
Butter

Preheat oven to 350°. Cook spinach according to directions, slightly undercooked. Drain cooked spinach thoroughly (must be dry). Season to taste with butter, salt, and pepper. Grease 8- by 9-inch square or 9- by 13-inch oblong casserole. Spread cooked spinach even in casserole. Sprinkle grated cheese over chopped spinach. Cover spinach and cheese mixture with pie crust, rolled thick. Brush crust with beaten egg and butter. Bake until crust is golden brown.

This is one of the delicious dishes served by the Dietetic Division to the staff of the Wilmington Medical Center, Wilmington Division.

Georgiean George, Wilmington Medical Center

BELLE'S SQUASH CASSEROLE

Serves 8

2 pounds yellow squash, sliced
1 small onion, chopped
½ green pepper, chopped
⅓ cup butter
2 eggs, slightly beaten
½ cup milk

½ cup grated sharp Cheddar
   cheese
1 teaspoon sugar
6 crackers, crumbled
Salt and pepper to taste

Cook squash in salted water until tender. Drain and set aside. Sauté onion and green pepper in butter till tender. Add to cooked squash; add eggs, milk, cheese, sugar, and ⅔ of the crushed crackers. Season with salt and pepper. Spoon into buttered casserole; top with additional crushed crackers. Bake at 325° for 1 hour.

Can be frozen before baking.

Elizabeth Young, Newark, Del.

SOUR CREAM PATTY PAN

Serves 4

2 pounds fresh Patty Pan
  squash or your favorite
  summer squash
4 tablespoons butter
2 tablespoons water
½ teaspoon basil, fresh if
  possible

1 garlic clove, mashed
Salt and pepper to taste
1 tablespoon flour
1 cup sour cream

Trim ends of washed squash. Shred coarsely, using largest holes of your grater. (You should have about 8 cups.) In a frying pan with tight-fitting lid, combine butter, water, basil, garlic, salt, and pepper. Over high heat, add the squash, mix in; then cover and cook until squash is just tender (about 5 minutes). If necessary, remove cover for the final 2 minutes, so that nearly all liquid is evaporated. Add flour, stirring in well; bring to boil. Remove pan from heat, add the sour cream, mix well and serve.

Patty Pan is a white flat squash that makes a perfect summer side dish and a favorite of the men folk.

Bernice Coulsting, Wilmington, Del.

DELAWARE SUCCOTASH

Serves 6

2 thin slices salt pork
Water
1 pint shelled (2 pounds
  unshelled) lima beans (or 1
  package, 2 cups yield, frozen,
  thawed lima beans)
8 ears corn (or 1 package, 2
  cups yield, frozen, thawed
  corn)

1 large ripe tomato, sliced and
  cubed
1 teaspoon salt
¼ teaspoon pepper
Dash of nutmeg

Lay slices of salt pork in bottom of a 4- to 6-quart saucepan and cover with lima beans. Add enough water to cover, and cook over a low heat until the beans are tender. Cut the kernels from fresh corn and combine with beans, tomato, and seasonings. Cover and continue cooking over a low heat for 10 to 15 minutes. Stir frequently to prevent scorching.

Originally, succotash—or *misickquatash*, as the Narragansett Indians called it—was made of corn and kidney beans, and cooked in bear grease. One of the early settlers wrote of misickquatash, "In winter (the Indians) esteem their Corne being boyled with Beanes for a rare dish."

The American Heritage Cookbook

© American Heritage, a division of Forbes Inc. Reprinted with permission from *The American Heritage Cookbook*.

DELAWARE FRIED TOMATOES AND MILK GRAVY

Serves 4

3 Delaware tomatoes, hard
  ripe
Flour
Salt and pepper
Bacon

2 tablespoons bacon fat
Sugar
2 tablespoons flour
1½ cups milk

Slice tomatoes ½ inch thick. Roll them in flour, salt, and pepper.

Fry several strips of bacon until crisp. Remove bacon and drain. Pour out most of bacon fat and reserve. Fry the tomatoes in some of the fat until brown. Sprinkle sugar on tomatoes to suit taste.

Put 2 tablespoons bacon fat in the pan. Add 2 tablespoons flour; blend. Then add milk; add salt, pepper, and sugar to taste. Crumble in bacon slices. Pour over tomatoes and serve.

Delaware Council of Farm Organizations

RIPE THANKSGIVING TOMATOES

Pick as many tomatoes as desired while still green, having them free from blemish. Wrap each one in tissue paper by itself, and arrange on a dry board in a cool place. They will ripen so gradually that they will be ready for slicing for Thanksgiving. It is better to gather tomatoes in late September or early October.

Taken from a 1927 newspaper.

THREE DAY CASSEROLE

Serves 4

1 pound green peppers, chopped

1 stalk celery, chopped

1 pound onions, coarsely sliced

2-ounce bottle green olives stuffed with pimento

1 pound fresh mushrooms (or 6-ounce can)

1 garlic clove

1 pound ground beef, lean

½ pound butter, or ¼ pound each margarine and butter

10¾-ounce can tomato soup (undiluted)

12-ounce can tomato mushroom sauce

1-pound package ½-inch wide noodles

½ pound American cheddar cheese, grated

Fry peppers, celery, onions, olives, mushrooms, garlic, and beef each *separately in order given* in the ½ pound of butter. Do not overcook.

Cook noodles according to package directions and drain. Add fried ingredients, sauce, and soup to noodles. *Cook and stir* mixture for 3 minutes. Place in casserole and, when cool, top with grated cheese.

Cover and refrigerate for *3 days* before cooking. Casserole may be frozen *after* being refrigerated for 3 days. Heat at 325° in a covered casserole dish about 1 hour. *Remove cover for last 15 minutes.*

Lib Andrews, Laconia, N.H.

SALTLESS SURPRISE

2 teaspoons garlic powder
1 teaspoon dried basil
1 teaspoon anise seed

1 teaspoon dried oregano
1 teaspoon powdered lemon rind

Put ingredients into blender and mix well. Store in labeled glass container, and add rice to prevent caking.

PUNGENT SALT SUBSTITUTE

3 teaspoons fresh basil
2 teaspoons fresh savory
  (summer savory is best)
2 teaspoons celery seed

2 teaspoons ground cumin seed
2 teaspoons fresh sage
1 teaspoon fresh lemon thyme
2 teaspoons fresh marjoram

Mix well and then powder with mortar and pestle.

These recipes can be placed in shakers and used instead of salt.

Suggestions from the U. S. Department of Health, submitted by Dr. Roger Rodrigue, Wilmington, Del.

DESSERTS

APPLE BROWN BETTY

Serves 6

3 cups flour
1 cup sugar
Melted butter
½ to 1 cup sugar
¼ teaspoon cinnamon
¼ teaspoon nutmeg

¼ teaspoon salt
3 cups sliced or chopped apples
¼ cup water
Juice and grated rind of 1 lemon
3 tablespoons butter

To make a crumb mixture, combine flour, 1 cup sugar, and enough melted butter to moisten.

Preheat oven to 350°. Mix sugar, spices, and salt. If apples are very tart, use additional sugar up to 1 cup. Grease a 1½-quart casserole. Put in a third of the crumbs, half of the apples. Sprinkle half of the sugar mixture. Repeat.

Mix water, lemon juice, and rind; pour over contents of casserole. Put remaining crumbs on top and dot with butter. Cover and bake for 1¾ hours.

Rhubarb, peaches, pineapple, bananas, or cherries may be used instead of apples.

Rose Messick, The Governor's House, Dover, Del.

OCTAGONAL
SCHOOL HOUSE

CHOCOLATE MOUSSE

Serves 10

½ pound semisweet chocolate
2 tablespoons butter
10 tablespoons sugar

10 eggs, separated
Heavy cream, whipped
Fresh strawberries, sliced

Melt chocolate in double boiler. Add butter. After butter is melted, remove from heat. Add sugar and mix well until smooth. Add 10 egg yolks to mixture and beat well. Beat egg whites until stiff. Fold in egg whites. Pour into compote and refrigerate overnight. Serve with whipped cream and fresh sliced strawberries.

Compliments of Winterthur Archives

CHOCOLATE SOUFFLÉ

Serves 12

2 envelopes unflavored gelatin
2¼ cups milk
1 cup canned chocolate syrup
6 egg yolks
3 tablespoons butter

1½ teaspoons vanilla
¼ teaspoon cream of tartar
6 egg whites
¾ cup superfine sugar
2½ cups heavy cream

Sprinkle gelatin over ½ cup milk; let stand 3 to 4 minutes to soften. In a saucepan combine 1¾ cups milk and gelatin mixture; add chocolate syrup and slightly beaten egg yolks. Place over moderate heat and stir constantly until it just reaches boiling point. Remove from heat. Stir in butter and vanilla. Let cool. Cover and chill in refrigerator until just stiff enough to mound when dropped from a spoon.

Meanwhile, make a meringue. Sprinkle cream of tartar over egg whites in mixing bowl; beat to a froth, then add and beat in sugar by tablespoonfuls until mixture is stiff enough to hold its shape when dropped. Pour chilled chocolate mixture into mixing bowl and beat until smooth; fold in meringue, blending well. Whip 1½ cups heavy cream. Carefully fold in whipped cream. Pour mixture into 1-quart souffle (or other straight-sided dish) around which you have pinned a 2-inch foil collar. Chill for several hours or overnight. Remove collar to serve. Whip remaining cup of heavy cream. Serve soufflé with whipped cream garnish.

Don't be afraid to try your hand at soufflés. They're not "as easy as pie." They're much easier—no crust to roll.

Louisa Martin

CRUNCHY CUSTARD

Serves 6

¾ cup grape-nuts cereal
¼ cup salted butter
½ cup sugar
3 eggs, well beaten
2 cups milk

¼ cup raisins (optional)
1 teaspoon vanilla
⅛ teaspoon nutmeg
⅛ teaspoon salt

Preheat oven to 375°. Mix cereal with butter. Blend sugar into eggs; add cereal mixture and remaining ingredients. Mix well. Pour into 1-quart baking dish; place in pan of hot water. Bake for 30 minutes, stir well. Bake about 10 to 15 minutes longer, or until knife inserted 1 inch from center comes out clean. Serve warm or cooled.

Catherine Downing, Milford, Del.

CHRISTMAS PUDDING

Yield: 1 pudding (1 quart)

1 cup bread crumbs
1 cup grated beef suet
1 cup flour
1 heaping teaspoon baking
  powder
1½ cups diced citron
1½ cups raisins

½ teaspoon nutmeg
½ teaspoon cinnamon
1 teaspoon salt
1 teaspoon baking soda
1 cup molasses
1 cup milk
2 eggs, beaten

Combine bread crumbs, suet, flour, baking powder, citrons, raisins, spices, and salt. Beat baking soda into molasses. Add egg and milk. Pour liquid into dry ingredients and mix well. Butter a 1-quart mold. Spoon pudding into mold. Put covered mold on a rack in a pan of boiling water and steam for 4 hours. To reheat, steam again 2 hours.

SAUCE

1 egg
1 pound confectioner's sugar
¼ pound butter

½ cup brandy or to taste
1 pint heavy cream

In a bowl or the top pan of a double boiler, beat egg and mix in sugar. Be sure all egg is absorbed. Add butter cut in pieces and cook over boiling water until butter melts. Stir constantly for about 10 minutes. This may be made a day or so ahead. When ready to use, add brandy to taste, mixing well. Whip cream. Blend sauce into whipped cream.

This is a favorite recipe of the Cannon family. It can be made well ahead of use and put in the refrigerator.

Submitted by the descendants of Delaware's forty-first governor, William Cannon, 1863-1865

C. L. Cannon, Bridgeville, Del.

HOMEMADE BANANA ICE CREAM

Yield: 1½ gallons

2 tablespoons flour
2 cups sugar
½ teaspoon salt
2 eggs
4 cups scalded milk

2 quarts half and half
2 tablespoons vanilla
8 bananas (other fruits may be
    used)

Mix flour, sugar, and salt; add eggs, slightly beaten, and milk. Gradually cook over hot water in a double boiler for 10 minutes, stirring constantly. Should custard have curdled appearance, it will disappear in freezing. Let cool. Add cream and flavoring. Mash bananas and stir in.

For a sensational, old-fashioned social, freeze ice cream in hand-turned freezer. (Use small chips of ice packed in layers with rock salt. Turn slowly and pour off water as ice melts. Handle will gradually become harder to turn. Remove ice cream container, cover, and let stand briefly.) Serve to delighted guests!

Much love and fellowship is built into the process of making ice cream in a hand-turned ice cream maker.

J. Christine Held, Hockessin, Del.

ICE CREAMY CAKE

Yield: 1 cake

1¼ cups all-purpose flour
1 cup chopped nuts
¼ pound margarine
16-ounce container whipped
  topping
8-ounce package cream cheese

1 cup confectioner's sugar
3-ounce box instant vanilla
  pudding
3-ounce box instant chocolate
  pudding

Preheat oven to 375°. Combine flour, nuts, and margarine and spread in a 9- by 13- by 2-inch oblong pan. Bake 20 minutes.

Blend together ½ of the whipped topping, the cream cheese, and sugar. Spread over nut mixture. Prepare instant puddings according to package directions. Spread in layers over the whipped topping. Top with remaining whipped topping. Garnish with additional chopped nuts, if desired. Store in refrigerator. Tastes just like ice cream.

Peg Evans, New Castle, Del.

LADYFINGER DESSERT

Yield: 8-inch cake

2 packages ladyfingers
12-ounce bag chocolate chips
2 tablespoons sugar
1 teaspoon water

2 eggs, separated
1 teaspoon vanilla
Whipped cream

Line an 8- by 8-inch pan with half of the lady fingers. Melt chocolate chips. Add vanilla, sugar, water, and egg yolks. Make into a paste. Beat egg whites until stiff and fold into the chocolate paste. Pour onto ladyfingers, top with rest of ladyfingers and garnish with whipped cream.

Very easy and very good.

Barbara du Pont, Montchanin, Del.

PEACHY APPLE DUMPLIN'

Serves 6 to 8

6 to 8 medium-sized tart
   apples
Water
6 to 8 peaches
Lemon juice

¾ to 1¼ cups sugar
1 teaspoon vanilla
1 cup biscuit mix
⅓ cup milk

Pare apples and cut into chunks. Cook over low heat with enough water to keep apples from burning on bottom until a chunky applesauce is formed. Stir occasionally. Pare and slice peaches, sprinkle with ascorbic acid or lemon juice, and add to apples. Sweeten mixture to taste and add vanilla. Continue cooking at slow boil for 1 minute.

Mix with a fork the biscuit mix and milk. Spoon dough onto boiling fruit. Cook uncovered over low heat for 5 to 10 minutes; cover and cook 5 to 10 minutes longer. Allow to cool slightly and serve with milk or cream.

Helen Fifer, Wyoming, Del.

BAKED PINEAPPLE

Serves 6

6 slices white bread, cubed
3 eggs, beaten
½ cup milk

20-ounce can crushed pineapple
¾ cup sugar
½ cup butter or margarine

Preheat oven to 375°. Mix all ingredients together. Bake in buttered 1½-quart casserole for about 1 hour.

Serve hot or as a cold dessert with a splash of whipped cream.

Also a good meat accompaniment.

Emilie Truman, Clifton Heights, Pa.

PINEAPPLE CREAM DESSERT

Serves 12

Approximately 1 cup crushed vanilla wafers	*2 eggs*
1½ cups confectioner's sugar	*20-ounce can crushed pineapple, very well drained*
¼ pound butter	*1 cup heavy cream*

Line a 7- by 11-inch or 8- by 10-inch pan with waxed paper. Cover paper with a layer of crushed vanilla wafers.

Cream sugar, butter, and eggs. Spread on crushed wafers. Cover with layer of pineapple. Whip the heavy cream, sweetening to taste. Last, spread with layer of whipped cream. Cover with plastic wrap and chill in refrigerator 24 hours.

A make-ahead dessert to chill until time to serve your guests. Delightful on a hot summer day.

Mrs. Norris Kirchner, Bethel, Del.

PLUM PUDDING

Serves 12 to 14

1 cup raisins
1 cup currants (or omit currants
    and use 2 cups raisins)
1 cup molasses
3½ cups milk
4½ cups plus 1 tablespoon flour
1 teaspoon baking soda
1 tablespoon lard (or 1 heaping
    tablespoon shortening or
    margarine)

1 cup sugar
1 egg
1 heaping tablespoon butter
2 tablespoons cold water
1 teaspoon vanilla

Combine the raisins, currants, molasses, 1½ cups of the milk, 4½ cups of the flour and the baking soda. Melt the lard or shortening and stir in. Pour into a greased mold and steam for 2 hours. Allow to cool before serving.

Make a sauce by beating together the sugar, egg, butter, the remaining tablespoon of flour, and the water. Scald the remaining 2 cups of milk in the top of a double boiler. Slowly add the sugar and egg mixture; stirring until thickened. Stir in vanilla. To serve, pour hot sauce over cold pudding. Note: sauce is also good poured over thinly sliced applesauce cake.

Mrs. F. F. Bradley, Seaford, Del.

ENGLISH TRIFLE—
The Real Thing

Serves 10 to 12

3 7- or 8-inch sponge cakes	Strawberry jam
6 macaroons	½ pint egg custard, freshly
1 ounce ratafias (if unobtainable,	made
use macaroons)	½ cup heavy cream
½ cup cooking sherry	4 teaspoons sugar
3 tablespoons brandy	1 egg white
A little grated lemon rind	1 teaspoon cooking sherry
½ cup blanched slivered almonds	Crystallized fruits, for garnish

Place sponge cakes, macaroons, and/or ratafias in an 8- or 9-inch glass dish. Mix sherry and brandy and pour over them. Over this, put the lemon rind, almonds, and a layer of jam. Make fresh custard or use packaged custard mix. When the custard is cool, pour it over the trifle.

Whisk together the heavy cream, sugar, and egg white, and sherry until the bulk is nearly doubled. The egg white lightens the cream. Heap the whipped mixture lightly over the trifle. Garnish with the crystallized fruits.

Graciously sent by Lady Wright, British Embassy, Washington, D. C.

WATERMELON POPSICLES

Yield: 36 small popsicles

3 cups watermelon juice
½ cup sugar

½ cup water
2 teaspoons fresh lemon juice

To make watermelon juice, cut watermelon into cubes and rub through a strainer to remove seeds. In small saucepan, mix together sugar and water; simmer 3 minutes. Remove from heat; stir in watermelon juice and lemon juice. Turn into two ice cube trays with dividers. Freeze until very mushy, then insert a popsicle stick in each cube. Freeze until solid.

Compliments of Mar-Del Watermelon Association

RICE PUDDING

Serves 4 to 6

½ cup uncooked rice, washed
2 quarts milk
1½ cups sugar

1 heaping tablespoon butter
2 teaspoons vanilla
Raisins (optional)

Preheat the oven to 400°. Put all except vanilla in pan on top of stove and cook on low fire until rice is practically done (approximately 1 hour). Stir occasionally. Pour into 3 or 4-quart casserole. Add vanilla and fold in raisins, if desired. Bake for about 10 minutes; stir. Do this 3 times. Take out after it has browned the fourth time. Don't stir the last time.

Senator Richard S. and Mary Jane Cordrey, Millsboro, Del.

WUTTASHIMNEASH
(Strawberry Shortcake)

Serves 4 to 6

2 cups all-purpose flour
4 teaspoons baking powder
½ teaspoon salt
½ cup sugar plus 1 tablespoon
½ cup shortening

1 egg
Milk
4 cups perfect strawberries
Cream, plain or whipped

Preheat oven to 450°. Sift together flour, baking powder, salt, and 1 tablespoon sugar. Add shortening and work in with fingertips to make very fine crumbs. The finer the better. Break egg into measuring cup, stir with fork to mix, and add milk to make measure ¾ cup. Pour into crumbs and stir quickly with the fork.

Turn out on floured surface and knead for 1 minute and then pat it out to fit in a buttered 8-inch round cake pan. Place pan in oven and bake about 25 minutes until it tests done and is golden brown. Turn out carefully on a rack and let cool a little, then cut in half and butter each side.

Meanwhile, have the strawberries picked over. Set aside 8 or 10 big ones for garnishing and cut the others in half. Mix with the half cup of sugar in a saucepan. Place over the lowest possible heat. Do not actually cook the berries, but simply warm them.

At serving time, place half the shortcake on a serving platter, cover with warm berries. Top with the other half of cake and arrange reserved berries on top. Serve with plain or whipped cream or ice cream.

The Indians called these berries Wuttashimneash. They cultivated this berry and would bruise it with meal in a mortar to make strawberry bread.

Frances Blackwood, *Philadelphia Evening Bulletin* "1965"

PIES AND PASTRIES

So many pie recipes call for unbaked pie shells, baked pie shells, or frozen pie shells that we have included a sprinkling of homemade, easy to do, pie crust recipes. Pie-making success depends upon a tender, flaky crust. A pie is only as good as its pastry: the choice is yours.

PLAIN PASTRY

Yield: double crust for 9-inch pie

½ cup lard
¼ cup butter
¾ teaspoon salt

2½ cups flour
⅓ cup ice water

With a wire pastry blender or two knives cut lard and butter into salt and flour until mixture looks like coarse meal. Sprinkle with water, using enough to moisten. Gather into a ball with a fork. Divide dough in half and roll on lightly floured board to about ⅛-inch thickness.

SWEET PASTRY

Yield: single crust for 9-inch pie

1 cup flour
½ teaspoon salt

2 tablespoons sugar
½ cup softened butter

Toss flour, salt, and sugar to mix. Add butter and work to a paste. Press paste against bottom and sides of a 9-inch pie plate. Great for open-faced fruit pies. If using for chiffon and other cooked fillings, chill, prick, and bake in a hot (400°) oven about 15 minutes, until golden brown, before filling.

NEVER-FAIL PIE CRUST

Yield: crust for two 9-inch pies

2 cups self-rising flour
⅔ cup butter, softened
1 egg yolk

¼ cup water
2 teaspoons lemon juice

Place flour in a bowl; cut in butter until mixture resembles small crumbs. Combine egg yolk, water, and lemon juice; beat lightly. Sprinkle egg mixture over flour, stirring gently with a fork to combine. Mix just until a ball is formed. Divide dough in half. Roll out half of dough on floured surface to a circle that is 1½ inches larger than a 9-inch pie pan. Fix loosely into pie pan; add desired filling. Roll out remaining dough as above and place on top of filling. Seal edges by fluting.

CREAM CHEESE CRUST

Yield: crust for two 9-inch pies

2 cups flour
Pinch of baking powder
¾ teaspoon salt

3 3-ounce packages cream cheese
½ cup butter
½ cup solid vegetable shortening

Sift flour, baking powder, and salt together. Add cream cheese, butter, and shortening. Cut with two knives or pastry blender until thoroughly blended; wrap in foil and refrigerate overnight. Roll to a little more than ⅛-inch thickness on a light floured board.

ZWIEBACK PIE CRUST

Yield: single crust for 8½-inch shell

1 package zwieback   ½ cup sugar
½ cup butter, melted   2 teaspoons cinnamon

Roll zwieback with rolling pin until very fine. Reserve about 2 tablespoons and mix the rest with butter, sugar, and cinnamon. Butter pie plate and spread mixture on evenly to make a crust. Bake 15 minutes in preheated moderate oven (350°) before filling.

Very good filled with custard or used as crust for lemon meringue pie.

PECAN CRUST

Yield: single crust for 9-inch shell

2 cups ground pecans   3½ tablespoons unsalted butter,
   (approximately ½ pound   melted, cooled to room
   shelled)   temperature
⅓ cup sugar

Mix pecans and sugar in medium bowl. Drizzle butter over nuts. Stir and toss vigorously with fork until nuts are uniformly moistened. Spoon into pie plate. Press mixture firmly against pie plate with back of spoon. Refrigerate 20 minutes.

Meanwhile heat oven to 350°. Bake crust for 13 to 15 minutes until edges are light brown. Cool.

PAPER BAG APPLE PIE

Yield: 9-inch pie

1 unbaked 9-inch pastry shell
4 large baking apples (about 2½
   pounds)
1 cup sugar

½ cup plus 2 tablespoons flour
½ teaspoon cinnamon
2 tablespoons lemon juice
½ cup butter

Preheat oven to 425°. Make an unbaked pastry shell. Pare, core, and quarter apples, then halve each quarter to make chunks. Place in bowl. Combine ½ cup of sugar, 2 tablespoons of flour, and the cinnamon in a cup; sprinkle over apples, tossing to coat well. Spoon apples into pastry shell and sprinkle with lemon juice.

Combine ½ cup of sugar and ½ cup of flour in a small bowl, cut in the butter, and sprinkle over apples to cover top. Slide pie into a heavy brown paper bag, large enough to cover pie loosely. Fold open end over twice and fasten with paper clips; place on large cookie sheet for easy handling.

Bake for 1 hour (apples will be tender and top bubbly and golden). Split bag open; and cool pie on rack.

Thank the Pilgrims for mom's apple pie. They brought the apple seeds with them on the *Mayflower* and planted the first seeds in the colonies. This recipe captures the taste of America's heritage.

From *What's Cooking in Claymont, Delaware*-1971

Section a large orange and add the segments to your next apple pie. Bake as usual and enjoy the different flavor.

CHIPMUNK PIE

Serves 4 to 6

1 egg, well beaten
¾ cup sugar, granulated white
  or brown
½ cup flour
1 teaspoon baking powder

¼ teaspoon vanilla
Pinch of salt (⅛ teaspoon)
1 cup pared tart cooking apples,
  chopped
½ cup nuts, chopped

Preheat oven to 350°. Mix together in order given. Pour into a greased 8-inch pie pan and bake for 25 minutes.

This unique dessert is served often at our covered dish dinners at Bethany Church of the Brethren.

Celia Miller, Farmington, Del.

READ HOUSE

APPLE MINCE PIE

Yield: 10-inch pie

Pastry for 10-inch pie
¾ cup brown sugar
⅓ cup flour
5 cups peeled, sliced apples

2 cups mincemeat
8 peeled, cored apple rings
2 tablespoons butter

Preheat oven to 425°. Prepare pie shell. Combine sugar with flour, sprinkle 3 tablespoons over shell. Place sliced apples in layers in shell, sprinkling each layer with sugar-flour mixture, reserving 3 tablespoons.

Spread top with mincemeat, reserving ½ cup. Arrange apple rings on top. Fill apple centers with remaining mincemeat. Sprinkle with remaining sugar-flour mixture; dot with butter. Bake about 40 minutes.

Homemade pies take longer, taste better.

Toni Weidel, Claymont, Del.

JANE'S PUMPKIN PIE

Yield: 2 10-inch pies

Pastry for 2 pies
3 cups mashed pumpkin
1½ cups milk
5 eggs separated
¾ cup sugar

1⅞ teaspoon cinnamon
⅜ teaspoon cloves
⅜ teaspoon ginger
⅜ teaspoon nutmeg
1½ teaspoon salt

Mix pumpkin and milk together; add 5 yolks, beaten. Add sugar mixed with spices and salt. Mix well. Fold in stiffly beaten egg whites. Turn into prepared pie shells. Bake in 450° over for 10 minutes; reduce heat to 375° and bake 20 minutes longer or until filling is firm.

Jane Taylor, Wilmington, Del.

COLONIAL INNKEEPER'S PIE

Serves 8

1½ squares unsweetened
  chocolate
½ cup water
⅔ cup plus ¾ cup sugar
¼ cup butter
2 teaspoons vanilla
1 cup sifted flour
1 teaspoon baking powder

½ teaspoon salt
¼ cup soft shortening
½ cup milk
1 egg
1 unbaked pie shell with high
  rim
½ cup chopped walnuts

Melt chocolate in water; add ⅔ cup of the sugar. Bring to boil, stirring constantly. Remove from heat. Stir in butter and 1½ teaspoons vanilla. Set aside. Sift together flour, ¾ cup of the sugar, baking powder, and salt. Add shortening, milk, and ½ teaspoon vanilla. Beat 2 minutes. Add egg; beat 2 minutes.

Pour batter into 9-inch pie shell. Stir chocolate sauce and pour carefully over batter. Sprinkle top with nuts. Bake in a 350° oven for 55 to 60 minutes or until cake tester stuck in center comes out clean. Garnish with whipped cream.

Ruth Hoffman, Claymont, Del.

CRANBERRY PEACH PIE

Yield: 9-inch pie

¾ cup sugar
2 tablespoons flour
1 teaspoon grated lemon rind
½ teaspoon ground cinnamon
9-ounce box pie crust mix for
    double crust
1 egg, well beaten

½ cup confectioner's sugar
2 teaspoons water
2 cans (about 1 pound each)
    sliced cling peaches, drained
2 cups fresh cranberries, washed
    and stemmed

Preheat oven to 400°. Mix all ingredients except peaches and cranberries. Add peaches and cranberries. Toss lightly to coat fruit. Prepare pie crust mix. Line 9-inch pie pan with crust. Spoon mixture into pastry shell. Cover with other pie crust. Cut several slits near center to let steam escape. Bake for 45 minutes.

This pie combines the tartness of cranberries with the sweetness of peaches—one of my favorites from home in New England. Also a Delaware 1972 Fair prize winner.

Pamela T. Nichols, Wilmington, Del.

CRANBERRY PIE TANGIER

Serves 6

2 cups fresh or frozen
  cranberries
½ cup sugar
½ cup chopped pecans
2 eggs
1 cup sugar

½ cup butter or margarine,
  melted
¼ cup shortening, melted
1 cup all-purpose flour
1 pint vanilla ice cream

Preheat oven to 325°. Grease well a 10-inch pie pan. Spread cranberries over the bottom. Sprinkle with sugar and pecans. Beat eggs well. Add sugar, butter, and shortening. Beat well and gradually add flour. Pour batter over cranberries. Bake for 60 minutes or until crust is golden brown.

Cut in wedges and serve either warm or cold with generous scoops of vanilla ice cream.

News Journal First Prize Winner, 1971

Nellie S. Collison, Newport, Del.

CREAMY EGGNOG PIE

Serves 6

1 cup uncooked quick oats	½ cup cold water
⅓ cup wheat germ (or unprocessed bran or finely chopped nuts)	2½ cups cold eggnog
	1 tablespoon brandy extract
	1½ cups heavy cream
¼ cup butter or margarine, melted	¼ cup granulated sugar
	Nutmeg
½ teaspoon cinnamon	Pecan halves
⅛ teaspoon nutmeg	
2 envelopes unflavored gelatin	

Preheat oven to 375°. Mix together oats, wheat germ, butter, and spices. Roll out dough to fit 8-inch pie pan. Bake for about 8 minutes or until golden brown. Cool.

Soften gelatin in cold water; stir over low heat until dissolved. Gradually add to combined eggnog and brandy extract mixture and mix well. Chill about 5 minutes or until mixture is very thick but not set.

Beat together cream and sugar until stiff peaks form. Beat gelatin mixture at high speed with electric mixer about 2 minutes or until mix is slightly fluffy. Fold in whipped cream. Chill 15 or 20 minutes or until mix mounds when dropped from a spoon.

Mound into crust. Chill until firm. Garnish with nutmeg and pecan halves.

Mabel M. Evans, Laurel, Del.

FRUIT PIE MARVEL

1 cup flour
¼ cup sugar
½ cup butter or margarine
½ cup chopped nuts
8 ounces cream cheese, softened
1 cup confectioner's sugar
9-ounce container frozen whipped
  topping

3-ounce package strawberry
  flavored gelatin
1 cup hot water
1 pint fresh strawberries, sugar
  to taste

Preheat oven to 325°. Mix together flour, sugar, butter, and nuts. Spread on bottom and up sides of 9- or 10-inch round pie pan. Bake for 15 to 20 minutes; cool.

Mix together cream cheese and sugar. Beat until fluffy. Fold in thawed whipped topping. Spoon into cooled crust.

Dissolve flavored gelatin in hot water. Cool until slightly thickened. Sprinkle whole strawberries with sugar if desired. Dip strawberries into flavored gelatin to coat. Arrange glazed strawberries on top of filling.

Note: You can also use any fresh fruit in season such as blueberries, peaches, or a combination of fruits. If you are using peaches, add a little lemon juice to the flavored gelatin.

A beautiful dessert for special occasions.

Amy Arimoto, Newark, Del.

LEMON SOUFFLÉ PIE

Yield: 9-inch pie

12-ounce box vanilla wafers
1 packet unflavored gelatin (1
   tablespoon)
¼ cup water
¾ cup sugar
½ cup lemon juice

½ teaspoon salt
4 eggs, separated
1 cup heavy cream
3 tablespoons confectioner's
   sugar
1 teaspoon vanilla

Line sides of 9-inch pie pan with whole vanilla wafers. Crush the rest of the wafers and line the bottom of the pan. (I put the cookies in a large ziploc bag, seal it, and crush cookies with a rolling pin.)

Dissolve gelatin in water; easier if water is first boiled. In the top of a double boiler, mix ¼ cup sugar, lemon juice, salt, and 4 beaten egg yolks. Add the dissolved gelatin. Stir over boiling water until the consistency of custard. Cool. To cool quickly, place pan in a bowl of ice cubes in refrigerator.

Whip 4 egg whites until stiff. Slowly beat in ½ cup sugar. When custard is cool, beat until fluffy. Slowly fold in the beaten egg whites.

Either pour custard-egg white mixture into pie pan. Beat heavy cream until stiff. Fold in confectioner's sugar and vanilla. Spoon whipped cream over pie. Chill until set; or you can beat heavy cream until stiff. Fold in confectioner's sugar, vanilla, and custard-egg white mixture. Pour into pie crust. Chill till set. May take several hours.

Lemon peel can be used as a decoration.

Note: Shortcuts such as artificially prepared whipped cream or non-dairy whipped toppings are not recommended. Bottled lemon juice is acceptable, but not as good as freshly squeezed lemon juice.

Kate Wheeler, Dover, Del.

LETTERBANKET

PUFF PASTRY

¼ pound sweet butter   ¼ cup (or more) ice water
1 cup sifted all-purpose flour   Pinch salt

Using sweet butter, flour, ice water, and salt, make puff paste dough following basic cookbook directions.

ALMOND PASTE FILLING

¼ pound blanched almonds   Grated peel of 1 lemon
½ cup sugar   Pinch of salt
1 egg, beaten

While puff pastry chills, prepare the almond paste. Grind the blanched almonds and mix with the sugar, beaten egg, grated lemon peel, and pinch of salt. Grind this mixture once more. On a floured board, roll it into a number of "sausages" about 1 inch in diameter. Wrap in waxpaper and chill for about 1 hour. Preheat oven to 425°.

After the final chilling period, roll out the dough into a strip 3½ inches wide and ⅛ inch thick. Place "sausages" end to end along the center, fold dough lengthwise and seal top and ends with water. Shape into your family's initial and place it, seam side down, on a floured cookie sheet. Brush with beaten egg diluted with water. Bake 30 to 35 minutes. Cool on a rack.

To make a Christmas wreath, shape the filled strip into a ring, sealing ends together. Bake as above; cool. Spread with confectioner's icing and decorate lavishly with red and green glacéed cherries and "leaves" cut from candied citron.

This renowned Dutch pastry, made of puff paste with an almond paste filling, is traditional both on Sinterklaas Eve and at Christmas. At Sinterklaas it is shaped in the family initial(s); at Christmas it is given the form of a wreath and decorated with glacéed fruit.

Compliments of Zwaanendael Museum, Lewes, Del.

PEACH CHEESE PIE

Yield: 9-inch pie

¾ cup flour
1 teaspoon baking powder
½ teaspoon salt
3-ounce package vanilla pudding, not instant
1 egg
3 tablespoons soft butter
½ cup milk

15- to 20-ounce can sliced peaches
8 ounces cream cheese
½ cup plus 1 tablespoon sugar
3 tablespoons peach juice
½ teaspoon cinnamon

Preheat oven to 350°. Combine first 7 ingredients; beat 2 minutes with electric mixer on medium speed. Put into deep 9-inch pie plate. Drain peaches reserving juice. Place peach slices on top of batter.

In bowl mix cream cheese, ½ cup sugar, and peach juice at medium speed; spread over batter to within 1 inch of edge.

Combine 1 tablespoon sugar and cinnamon and sprinkle on top. Bake for 30 to 35 minutes. Cool. Refrigerate about 2 hours before serving.

Delicious.

Frannie Donavan, Havertown, Pa.

PEACHES AND CREAM PIE

Yield: 9- or 10-inch pie

4 cups fresh sliced peaches
9- or 10-inch pie crust, unbaked
1 cup sugar
4 tablespoons flour

Dash of salt
1 cup heavy cream
4 drops vanilla

Preheat oven to 400°. Place peaches in pie crust. Mix sugar, flour, and salt together; stir in cream and vanilla. Pour over peaches and bake for 50 to 60 minutes.

Dolores Dineen, Claymont, Del.

BLUE COAT INN PEANUT BUTTER ICE CREAM PIE

Serves 8 to 10

1 quart vanilla ice cream,
    slightly softened
½ cup chunky peanut butter
½ cup crushed unsalted peanuts

1½ tablespoons vanilla
10-inch graham cracker crust
Whipped cream
Maraschino cherries

Combine ice cream, peanut butter, ¼ cup peanuts, and vanilla in large bowl and mix well. Turn into crust and sprinkle with remaining peanuts. Freeze. Decorate with whipped cream and maraschino cherries, if desired.

Blue Coat Inn, overlooking Silver Lake, Dover, Del.

PINEAPPLE CHEESE TARTS

Yield: 10 to 12 tarts

¼ pound butter or margarine
3 ounces cream cheese
Pinch salt

1 cup flour
12 teaspoons pineapple jam

Preheat oven to 375°. Cream butter and cream cheese. Add salt and flour. Mix well with fork. Chill. Roll out, cut into squares and fill each square with 1 teaspoon pineapple jam. Fold over, press edges together, prick with fork. Bake on cookie sheet until golden brown about 12 to 15 minutes.

> When you find a special recipe
> And others like it, too
> Make one to share with someone nice
> And another just for *you*!

Mrs. Nelson Spence, Bethel, Del.

GRANDMA'S PUMPKIN PIE

Yield: 1 large pie, plus. Extra filling baked in custard cups.

30-ounce can pumpkin
1½ cups milk
1 cup sugar
3 eggs
2 tablespoons flour

½ teaspoon each ginger, cloves,
nutmeg, cinnamon
3 ounces rye whiskey
Pie shell, unbaked

Preheat oven to 450°. Mix all ingredients together. Put in pie shell. Bake at 450° for 15 minutes, then lower oven temperature to 350° and bake for approximately 45 minutes or until knife comes out clean.

Ruthie Upham, Saunderstown, R.I.

PUMPKIN MINCE PIE

Yield: 10-inch pie

1 package dry mincement
1 cup water
1½ cups canned pumpkin
¾ cup light brown sugar
12-ounce can evaporated milk
2 tablespoons butter

½ teaspoon nutmeg
¼ teaspoon cinnamon
1 teaspoon vanilla
2 eggs, slightly beaten
10-inch pastry

Preheat oven to 500°. Break up mincemeat in a saucepan. Add water; cook 3 minutes, stirring. Cool.

In another saucepan combine pumpkin, sugar, milk, butter, spices, and vanilla. Heat until butter melts. While stirring, pour slowly into beaten eggs, folding them in. Cool. Line a 10-inch pie pan with the pastry. Spread mincemeat on bottom. Pour pumpkin mixture over top. Bake at 500° for 5 minutes; reduce heat and continue baking at 350° about 30 minutes more or until set.

A spicy layer of mincement baked under a luscious, creamy pumpkin custard.

John J. Williams, Delaware State Senator, 1947-1971

RASPBERRY RIBBON PIE

Yield: 9-inch pie

3-ounce package raspberry
  gelatin
¼ cup granulated sugar
1¼ cups boiling water
10-ounce package frozen red
  raspberries
1 tablespoon lemon juice

3-ounce package cream cheese
⅓ cup confectioner's sugar
Dash of salt
1 teaspoon vanilla
1 cup heavy cream, whipped
9-inch baked pastry shell

Dissolve gelatin and sugar in boiling water. Add raspberries and lemon juice. Stir until berries thaw. Chill until partly set. Meanwhile blend cream cheese, confectioner's sugar, salt, and vanilla. Fold in small amount of whipped cream. Fold in remainder of whipped cream. Spread ½ cup cream cheese mixture in bottom of pastry shell. Top with ½ cup raspberry mixture, then a layer of remaining cream cheese mixture, ending with a final layer of the raspberries. Chill for 2 to 3 hours before serving.

Anne Kappel, Claymont, Del.

RITZ CRACKER PIE

Yield: 8½-inch pie

3 egg whites
1 cup sugar
1 teaspoon baking powder

¾ cup chopped walnuts
20 crushed Ritz crackers
Whipped cream

Preheat oven to 325°. Beat egg whites until stiff. Fold in remaining ingredients. Bake in buttered pie pan for 30 minutes or until firm in center. Top with whipped cream.

Easy and delicious.

Ruth Ross, Claymont, Del.

SHOOFLY PIE

Serves 8 to 12

1 cup flour
⅔ cup brown sugar
1 tablespoon vegetable shortening
1 cup molasses

1 egg
1 cup hot water
1 teaspoon baking soda

Preheat oven to 400°. Mix 1 cup of flour, the brown sugar and 1 tablespoon shortening together. Reserve ½ cup crumbs for topping. To remainder of crumbs, add molasses, egg, and ¾ cup hot water; blend. Mix soda in ¼ cup hot water and blend it into above mixture. Pour into unbaked pie crust; sprinkle the reserved crumbs on top. Bake at 400° for 10 minutes; then reduce oven to 325° and bake for 30 minutes.

The Hostess House is a delightful remodeled old farm house serving Pennsylvania Dutch food.

Esther Swartzentruber, The Hostess House, Greenwood, Del.

STRAWBERRY PIE

Yield: 8- or 9-inch pie

1 quart strawberries
1 cup sugar
3 tablespoons cornstarch
Few drops lemon juice (optional)

8- or 9-inch crust, baked
3-ounce package cream cheese
½ pint heavy cream

In a saucepan, mash *only half* of the berries, bring to a boil and stir in sugar, cornstarch, and lemon juice. Boil slowly 10 minutes. Spread cream cheese in bottom of baked crust. Arrange whole berries on top of cream cheese. Pour *cooled* cooked mixture on top. Garnish with whipped cream and fresh whole strawberries. Serve very cold. Chill several hours before serving.

Great—guests ask for more.

Virginia Scheiber, Wilmington, Del.

RIDGELY HOUSE

STRAWBERRY RHUBARB PIE

Yield: 9-inch pie

1 cup sugar	3 cups cut fresh rhubarb
2 tablespoons quick cooking tapioca	1 recipe pastry or 9-inch frozen pie shell
¼ teaspoon salt	1 cup sliced strawberries
½ teaspoon nutmeg	1 tablespoon butter or margarine
¼ cup orange juice	

Preheat oven to 400°. Combine sugar, tapioca, salt, nutmeg, orange juice, and rhubarb. Place in 9-inch pie pan lined with pastry. Top with strawberries; dot with butter. Put on top crust. Bake for 40 to 50 minutes.

Norma Ferguson, Elkton, Md.

SWEET POTATO CUSTARD PIE

Yield: 9-inch pie

2 cups mashed sweet potatoes
  (canned or cooked fresh)
2 cups milk
3 eggs
1 cup sugar

Juice of 1 lemon
Pinch of salt
1 teaspoon nutmeg
Pumpkin pie spice (optional)
9-inch unbaked pastry shell

Preheat oven to 350°. Combine all ingredients in order listed and pour into pastry shell. Bake for 40 minutes.

Wayside Inn, Smyrna, Del.

VICTORY KRINGLE BARS

1 cup butter (or ½ cup butter
  and ½ cup solid vegetable
  shortening)
2 cups flour
1 cup plus 2 tablespoons cold
  water

3 eggs
1 teaspoon almond extract
1 cup confectioner's sugar
1 tablespoon butter

Preheat oven to 350°. Mix ½ cup butter, 1 cup of flour, and 2 tablespoons of cold water as for a pie crust. Divide dough into 2 parts and roll out to 3 inches wide and 12 to 14 inches long. Place the two parts on a cookie sheet. Bring to a boil ½ cup butter and 1 cup water. Remove from heat and add 1 cup flour, eggs, and ½ teaspoon almond extract. Spread on dough and bake for 1 hour.

Make frosting by combining confectioner's sugar, 1 tablespoon butter, and ½ teaspoon almond extract and thin with about 2 tablespoons milk. Frost pastry.

This recipe is being shared with us by the Scandanavian galley chef from the cruise ship *Victory Chimes*. The ship was formerly known as the *Edward and Maude*, a ram, built in Bethel, Delaware, in 1902.

COOKIES

CHRUSCIK
(Polish Pretzels)

Yield: approximately 2 dozen

½ teaspoon salt
2 eggs, whole
4 egg yolks
½ cup confectioner's sugar

¼ cup butter
1 jigger rum
2 cups flour

Add salt to whole eggs and yolks; beat until thick and lemon colored. Add sugar, butter, and rum and continue to beat. Fold in flour and knead until dough blisters. Cut in halves and roll very thin. Cut into strips 1½ inches wide and 4 inches long. Slit center of strip and slip one end through the slit. Fry in hot oil until lightly browned. Drain on absorbent paper and sprinkle with powdered sugar.

These will keep, if hidden!

Rocky Gentkowski, Wilmington, Del.

CREME DE MENTHE BROWNIES

Yield: 18 to 24

First Layer:
1 cup sugar
½ cup soft butter
4 eggs, beaten

1 cup flour
1 can chocolate syrup
1 teaspoon vanilla
Nuts (optional)

Preheat oven to 350°. Line 9- by 13-inch pan with foil; grease lightly. Mix all ingredients and pour into prepared pan. Bake for 30 minutes. Cool completely.

Second Layer:
2 cups confectioner's sugar
½ cup soft butter

2 tablespoons creme de menthe
* liqueur*

Mix together well confectioner's sugar, ½ cup butter, and liqueur. Spread over first layer.

Third Layer:
6 tablespoons butter

6 ounces chocolate chips

Melt together 6 tablespoons butter and chocolate chips in double boiler; pour over creme de menthe layer. Cut into squares.

They'll melt in your mouth.

Mary Wallace, Wilmington, Del.

SWEDISH WHITE BROWNIES

Yield: 24

2 eggs
1 cup plus 1 tablespoon sugar
Pinch of salt
½ cup melted butter

1 cup flour
1 teaspoon almond extract
1½ to 2 tablespoons slivered
　　almonds

Preheat oven to 325°. Beat eggs, 1 cup of sugar, salt, butter, flour, and almond extract together. Spread in greased, square 9-inch pan. Sprinkle top generously with about 1 tablespoon sugar and nuts. Bake about 30 minutes. Cool. Cut into squares.

Absolutely delicious.

Sandy Pierson, Wilmington, Del.

CREAM CHEESE COOKIES

Yield: approximately 5 dozen

1 cup butter
8 ounces cream cheese

2 cups flour
10-ounce can apricot filling

Preheat oven to 350°. Blend butter, cheese, and flour together to handle. Shape into walnut-sized balls. Hollow center to hold a small amount of filling. Bake for 15 minutes or until barely brown on bottom.

Why not make two batches—one for you and one for a friend?

Bryan Mumford, Summerland, Cal., formerly of Claymont, Del.

EASY GERMAN COOKIES

Yield: approximately 2 dozen

4 eggs, well beaten
1-pound brown sugar
2 cups flour
1 teaspoon cinnamon
1 teaspoon vanilla
1 cup raisins

1 cup walnuts, chopped
  (approximately ¼ pound)
½ to 2 cups confectioner's sugar
¼ cup orange juice
½ tablespoon grated orange rind
  (2 to 3 large oranges)

Preheat oven to 275°. Mix eggs, brown sugar, flour, cinnamon, vanilla, raisins, and nuts and spread thin in cookie sheet with sides or 11- by 14-inch glass dish. Bake for 25 minutes.

When cool, frost cookies with powdered sugar frosting or make orange frosting by mixing confectioner's sugar, orange juice, and rind in top of a double boiler, cook for 10 to 15 minutes. Remove from over boiling water; beat icing until cool and thick enough to spread. This is particularly nice with its fruity flavor.

Cookie of the Week Winner, 1959.

Mrs. Marion Howard Neal, Claymont, Del.

NO-BAKE COOKIES

½ cup crunchy peanut butter
2 teaspoons vanilla
3 cup quick oatmeal
  heaping pinch of salt

2 cups sugar
¼ pound oleo
½ cup milk
3 tablespoons cocoa

Before cooking have ready the first 4 ingredients. Cook together, boiling for 2 minutes, the sugar, oleo, milk and cocoa. Remove from heat and add peanut butter, oatmeal, vanilla and salt. Drop on waxed paper by teaspoon. *Do not bake.*

An easy recipe that takes about ½ hour to prepare.

Mary Morgan, Milton, Del.

GINGER CAKES

Yield: approximately 2 dozen

2 cups lard or vegetable   2 cups dark molasses
  shortening   2 tablespoons baking soda
1 cup sugar   2 tablespoons ginger
1 cup sour cream   ½ teaspoon salt
3 eggs   6½ to 7 cups flour, sifted

Preheat oven to 350°. Cream lard, sugar, eggs, and sour cream. Add molasses and dry ingredients alternately to first mixture. Roll out about ½-inch and cut in shapes of your choice. Sprinkle sugar on top. Bake for 12 to 15 minutes.

Recipe may be halved.

E. Bernice Seymour, Hockessin, Del.

GINGERBREAD BOYS AND GIRLS

1 cup solid vegetable
  shortening
1 cup sugar
1 egg
1 cup dark molasses
2 tablespoons cider vinegar

5 cups sifted flour
1½ teaspoons baking soda
1 tablespoon ginger
1 teaspoon ground cloves
1 teaspoon cinnamon

Cream together shortening and sugar. Add egg, then molasses and vinegar. Combine dry ingredients in a bowl and add to above mixture.

Divide and wrap in wax paper. Chill in refrigerator 3 or 4 hours. Preheat oven to 370°. Remove one batch at a time, kneading slightly on floured board. Roll out to ½-inch thick. Bake on lightly greased cookie sheet for 8 to 10 minutes (watch carefully).

More joy than job.

Gingerbread men were popular throughout the world. Not only children loved them, but adults too for they would not spoil when taken on long voyages.

This is a specialty of the Robinson House, sometimes referred to as Naamans Tea House in Claymont.

GINGERSNAPS

Yield: 4 to 5 dozen

2 cups flour
½ teaspoon salt
1 teaspoon ground cloves
1 teaspoon ground ginger
1 teaspoon cinnamon
3 teaspoons baking soda

¾ cup soft vegetable shortening
1 cup granulated sugar
1 egg
¼ cup light molasses
Granulated sugar

Preheat oven to 350°. Sift together dry ingredients. Cream shorteninng until light and fluffy, gradually adding sugar. Blend in egg and add molasses; then stir in flour mixture until well blended.

Shape dough into 1-inch balls. Roll in granulated sugar. Place 2 inches apart on ungreased cookie sheet. Flatten slightly with fingers. Bake 6 minutes. Let stand a minute before removing from sheet.

A yearly winner. This recipe dates back to the '50s and every year one of our children would enter this recipe in the Unionville Fair, and every year it won first prize.

Nora Hug, Chadds Ford, Pa.

HOBNAILS

Yield: approximately 2 dozen

1 cup light brown sugar
½ cup shortening
1 egg, beaten
1 teaspoon vanilla
1½ cups flour

½ teaspoon baking soda
½ teaspoon salt
½ cup chocolate chips (or ½ cup
  raisins plus 1 teaspoon
  cinnamon)

Preheat oven to 375°. Cream sugar and shortening. Add next 6 ingredients and drop in small balls on greased cookie sheet. Bake for 12 to 15 minutes.

I added this cookie recipe to my recipe box over 30 years ago after testing them in Virginia.

Mary Edith Farlow, Selbyville, Del.

JEWISH COOKIES

Yield: 3 dozen

2 3-ounce packages cream
  cheese
1 cup solid vegetable shortening
1 cup sugar

2 cups flour
½ teaspoon salt
Jelly or preserves

Preheat oven to 350°. Beat together the cream cheese, shortening, and sugar until fluffy. Add flour and salt. Drop by teaspoonful onto a greased cookie sheet. Make a dent with a spoon in the top. Add a dab of jelly. Bake for 10 or 15 minutes.

Evelyn Patterson, Wilmington, Del.

LEMON COCONUT CHEWS

Yield: 4 dozen

2 cups flour
1 cup sugar
1 teaspoon salt
½ teaspoon baking soda

¾ cup butter, softened
1 cup canned coconut
21-ounce jar lemon pie filling

Preheat oven to 375°. Combine flour, sugar, salt, baking soda, and butter at low speed in electric mixer. Scrape bowl often until mixture is crumbly for 2 to 3 minutes. Stir in coconut. Reserve 1½ cups of crumb mixture for topping.

Press remaining crumbs into greased and floured 13- by 9- by 2-inch pan. Spread lemon filling over crust. Sprinkle with reserved crumb mixture. Bake near center of oven until golden brown for 25 to 35 minutes. Cool. Cut in bars. The lemon filling bakes on top of a buttery cookie crust.

A cake sale success.

Robin Santobianco, Claymont, Del.

PECAN NUT CUPS

Yield: 24

¼ *pound butter*
1 *cup flour*
3 *ounces cream cheese, room*
  temperature
1 *large egg*

1 *cup light brown sugar*
Pinch of salt
1 *teaspoon vanilla*
¾ *cup chopped pecans*
1 *tablespoon melted butter*

Mix together ¼ pound butter, flour, and cream cheese with a fork. Divide dough into 24 balls. Place balls into cups of small muffin tins. Press dough evenly to line cups.

Preheat oven to 350°. Mix together egg, brown sugar, salt, vanilla, pecans, and melted butter. Put 1 teaspoon mixture into each cup. Bake for 20 minutes. When cooled, sprinkle with confectioner's sugar (optional).

Cookies lend themselves beautifully to easy, friendly hospitality.

Jan Wrigley, Wilmington, Del.

PREACHER COOKIES

Yield: 24

2 *cups sugar*
¼ *pound butter or margarine*
½ *cup milk*
2 *cups quick rolled oats*

½ *cup cocoa or 1 cup semisweet*
  chocolate chips
1 *teaspoon vanilla*
½ *cup walnuts*

In a saucepan cook sugar, butter, and milk for 2 minutes, stirring constantly. While boiling, add last 4 ingredients. Stir until chocolate melts. Drop by teaspoonsful on waxed paper.

In a hurry? Try these.

Marge Weir, Winter Haven, Fla., formerly of Claymont, Del.

PRINGLE COOKIES

Yield: 6 to 8 dozen

1 cup sugar
2 cups butter or margarine (1
   pound)
2 teaspoons vanilla
4 cups all-purpose flour, sifted
1 cup (about ⅔ can) crushed
   Pringle potato chips

1 cup chopped walnuts or pecans
   (optional)
Red and green sugar for coating
   cookies

Preheat oven to 350°. Cream sugar, butter, and vanilla. Add flour and mix well. Stir in Pringles and chopped nuts. Combine thoroughly.

Form in 1-inch balls. Roll in either red or green sugar. Place on ungreased cookie sheets. Flatten with bottom of glass dipped in sugar. Bake for 14 to 16 minutes or until lightly browned on edges.

Scrumptious—they'll melt in your mouth.

Margaret Jordan, Elkton, Md., formerly of Claymont, Del.

RAISIN COOKIES

1 cup sugar	*1 teaspoon nutmeg*
1 cup butter	*1 teaspoon salt*
2 eggs, beaten	*2 teaspoons baking soda*
3½ cups flour	*2 cups raisins*
1 teaspoon cinnamon	*1 cup walnuts or pecans*
1 teaspoon allspice	*(chopped about ¼ pound)*

Preheat oven to 325° to 350°. Cream sugar and butter. Add eggs. Sift flour, cinnamon, allspice, nutmeg, salt, and baking soda. Set aside. In a saucepan, cover raisins with water and cook until raisins are soft (will puff up). Drain off liquid (at least 1 cup) and add it alternately with dry ingredients to sugar and butter mixture. Add nuts.

Spread very thinly on greased cookie sheet with sides. Bake 25 minutes. Ice with cookie icing of your choice and cut in squares.

Mayor Al Stango, Lewes, Del.

SEVEN LAYER COOKIES

Yield: 24

¼ pound butter or margarine	*6-ounce package butterscotch*
1 cup graham cracker crumbs	*chips*
1 cup canned flaked coconut	*14-ounce can condensed milk*
6-ounce package chocolate chips	*1½ cups chopped walnuts*

Preheat oven to 350°. Melt butter in 13- by 9-inch pan. Add each layer of ingredients evenly in order listed. Bake for ½ hour. Cut into squares when cooled.

Rich and luscious.

Dorothy Poteet, Wilmington, Del.

SNICKERDOODLES

Yield: approximately 100

1½ cups sugar
1 cup soft shortening (half
   butter and half solid
   vegetable shortening)
2 eggs
2¾ cups flour

1 teaspoon baking soda
½ teaspoon salt
2 teaspoons cream of tartar
3 tablespoons sugar
3 teaspoons cinnamon

Preheat oven to 400°. Cream sugar and shortening together. Add eggs and beat well. Stir in flour, baking soda, salt, and cream of tartar. Chill for 1 hour. Roll dough into small balls and roll these in a mixture of 3 tablespoons sugar and 3 teaspoons cinnamon. Bake on *ungreased* cookie sheets for 8 to 10 minutes. Snecken noodles, so-called by the Dutch, are an all-time favorite.

Great recipe for holidays and afternoon tea.

Mildred Quigley, Claymont, Del.

Be sorry for people
  Whoever they are
Who live in a house
  Where there's no cookie jar!

SPECULAAS

Yield: approximately 2 dozen

2 cups flour
Pinch of salt
1 tablespoon baking powder
2 teaspoons cinnamon
¾ teaspoon ground cloves
¼ teaspoon nutmeg
¼ teaspoon aniseed (ground) or
   anise extract

½ pound butter
¾ cup brown sugar
1 large egg, beaten
Pinch of cocoa
Pinch of pepper
Drop of almond extract
½ teaspoon lemon peel
Ginger pieces or almonds

Preheat oven to 350°. Mix flour, salt, baking powder, cinnamon, cloves, and aniseed. In a separate bowl, beat butter and sugar together until fluffy. Add egg. Gradually add dry ingredients, adding cocoa and pepper; then the almond extract, lemon peel, and ginger pieces. You can use almonds as well if they are in thin slices. Form dough into a ball and knead it well.

Roll dough into a flat cookie sheet, ¼-inch thick. Press dough into cookie boards or use cookie cutters. Let dough rest for 1 hour. Unmold cookies and place on buttered cookie sheet. Bake for 25 minutes. Let cool on rack.

These are Dutch cookies made for St. Nicholas Day and Christmas in France, Belgium, and Holland. "Speculaas" came from the Latin word Speculum or mirror, because the dough is pressed into wooden cookie boards and thus gives a mirror image of the carved molds. We serve this Christmas treat at Christmas time at the Newcastle Inn Restaurant.

Claudie J. Brock, New Castle, Del., and Newtown Square, Pa.

SWEDISH PIZZELLES

Yield: 4 to 5 dozen

½ pound butter
1¼ cups sugar
2 teaspoons vanilla
2 extra large eggs
½ cup light cream

4 cups flour
2 tablespoons baking powder
1 teaspoon salt
Confectioner's sugar

Mix the butter, sugar and vanilla. Add the remaining ingredients.

Follow baking instruction of the pizzelle iron. Sprinkle pizzelles with confectioner's sugar while still warm.

Ann Tenuto, Chester, Pa.

WELSH COOKIES

Yield: approximately 3 dozen

4 cups flour
3 teaspoons baking powder
3 teaspoons nutmeg
¼ teaspoon salt
½ pound margarine

2 cups sugar
2 eggs
¼ to ½ cup milk
1 cup raisins

Sift together flour, baking powder, nutmeg, and salt. Cream margarine, sugar, and eggs adding flour mixture plus ¼ to ½ cup of enough milk to keep batter from being sticky. Add the raisins; roll out to ¼ inch thick. Cut to any size. Cook in electric fry pan at 330°. Shortening is not needed in the frying pan as there is sufficient in the batter.

Diane Evans, Claymont, Del.

FILLED CRESCENT COOKIES

Yield: 4 dozen

1 *package yeast*	1 *cup butter, softened*
¼ *cup lukewarm milk*	4 *hard-boiled egg yolks (sieved)*
1 *teaspoon vanilla*	*Preserves, of your choice, level*
1 *tablespoon sugar*	*tablespoon*
3 *cups flour*	*Confectioner's sugar*

Preheat oven to 375°. Dissolve yeast in lukewarm milk. Add vanilla and sugar. In separate bowl, blend flour with softened butter and egg yolks. Add liquid mixture. Work well together into a smooth dough. Divide dough into 8 sections. Roll each section into a thin circle (between 2 sheets of waxed paper). Divide each circle into wedges. Place preserve filling at wide end of wedge and roll towards point. Bend to crescent shape. Bake for 20 minutes. Sprinkle with confectioner's sugar before serving.

Carol A. Day, Wilmington, Del.

CANDY

HEALTH CEREAL

Yield: approximately 9 to 10 cups

7 cups quick oats
1 cup wheat germ
¼ cup sesame seeds
¼ cup ground pecans
¼ cup sliced almonds
¾ cup honey

⅓ cup safflower oil
½ of 15-ounce box of raisins
½ of 8-ounce package of dried
  apricots, finely chopped
4 ounces dates, finely chopped

Preheat oven to 350°. Mix all ingredients, except the fruits, in a soup pot. Turn onto a cookie sheet with sides. Bake for 30 minutes. Stir in dried fruit after baking. When cool, store in an airtight container.

"These delights won't linger very long."

Nancy Zippe, Wilmington, Del.

CHOCOLATE FUDGE

Yield: 16 pieces

¼ pound margarine
½ cup cocoa
3 cups sugar
½ cup corn syrup

7 ounces evaporated milk
⅛ teaspoon salt
1 teaspoon vanilla

Melt margarine in 2 quart saucepan and add cocoa; blend well. Add sugar, syrup, milk, and salt. Mix well and place over medium heat. Stir occasionally until sugar dissolves and mixture is boiling. Turn heat to low, cover, and let cook until mixture reaches the soft ball stage. Remove from heat and let cool to room temperature. Then add vanilla extract and beat until mixture thickens. Pour fudge in 8-inch pan greased with margarine and let cool. Then cut to desired pieces.

Maxine W. Mann, Claymont, Del.

HEALTHFUL FUDGE

Yield: 2½ pounds

1 cup honey
1 cup peanut butter
1 cup carob powder
1 cup sunflower seeds, shelled

½ cup toasted sesame seeds
½ cup canned flaked coconut
½ cup walnuts, chopped
½ cup raisins

In large saucepan heat honey and peanut butter, stirring constantly until smooth. Remove from heat. Stir in carob powder. Mix well. Stir in sunflower seeds and remaining ingredients. Press into buttered 8-inch square dish or pan. Chill, covered, several hours. Store in refrigerator.

Maggie Houser, Claymont, Del.

HOLIDAY FUDGE

Yield: approximately 16 pieces

3 cups semisweet chocolate
* chips*
14-ounce can condensed milk

Pinch salt
1½ teaspoon vanilla
½ cup ground nuts, optional

Melt chocolate chips in top of double boiler over hot water. Stir occasionally. Remove from heat and add condensed milk, salt, vanilla, and nuts. Stir until smooth. Turn into waxed-paper-lined 8-inch square pan. Spread evenly. Place in refrigerator 2 hours or until firm. Turn candy onto cutting board, peel off paper. Cut fudge into serving pieces. Store in airtight container.

"And he who gives a child a treat makes joy bells ring in heaven's street." —JOHN MASEFIELD (1878-1967)

Amy Hanchey, Wallace, N. C., formerly from Claymont, Del.

PEANUT BUTTER FUDGE

Yield: 35 to 40 pieces

¼ pound butter
3 cups sugar
Pinch of salt
⅔ cup evaporated milk

7½-ounce jar marshmallow
   creme
8-ounce jar peanut butter

Cook the above until it comes to a soft boil, approximately 12 minutes. Beat in marshmallow and peanut butter.

Pour in greased 9- by 13-inch pan; let cool.

Kathleen Holland, Claymont, Del.

VELVETY FUDGE

Yield: 4 pounds

4 pounds confectioner's sugar
1 cup cocoa
1 pound Velveeta cheese

1 pound butter or margarine
1 tablespoon vanilla
2 cups chopped nuts (optional)

Sift sugar and cocoa together and set aside. Cut up cheese and butter into pieces and melt together over low heat. (*Do not* let it boil or cheese may curdle.) Turn off heat. Add cocoa mixture to this, a cupful at a time. Add vanilla and nuts, keeping a few nuts to sprinkle over top and press in.

Pour into buttered 9- by 13-inch dish. Cool and cut.

Recipe may be halved.

Sue Coyle, Wilmington, Del.

CHOCOLATE COVERED PRETZELS

Yield: 30

5 ounces semisweet chocolate
 chips
2 tablespoons corn syrup

2 tablespoons butter
1½ teaspoons water
30 pretzels

n the top of a double boiler, over hot but not boiling water, combine chocolate, syrup, butter, and water. Stir until chocolate melts. Remove from heat, but keep over hot water. One at a time, dip pretzels into chocolate sauce. Place on wire rack. Chill 10 minutes to set coating. Remove to firm at room temperature.

Mary Swider, Claymont, Del.

CHOCOLATE SALTINES

Yield: 40

Margarine for greasing foil
Saltines, approximately 40
¼ pound butter or margarine
1 cup brown sugar

12-ounce package semisweet
 chocolate chips
½ cup chopped pecans

Preheat oven to 350°. Line an 11- by 15-inch pan with aluminum foil and grease foil with margarine. Spread a single layer of saltines on the coated foil.

In a small pan, combine butter and brown sugar; bring to a boil and boil for 3 minutes, stirring constantly to prevent sticking. Pour this mixture over the layer of saltines and bake in oven for 5 minutes. Remove from the oven and scatter the chocolate chips over the surface. Let soften, then spread to coat the saltine base. Scatter the pecans over the top. Score with knife. Chill ½ hour. Carefully break or cut apart to serve. Store in refrigerator.

Ellen B. DiTeodoro, New Castle, Del.

CHOCOLATE PEANUT BUTTER CRISPIES

Yield: about 4 dozen

1 cup (6-ounce package)
  semisweet chocolate chips
1 cup (6-ounce package) peanut
  butter chips

2 tablespoons vegetable oil
1⅓ cups crisp rice cereal
½ cup chopped walnuts

Combine chocolate chips, peanut butter chips, and oil in top of double boiler over boiling water. Stir until chips are completely melted and well blended. Remove from heat; stir in cereal and nuts. Cool slightly; drop by tablespoons into paper nut cups. Chill until firm. Store in covered container in refrigerator.

Compliments of the Hershey Chocolate Company, Hershey, Pa.

KRISPIE BALLS

Yield: 80

½ pound butter
1½ cups sugar
1 pound dates
2 eggs
2 tablespoons milk

¼ teaspoon salt
1 teaspoon vanilla
4 cups Rice Krispies
2 cups pecans, broken
2 cups canned flaked coconut

Melt butter and sugar in a skillet. Stir in dates. Boil 2 minutes; let cool. Beat eggs; mix with milk, salt, and vanilla. Add 2 tablespoons of date mixture to egg and milk mixture. Then add this to date mixture in skillet and boil 2 more minutes. Let cool while you prepare the Rice Krispies and pecans. Mix with first mixture in large bowl. Form into small balls; roll in coconut.

Ruth Jensen, Milton, Del.

OLD FASHIONED PEANUT BRITTLE

Yield: 1 pound

cups sugar   1 cup dry roasted peanuts

In a large, heavy skillet, stir sugar over medium heat until it dissolves and becomes a caramel-colored syrup. Guard against burning. Remove pan from heat and quickly stir in the nuts. Pour *immediately* onto lightly oiled cookie sheet, spreading the brittle as thin as you wish. Cool and break into pieces. Keep in a tightly covered container in a cool place.

A favorite at church and school functions.

Kay Herr, Claymont, Del.

PEANUT BUTTER BALLS

Yield: approximately 50 balls

12 ounces peanut butter   1 teaspoon vanilla
¼ pound margarine   12 ounces chocolate chips
1 pound confectioner's sugar   ½-inch slice paraffin wax

Mix together peanut butter, margarine, sugar, and vanilla and form into balls. In a double boiler, melt chocolate chips and wax. Dip ball in the melted chocolate. Cool on waxed paper.

They freeze beautifully.

Pat Gennaria, Claymont, Del.

PEANUT BUTTER CUPS

2 cups peanut butter, creamy or
   chunk style
½ cup plus 1 tablespoon melted
   butter

2¾ cups confectioner's sugar
12-ounce package chocolate chips

Stir together peanut butter, ½ cup melted butter, and confectioner's sugar. Press mixture into bottom of 9-inch square dish. Melt chocolate chips and stir together with remaining tablespoon butter; spread on top. Refrigerate for *10 minutes* to set chocolate. Store at *room temperature*. Cut into small squares

Note: Mixture also may be pressed into small baking cups. Especially colorful in "holiday cups."

Linda Schupp, Newark, Del.

SALT WATER TAFFY

1 cup sugar
¾ cup light corn syrup
⅔ cup water
1 tablespoon cornstarch

2 tablespoons butter or
   margarine
1 teaspoon salt
2 teaspoons vanilla

Mix sugar, syrup, water, cornstarch, butter and salt in 2-quart pan. Cook over medium heat, stirring with wooden spoon till 256°. Stir in vanilla and pour into buttered 8-inch pan. When cool, pull till light in color and stiff. Cut into small pieces and wrap in wax paper.

Bring the seashore to your home and treat your family to a homemade batch.

Brenda Coulsting, Wilmington, Del.

CAKES AND FROSTINGS

APPLE CAKE

Serves 12

3 eggs
2 cups sugar
1½ cups vegetable oil
3 cups flour
1 teaspoon baking soda
1 teaspoon salt
1 teaspoon cinnamon

2 teaspoons vanilla
1 cup walnuts, chopped
3 cups apples, peeled and
  chopped
¼ cup margarine
1 cup brown sugar
¼ cup evaporated milk

Preheat oven to 325°. Beat eggs, add sugar, and mix thoroughly. Add remaining 8 ingredients. Bake in greased 10-inch tube pan lined with wax paper for 1 hour and 15 minutes. (Bake only 1 hour if batter is divided in two pans.)

Make topping by mixing together margarine, brown sugar, and evaporated milk in a saucepan. Boil 2 or 3 minutes. Pour over cooled cake.

Marion Griffith, Seaford, Del.

ELSIE'S TOSS APPLE CAKE

¼ pound margarine
2 eggs
1 teaspoon vanilla
1½ cups flour
1¼ cups sugar
½ teaspoon salt
1 teaspoon baking soda

1 teaspoon baking powder
1 teaspoon cinnamon
4 cups apples, peeled, and diced
   (4 to 5 large apples)
½ cup chopped walnuts
   (optional)

Preheat oven to 350°. Melt margarine in small pan over low heat. Beat eggs and vanilla in small bowl and set aside. In a large bowl, sift together flour, sugar, salt, baking soda, baking powder, and cinnamon. Add the melted magarine and the eggs and mix with a wooden spoon. Add apples and walnuts.

Grease and flour a 9- by 12- by 2-inch pan and spread out batter. It will be a thin layer, but bakes nicely. Bake for 40 to 45 minutes.

Cake is moist and delicious. Best make two. The "kids" will eat the first one while still warm.

Elsie Toth

ONE QUART APPLESAUCE CAKE

Serves 12

4½ teaspoons baking soda
1 quart applesauce
2½ cups sugar
½ cup butter, melted
4 cups flour

2 teaspoons cinnamon
1 teaspoon nutmeg
2 cups raisins
½ cup black walnuts

Preheat oven to 300°. In a large bowl beat baking soda into applesauce. Stir in sugar. Melt butter and add. Stir in flour and mix well by hand. Add remaining ingredients. Pour ingredients into greased and floured 10-inch tube pan (if using a Teflon pan, do not grease and flour). Bake 1 hour and 15 minutes.

Ginny Austin, Blades, Del.

APPLE UPSIDE-DOWN CAKE

Yield: 9-inch cake

¼ cup butter
1 cup brown sugar
2 large baking apples
½ cup raisins
1½ cups cake flour
½ teaspoon salt
3 teaspoons baking powder

⅓ cup solid vegetable shortening
⅓ cup sugar
2 eggs, well beaten
1 teaspoon vanilla
⅔ cup water
Whipped cream

Preheat oven to 350°. Melt butter in 9-inch baking pan. Add brown sugar and stir until melted. Cool. Peel, core, and slice apples; place on sugar in pan. Sprinkle with raisins. Sift flour, salt and baking powder together. Cream shortening with sugar until fluffy. Add eggs and vanilla and beat thoroughly. Add sifted dry ingredients and water alternately in small amounts, beating well after each addition. Pour over apples. Bake 40 minutes. Turn onto plate immediately. Serve with whipped cream.

Ronnie Swafford, Wilmington, Del.

FROSTED BANANA FINGERS

Yield: 14 or 15 fingers

1⅜ cups cake flour
1 teaspoon baking powder
⅛ teaspoon baking soda
⅜ teaspoon salt
¼ cup vegetable shortening
½ cup sugar
1 egg
1 teaspoon vanilla
½ cup plus 2 tablespoons
  mashed ripe banana (1 to 2
  large bananas)

1 tablespoon milk
¼ teaspoon lemon juice
2 tablespoons butter
1¼ cups confectioner's sugar
Few drops yellow food coloring
1 square unsweetened chocolate

Peheat oven to 350°. Sift the cake flour. Sift together cake flour, baking powder, baking soda, and salt. Set aside. Cream shortening and sugar; add egg and beat well. Mix together vanilla, ½ cup bananas and milk. Alternately add dry and liquid ingredients to shortening.

Grease cornstick pans well. Fill pan with batter ¾ full. Bake for 20 minutes. Cool before frosting.

While fingers bake, make frosting by combining 2 tablespoons mashed banana and lemon juice. Add the butter and confectioner's sugar and beat with a mixer. Add enough yellow food coloring to make the frosting banana colored. Blend well and mix until fluffy.

Turn cakes from pan. Frost the bottom of the cakes. Melt the chocolate. With a toothpick or fork dipped into the chocolate, make dark lines on the frosting to make fingers look like bananas. Finished cakes may be wrapped well and frozen.

Mildred Woodall, Wilmington, Del.

CARROT CAKE

3 cups flour
2 cups sugar
2 teaspoons baking soda
2 teaspoons baking powder
2 7¼-ounce jars carrot baby food
1¼ cups vegetable oil
4 eggs

2 teaspoons cinnamon
Pinch of salt
¼ pound butter
1 pound confectioner's sugar
8 ounces cream cheese
1 teaspoon vanilla
¼ cup milk

Preheat oven to 350°. Mix together flour, sugar, baking soda, baking powder, carrots, oil, eggs, cinnamon, and salt. Pour into greased 10-inch tube pan and bake for 55 to 60 minutes.

CREAM CHEESE FROSTING:

Combine butter and confectioners's sugar. Add cream cheese and vanilla; stir in milk by tablespoonfuls until frosting is spreadable. Frost cake when cool.

So easy and so good. Carrots are native to England, and the colonists brought them to America.

Sandy Walker, Claymont, Del.

JIMMY CARTER CAKE

¼ pound plus 4 tablespoons
  margarine
1½ cups flour
¾ cup chopped nuts
8 ounces cream cheese
1 cup confectioner's sugar
⅓ cup peanut butter
1 cup frozen whipped topping

1 small box vanilla instant
  pudding
1 small box chocolate instant
  pudding
2½ cups cold milk
Chopped nuts
1.65-ounce milk chocolate candy
  bar

Preheat oven to 350°. Combine margarine and flour, add nuts, and pat into a 9- by 13-inch pan. Bake for 20 minutes. Cool.

Mix together cream cheese, sugar and peanut butter. Add thawed whipped topping. Spread in a layer over cooled crust.

Combine the vanilla and chocolate puddings and the milk. Pour over the peanut butter layer. Refrigerate until firm. Top with any leftover topping. Garnish with chopped nuts and grated chocolate bar. Refrigerate overnight.

Delicious. You can keep this cake for 2-3 days.

Jo Domenic, Wilmington, Del.

CHOCOLATE CREAM CHEESE CAKE WITH CHOCOLATE CREAM CHEESE ICING

Yield: 2 9-inch layers

2 3-ounce packages cream
  cheese, softened
½ cup plus 4 tablespoons butter
  or margarine, softened
1 teaspoon vanilla
6½ cups (1½ pounds) sifted
  powdered sugar
⅓ cup plus 1¼ cups milk, room
  temperature

4 squares (4 ounces) unsweetened chocolate, melted and
  cooled
3 eggs
2¼ cups all purpose flour
1 teaspoon baking powder
1 teaspoon baking soda
1 teaspoon salt

Preheat oven to 350°. Cream together cheese, ½ cup butter, and vanilla. Alternately beat in sugar and ⅓ cup milk. Blend in chocolate. Remove 2 cups of batter for frosting; cover and refrigerate. Cream together remaining chocolate mixture and 4 tablespoons butter. Add eggs, beat well. Stir together dry ingredients. Beat into creamed mixture alternately with the remaining milk. Turn into 2 greased and floured 9- by 1½-inch cake pans. Bake for 30 minutes. Cool in pans 10 minutes. Remove, cool on racks. Remove frosting from refrigerator 15 minutes before frosting cake. The frosting comes from part of the batter.

My family's favorite chocolate cake recipe.

Jill Biden, Wilmington, Del.

DELAWARE CHEESECAKE

Yield: 8-inch square cake

1¾ cups graham cracker
    crumbs
⅓ cup butter
¼ cup sugar
1 envelope Dream Whip

2 8-ounce packages cream cheese
3 cups confectioner's sugar
21-ounce can cherry or blueberry
    pie filling

Preheat oven to 350°. In an 8- by 8- by 2-inch square pan, combine graham cracker crumbs, butter, and sugar. Spread mixture as thinly as possible. Make sure to cover pan sides at least up to within ½ inch of the top. Bake for 8 minutes. Let cool.

In a bowl, mix Dream Whip thoroughly with an electric beater. In a separate bowl, mix the cream cheese and confectioner's sugar. Add to the Dream Whip. Spread in pan over cracker crust. Refrigerate at least 3 hours or overnight. Then spread fruit pie filling on top. Refrigerate at least 2 hours before serving. Cut in squares to serve.

Dr. Harold B. Hancock, receiver of the 1984 Governor's Award for Outstanding Contributions to Delaware History and Culture. Emeritus Professor, Otterbein College, Westerville, Ohio.

GREAT GRANDMA'S CHEESECAKE

Yield: 10-inch round cake

4-ounce box Zweiback crackers
1½ cups sugar
2 teaspoons cinnamon
1 heaping tablespoon butter
1 teaspoon vanilla
1½ pounds pot cheese or farmer cheese, or a combination of both

Pinch of salt
4 eggs
1 tablespoon flour
½ pint heavy cream

Preheat oven to 350°. Crush crackers into fine crumbs. Combine crumbs, ½ cup of the sugar, and cinnamon; cream in the butter and vanilla. Set aside.

Put cheese through food mill. Add salt, 1 cup sugar, eggs, and flour. Whip the heavy cream; add half the vanilla. Fold the whipped cream into the cheese mixture.

Take about half of the reserved cracker mixture and press into the bottom and partly up the sides of a springform pan. Pour cheese mixture in. Sprinkle rest of cracker mixture on top. Bake for 40 to 50 minutes. Let stand in the oven until oven and cake are cool. Chill overnight, if possible. Remove outside rim of pan to serve.

Lelaine Nemser, Wilmington, Del.

PUMPKIN CHEESECAKE

Graham cracker crust for
  springform pan
1 cup fruit juice, orange or
  pineapple
16-ounce can pumpkin
1 cup brown sugar

1 teaspoon cinnamon
½ teaspoon ginger
3 eggs
1 envelope unflavored gelatin
2 8-ounce packages cream cheese
1 teaspoon vanilla

Preheat oven to 350°. Line 10-inch springform pan with graham cracker crumbs made for a crust*. Bake for 10 minutes. Combine juice, pumpkin, sugar, spices, eggs, and gelatin in medium saucepan. Mix well, cover, and simmer gently for 30 minutes. Stir occasionally. Beat cream cheese and vanilla. Gradually beat in warm pumpkin mixture. Blend well. Pour into crust and refrigerate overnight. Serve with whipped cream.

*1¼ cup graham cracker crumbs
¼ cup sugar
¼ cup butter

Mix well with fork.

Delaware Senator Ruth Ann Minner, Dover, Del.

BLUE GOOSE
CHOCOLATE CAKE

Yield: 1 large cake or 2 9-inch layers

3 squares unsweetened choco-
    late or ¾ cup cocoa
¼ pound margarine
2 teaspoons instant coffee
1 cup water
2 cups flour, sifting optional

2 cups sugar
2 teaspoons baking soda
½ pint sour cream
2 eggs
2 teaspoons vanilla

Preheat oven to 325°. Melt chocolate (or cocoa), margarine, and instant coffee in 1 cup boiling water. Pour hot mixture over flour, sugar, and baking soda. Add sour cream, eggs and vanilla. Bake in 10½-inch tube pan for 50 to 60 minutes, or in 8- or 9-inch layer cake pans at 350° for 40 to 45 minutes. Enjoy. Needs no icing.

Quite a nice combination of qualities and you don't even need a mixer for this family favorite.

Fran Mayhew, Wilmington, Del.

CHOCOLATE CHERRY BARS

Yield: 20 to 24 bars

1 pound 2½-ounce box devil's
  food cake mix
15-ounce can cherry pie filling
1 teaspoon almond extract
2 eggs, well beaten

1 cup sugar
5 tablespoons margarine
⅓ cup milk
1 cup chocolate chips

Preheat oven to 350°. Grease and flour 10- by 14-inch jelly roll pan. Combine cake mix, cherries, almond extract, and eggs. Mix with wooden spoon; *do not use mixer*. Pour into pan. Bake 20 minutes or until done. Cool in pan.

In saucepan, combine sugar, margarine, and milk. Heat to boiling; boil and stir for one minute. Remove from heat; stir in chips until smooth. Pour over warm cake. Cut and serve.

Grace Millman, Milton, Del.

CHOCOLATE CHIP CAKE

Serves 12

¼ pound margarine
1 cup sugar
2 eggs
1 cup sour cream
1 teaspoon vanilla
2 cups sifted flour

1½ teaspoons baking powder
1 teaspoon baking soda
½ cup sugar
1 teaspoon cinnamon
6 ounces chocolate chips

Preheat oven to 350°. Cream margarine, sugar, and eggs together. Add sour cream, vanilla, flour, baking powder, and baking soda. In a separate bowl mix sugar, cinnamon, and chocolate chips. Into a greased 9- by 13-inch oblong pan, pour in about half the cake batter. Sprinkle on half the chocolate chip mix. Pour on remaining cake batter; top with balance of chips. Bake for 30 minutes.

Pauline Welch, Wilmington, Del.

COLA CAKE

Serves 10 to 12

2 cups sifted flour
2 cups sugar
1 teaspoon baking soda
¾ pound butter
6 tablespoons cocoa
1 cup plus 6 tablespoons cola
½ cup buttermilk

2 eggs, beaten
1 teaspoooon vanilla
1½ cups miniature marshmallows
1 pound confectioner's sugar (or
   more)
1 cup chopped walnuts
   (optional)

Preheat oven to 350°. Combine flour, granulated sugar, and baking soda in bowl. In a saucepan, heat ½ pound butter, 3 tablespoons cocoa, and 1 cup of cola to boiling. Pour over flour and sugar; mix well. Add the buttermilk, eggs, vanilla, and marshmallows. Batter will be thin with the marshmallows floating on top. Bake in a greased 9- by 13-inch pan for 30 to 35 minutes.

While cake bakes, make the icing. In a saucepan combine ¼ pound butter and 6 tablespoons cola. Heat until butter melts. Beat well. In a bowl, mix together 3 tablespoons cocoa and the confectioner's sugar. Pour in melted butter. Add nuts. Spread hot icing over hot cake.

Marjorie Parkin, Claymont, Del.

DAISY FLOWER CAKE

Serves 25

½ cup water
2 tablespoons gelatin
1 dozen eggs, separated
1½ cups sugar
3 tablespoons lemon rind, grated
  (approximately 6 to 8
  lemons)

1½ cups lemon juice
1½ cups fine sugar, for egg
  whites
1 Sponge Cake recipe

Soften gelatin in water. To make a custard, combine egg yolks, sugar, lemon rind, and lemon juice over low heat until mixture coats spoon. Remove from heat. Add softened gelatin. Beat the 12 egg whites until stiff. Add the last 1½ cups sugar to egg whites. Beat and fold into custard mixture.

SPONGE CAKE

16 egg yolks
1 cup cold milk
1 pound sugar

2 teaspoons vanilla
1½ pounds flour
Whipped cream

Preheat oven to 300°. Beat together the egg yolks and milk. Add the sugar gradually, beating until dissolved. Add vanilla. Sifting gradually, add the flour and beat until smooth. Pour batter into 14- by 6-inch pan lined with greased paper. Bake for 1 hour. Invert on board; tear off paper; cool. Break cake into small pieces. In 2 10-inch round pans, layer cake pieces alternately with custard. Chill or freeze. To serve, unmold and frost with unsweetened whipped cream.

Hubert M. Winkler, executive chef, Hotel Dupont, Wilmington, Del.

HARVEST CAKE

Serves 18 to 20

4 cups apples, peeled and diced   3 cups flour
2 cups sugar   ½ teaspoon salt
2 eggs, beaten   2 teaspoons baking soda
1 cup vegetable oil   1 cup walnuts
1 teaspoon vanilla   1 cup raisins

Preheat oven to 375°. Using apples that are not too juicy, add sugar and let stand 1 hour. Add eggs beaten in the salad oil and vanilla to the apple mixture. Add flour which has been sifted with salt and baking soda. Fold in walnuts and raisins. Mix well but do not beat hard. Bake in greased and floured 10- by 14-inch sheet pan for 45 minutes.

This makes a really different cake—moist and nice. Delicious with a glob of whipped cream and/or a mug of cider.

Gayle Hatz, Newark, Del.

ITALIAN CREAM CAKE

Serves 8

¼ *pound margarine plus 4*
  tablespoons
½ *cup vegetable shortening*
2 *cups sugar*
5 *eggs, separated*
2 *cups flour*
1 *teaspoon baking soda*
1 *cup buttermilk*

2 *teaspoons vanilla*
3½-*ounce can flake coconut*
1 *cup chopped pecans*
8-*ounce package cream cheese,*
  softened
1 *pound box confectioner's sugar*
Chopped pecans

Preheat oven to 350°. Cream ¼ pound of margarine with shortening. Add sugar and egg yolks, beating until mixture is smooth. Combine flour and soda and add to creamed mixture alternately with buttermilk. Stir in 1 teaspoon vanilla. Add coconut and chopped nuts. Fold in stiffly beaten egg whites. Pour batter into 3 greased and floured 8-inch cake pans. Bake for 25 minutes or until cake is done.

Make frosting by beating cream cheese and 4 tablespoons margarine until smooth. Add confectioner's sugar and mix well. Add 1 teaspoon vanilla and beat until smooth. Spread between layers, on top, and sides of cake. Sprinkle top with pecans.

What a treat for the old Claymont School District friends.

Gloria Treco, Claymont, Del.

MADELEINES

1 stick butter plus 6
  tablespoons, softened
½ cup sugar
2 eggs

½ teaspoon salt
1 cup sifted flour
1½ teaspoons vanilla
Confectioner's sugar

Preheat oven to 350°. Cream butter and sugar until light and fluffy. Add eggs, one at a time, beating well after each addition. Add salt and flour, mixing well. Add vanilla. Pour batter into buttered and floured Madeleine tins, ¾ full (a scant tablespoonful). No need to spread batter, heat takes care of that. Bake for 15 minutes or until lightly brown. Turn out on a rack and sprinkle with confectioner's sugar.

Scrumptious delights for high tea.

Friend of the Heritage Commission

MANDARIN ORANGE CAKE

Serves 8 to 10

18½-ounce package yellow cake mix without pudding
11-ounce can mandarin oranges, undrained
4 eggs
½ cup vegetable oil

15¼-ounce can crushed pineapple, undrained
9-ounce carton frozen whipped topping, thawed
3¾-ounce package vanilla instant pudding mix

Preheat oven to 350°. Combine cake mix, oranges, eggs, and oil; with electric mixer, beat for 2 minutes. Reduce speed to low; beat 1 minute. Pour batter into 3 greased and floured 9-inch round pans. Bake for 20 to 25 minutes or until it tests done. Cool in pans 10 minutes; remove from pans and cool completely.

Make frosting by combining crushed pineapple, whipped topping, and pudding mix; beat 2 minutes at medium speed. Let stand 5 minutes or until it reaches spreading consistency. Ice cake. Chill 2 hours before serving.

I've often wondered which was prettier, orange trees in bloom or laden with ripening fruit.

Mary Agnes Dennis, Wilmington, Del.

MEE CAKE

¾ pound butter (not margarine)
3 cups sugar
6 eggs, separated

3 cups all-purpose flour
¼ teaspoon baking soda
1 cup sour cream
2 teaspoons vanilla

Preheat oven to 325°. Cream butter and sugar until fluffy. Mix in egg yolks one at a time. Sift flour with baking soda and add alternately with sour cream. Stir in (don't beat) the vanilla. Beat the egg whites until stiff and fold in carefully (do not beat). Pour batter in a greased floured 10-inch tube pan.

Bake for 1½ hours. Let stand for 10 minutes before removing. While it's hot, sprinkle superfine sugar on top!!

This is a "super moist" cake and needs no frosting.

A Delaware First Prize, 1980 Winner

Carolyn Pendleton, Milford, Del.

MOM'S BIRTHDAY CAKE

Serves 12

½ cup margarine
1½ cups sugar
3 eggs
2¼ cups all-purpose flour
1 teaspoon salt

¼ teaspoon mace
3 teaspoons baking powder
⅔ cup milk
½ teaspoon vanilla
½ teaspoon lemon extract

Preheat oven to 350°. Cream shortening, sugar, and eggs. Mix and sift flour, salt, mace, and baking powder. Add alternately with milk to the creamed ingredients. Add vanilla and lemon extract and beat thoroughly. Pour into greased 10-inch tube pan and bake for 1 hour.

Sue O'Donnell, Claymont, Del.

ORANGE SLICE CAKE

1 pound gum orange slices, chopped
8-ounce package dates, chopped
2½ cups flour
½ pound margarine
2 cups sugar
4 eggs
¼ teaspoon salt
1 teaspoon vanilla
1 teaspoon rum extract
1 cup buttermilk
½ teaspoon baking soda
2 cups pecans, chopped
3½-ounce can flaked coconut (optional)
2 cups confectioner's sugar
½ cup orange juice

Preheat oven to 300°. Combine orange slices and dates; dust with ½ cup flour and set aside. In separate bowl, cream margarine, sugar, and eggs. Add salt, vanilla, and rum extract. Dissolve baking soda in buttermilk and add to creamed mixture. Stir in orange slices and dates. Add remaining 2 cups flour, gradually mixing well. Add nuts. Fold in coconut. Pour into well-greased and floured tube pan and bake for 1 hour and 50 minutes or until done. Remove from oven, run knife around sides to loosen. Dissolve the confectioner's sugar in the orange juice. Pour mixture over cake and cool in pan.

Mrs. Sidney Collison, Dover, Del.

PETIT FOURS

Yield: about 30

2 cups cake flour, sifted twice
3 teaspoons baking powder
¼ teaspoon salt
½ cup butter, softened
1 teaspoon vanilla
1 cup sugar
½ cup milk

4 egg whites, stiffly beaten
6 cups confectioner's sugar
5 tablespoons water
5 tablespoons corn syrup
1 teaspoon vanilla
3 drops food coloring

Preheat oven to 375°. Sift flour twice, then sift flour, baking powder, and salt together. Cream butter, 1 teaspoon vanilla, and sugar together until fluffy. Add dry ingredients and milk alternately. Fold in stiffly beaten egg whites. Pour into 2 greased 9-inch pans or an oblong pan. Bake about 25 minutes.

Cool, then cut into 2-inch squares or use cookie cutters. Brush off crumbs, arrange on wire racks and place racks on waxed paper.

Make fondant by combining confectioner's sugar, water, corn syrup, 1 teaspoon vanilla, and food coloring in top of double boiler. Heat until mixture is thin enough to pour. Pour melted fondant slowly over cakes. Cover cakes twice with fondant. Decorate as desired.

Irene Cole, Wilmington, Del.

PINEAPPLE CASHEW CAKE

1½ cups butter
1¼ cups sugar
1 teaspoon salt
1 teaspoon vanilla
4 egg yolks
2½ cups cake flour
3 teaspoons baking powder
¾ cup milk

9 ounces crushed pineapple,
   chopped
3 egg whites
3 cups confectioner's sugar
½ cup (4 ounces) coarsely
   chopped and toasted cashew
   nuts

Preheat oven to 350°. Cream ¾ cup butter, sugar, ½ teaspoon salt, and vanilla well. Add 3 egg yolks and continue creaming until light and fluffy. Sift flour and baking powder three times. Add alternately with milk. Add 5 ounces chopped crushed pineapple to batter, mixing until smooth. Whip 3 egg whites stiff, but not dry. Fold in lightly, but thoroughly. Divide into 2 greased 9-inch cake pans. Bake for 25 to 30 minutes in preheated oven.

Make icing by creaming ¾ cup butter, confectioner's sugar, and ½ teaspoon salt. Add 1 egg yolk and continue creaming until light and fluffy. Add remaining chopped crushed pineapple (slightly drained) and mix well. Ice cake and sprinkle with chopped and toasted nuts. Guests will ask for the recipe for this extra good flavor cake.

A favorite with my family taught to me by my father when I was a little girl. Enjoy!

Kim Roseman, Wilmington, Del.

PINEAPPLE UPSIDE-DOWN CAKE

Serves 8

2 tablespoons margarine
¾ cup brown sugar
7 slices pineapple
7 maraschino cherries
3 eggs, separated

1½ cups sugar
½ cup of boiling water
1½ cups sifted flour
1 teaspoon baking powder
¼ teaspoon salt

Preheat oven to 325°. Melt margarine in thick-bottomed 9-inch pan, 3½ inches high and a little curved where bottom and sides join. Add brown sugar, spread this mixture evenly over bottom of pan. Place 1 slice of pineapple in center and 6 slices around it with a cherry in center of each slice. Beat 3 egg yolks with electric beater until light and lemon colored. Add ½ cup sugar and beat again. Add ½ cup boiling water and beat until volume is 5 or 6 times greater than before and the batter falls in folds. Sift together 4 times 1 cup of sugar, sifted flour, baking powder, and salt; fold into the batter. Fold in the 3 egg whites that have been beaten to soft, moist peaks. Pour over pineapple slices in the pan. Bake for 45 minutes. Cool. Turn out onto cake plate.

Evelyn Tryon, Claymont, Del.

CATHERINE'S KENTUCKY POUND CAKE

Serves 12

1 cup butter
2 cups sugar
1 cup buttermilk
3 cups flour, sifted
½ teaspoon salt

½ teaspoon baking powder
½ teaspoon baking soda
4 eggs
1 teaspoon vanilla or lemon
  extract

Preheat oven to 350°. Cream butter and sugar. Add buttermilk, then sifted flour, salt, baking powder, and baking soda. Add the eggs. Beat, then add vanilla. Bake in greased 10-inch tube pan for 1 hour.

Use your favorite frosting. Dust a cake lightly with sifted confectioner's sugar before putting on icing, and it will keep the icing from running down the sides of cake.

Catherine Marsh

SOUR CREAM POUND CAKE

Serves 8 to 10

1 cup butter
2½ cups sugar
5 eggs
3 cups all-purpose flour
Dash salt

¼ teaspoon baking soda
1 cup sour cream
1 teaspoon vanilla
1 teaspoon lemon extract

Preheat oven to 350°. Cream butter and sugar. Add eggs, one at a time,, beating well after each addition. In a medium bowl, sift together flour, salt, and baking soda. With mixer on low speed, add flour mixture alternately with sour cream to butter mixture, beginning and ending with dry ingredients. Stir in vanilla and lemon extract. Pour batter into greased and floured 10-inch tube pan. Bake about 1 hour or until done. Cool in pan about 15 minutes, then remove and cool completely.

Freezes well!

Elinor Evans, Wilmington, Del.

BUTTERED RUM CAKE

1¼ cups plus 2 tablespoons
    butter, softened
3¾ cups sugar
6 eggs, separated
3 cups all-purpose flour
¼ teaspoon baking soda

8-ounce container sour cream
1 teaspoon vanilla
1 teaspoon lemon extract
3 tablespoons rum
3 tablespoons water
½ cup chopped walnuts

Preheat oven to 325°. Cream together 1 cup softened butter, gradually beating in 2½ cups sugar. Add egg yolks one at a time, beating well after each addition. Combine flour and baking soda. Add flour and sour cream alternately to the butter mixture, beginning and ending with the flour. Stir in flavorings. Beat egg whites at room temperature until foamy; gradually add ½ cup sugar, 1 tablespoon at a time, beating until stiff peaks form. Fold egg whites into batter.

Pour batter into a greased and floured 10-inch tube pan. Bake for 1½ hours or until a wooden pick inserted in center comes out clean. Cool cake in pan 10 to 15 minutes.

While cake is cooling, make the glaze by combining ¼ cup plus 2 tablespoons butter, rum, ¾ cup sugar, and 3 tablespoons water in a small saucepan; bring to a boil. Boil mixture, stirring constantly for 3 minutes. Remove from heat and stir in walnuts.

Remove still-warm cake from pan and place on a serving plate. Prick cake surface at 1-inch intervals with a wooden pick or meat fork. Pour warm butter rum glaze over cake. Let cake cool to room temperature before serving.

Mayor B. J. Hardin, Blades, Del.

SOUR CREAM CAKE

Serves 10 to 12

½ cup butter
1¼ cups sugar
2 eggs
2 cups flour, sifted
1 teaspoon baking soda
1 teaspoon baking powder

½ teaspoon salt
1 cup sour cream
1 teaspoon vanilla
⅓ cup brown sugar
½ teaspoon cinnamon
1 cup walnuts

Preheat oven to 350°. Cream butter and 1 cup sugar. Add eggs. Sift together flour, baking soda, baking powder, and salt. Add to butter alternately with sour cream. Add vanilla.

In separate bowl, mix brown sugar with remaining white sugar, cinnamon, and nuts. Spread ½ batter in greased and floured 13- by 9-inch pan; sprinkle with half the nut-sugar mixture. Cover with rest of the batter and top with remaining nut-sugar mixture. Bake for 35 minutes.

Grace Pryslak, Wilmington, Del.

SOUR CREAM TORTE

Serves 12 to 15

3 cups sifted flour   2 cups walnuts
¾ cup sugar   2 cups sour cream
1 cup butter or margarine   1½ cups confectioner's sugar
1 egg   1 teaspoon vanilla

Preheat oven to 350°. Mix flour and sugar together in bowl. Work in butter with pastry blender or knife until mealy. Stir in unbeaten egg and mix with hands until dough holds together. Divide dough into 7 parts. Roll each part into a 9-inch circle on a lightly floured and greased cookie sheet. Use a 9-inch pie pan as a guide. Bake 10 to 12 minutes or until the edges begin to brown lightly. Cool and remove from sheet with a spatula.

Make filling by mixing thoroughly together walnuts, sour cream, confectioner's sugar, and vanilla. Spread layer of filling between each layer of torte, piling the layers on top of each other. Sprinkle the top with additional confectioner's sugar. If Christmas, use the colored sugar. Let mellow in the refrigerator for 5 hours or longer. Cut into wedges and serve.

No need to improve on this old time treat.

Irene C. Cooley, Claymont, Del.

STRAWBERRY 7-UP CAKE

Serves 10 to 12

pound 2½-ounce box yellow
  cake mix
eggs
¼ cup vegetable oil
  cup 7-Up
  small box strawberry gelatin
  dessert mix
½ cup hot water

1¼ cups cold water
¼ cup frozen strawberries,
  chopped
¾ cup evaporated milk
1 package instant vanilla
  pudding
1 small frozen whipped topping

Preheat oven to 350°. Combine cake mix, eggs, oil, and 7-Up and mix thoroughly. Bake in 9- by 13-inch pan for 35 minutes. Cool; when cooled make holes in the cake with chopstick (or something that size) making holes 1 inch apart.

Dissolve gelatin mix in hot water, add ½ cup cold water and berries. Pour cooled solution into holes of cake and over entire cake.

Make frosting by mixing evaporated milk, ¾ cup cold water, and vanilla pudding thoroughly. Fold in thawed whipped topping. Frost the cake; decorate with strawberries.

Variation: Instead of pouring the strawberry gelatin mixture over the cake, melt a ¼ pound of butter and pour over the cake while still hot.

Lois Braden, Gurnee, Ill.

MARTHA WASHINGTON CAKE

Serves 8

1 cup solid vegetable
  shortening
2 cups sugar
4 eggs, separated
1 teaspoon vanilla

3 cups all-purpose flour
¼ teaspoon salt
3 teaspoons baking powder
1 cup milk

Preheat oven to 350°. Thoroughly cream shortening and sugar. Add egg yolks and vanilla, beating well. Sift dry ingredients together and add to batter with milk. Beat egg whites until stiff. Fold in egg whites. Bake in 3 8-inch round cake pans lined with waxed paper for 30 minutes.

Scrumptious is putting it mildly! Great with fresh strawberries and whipped cream.

Mrs. Harold Clouser, Sr., Wilmington, Del.

FROSTINGS AND ICINGS

CHOCOLATE PEANUT BUTTER FROSTING

Yield: frosting for 8-inch layer cake

½ cup peanut butter
¼ cup butter
 cups confectioner's sugar
 1-ounce squares unsweetened
 chocolate, melted

6 tablespoons light cream
1 teaspoon vanilla

Cream together peanut butter and butter. Slowly beat in confectioner's sugar and melted chocolate until smooth. Add cream and vanilla; beat until smooth.

Helen Reher, New Castle, Del.

SIMPLE CHOCOLATE ICING

Yield: icing for 8-inch cake

½ cups confectioner's sugar,
 sifted
 egg yolk (large egg)
 tablespoons butter

1 ounce (1 square) unsweetened
 chocolate, melted and cooled
3 tablespoons light cream
1 teaspoon vanilla

Combine all ingredients in a deep bowl and beat with electric mixer at medium speed until smooth.

E. Winn, Kent Co., Del.

SEVEN MINUTE COCONUT ICING

Yield: icing for 8-inch layer cake

2 egg whites	1½ teaspoons vanilla
1½ cups sugar	1 fresh coconut, grated
5 tablespoons water	

Combine unbeaten egg whites, sugar, and water in top of double boiler, mixing well. Place over boiling water and beat with beater for exactly 7 minutes. Remove from heat and stir in vanilla, beating until thick.

Ice one layer, sprinkling some of the freshly grated coconut over icing. Add second layer, ice and sprinkle remaining coconut on top and sides.

If cooked frosting becomes too sugary, add a little lemon juice.

Catherine Warner

FOUR MINUTE FUDGE FROSTING

Yield: frosting for two 8-inch layers

½ cup evaporated milk	¼ cup softened butter or
3 ounces unsweetened chocolate	margarine
3½ to 4½ cups confectioner's sugar, sifted	

Heat milk with chocolate until chocolate melts (about 3 minutes). Remove from heat. Add confectioner's sugar, 1 cup at a time, to spreading consistency. Stir in butter. Blend.

Rena Howard, Claymont, Del.

FLUFFY ORANGE ICING

Yield: icing for 10- or 12-inch cake

4½ ounces cream cheese (1½
   3-ounce packages)
2¼ cups confectioner's sugar,
   sifted

1½ tablespoons grated orange
   rind (about 2 oranges)

Cream cream cheese until light and fluffy. Gradually add confectioner's sugar. Beat well. Stir in grated orange rind. If too thick to spread, add a few drops of orange juice.

Mary Jane Reibsome

WHIPPED CREAM FROSTING

1 cup heavy cream
¼ cup sugar

½ to 1 teaspoon flavoring:
   vanilla, almond extract or
   orange extract (optional)

Combine cream with sugar. Chill in refrigerator at least 2 hours. Beat with rotary beater or electric mixer until stiff. Add flavorings of your choice if desired.

Anne Barr, Claymont, Del.

CHOCOLATE CREAM CHEESE FROSTING

Yield: frosting for 9-inch cake

3 ounces cream cheese
¼ cup milk
3½ cups confectioner's sugar

3 squares chocolate, melted
1 teaspoon vanilla
½ teaspoon salt

Soften cream cheese with half the milk. Beat until smooth. Add sugar and remainder of milk. Beat thoroughly. Add chocolate, vanilla, and salt. Beat until creamy.

Diane Clifford, Claymont, Del.

BUTTER, PICKLES, AND PRESERVES

FRIENDS
MEETING HOUSE

LEMON BUTTER

Yield: 3½ pints

½ pound butter
2 pounds sugar
6 lemons, rind and juice (should
   make 1½ cups of juice)

12 eggs

In the top of a double boiler melt butter; then add sugar, lemon rind, and juice; then add eggs. Stir with a wooden spoon; cook until thick.

Good on toast, biscuits, etc.

From our late member Mary Taylor, submitted by the Friends Meeting House

SUMMERTIME STRAWBERRY BUTTER

Yield: ¾ cup

3 tablespoons butter   6 tablespoons strawberry jam
3 tablespoons cream cheese

Cream butter and cheese until light and fluffy. Add jam. Stir until well blended and creamy. Place in covered dish and chill.

Makes enough for 12 slices of hot toast.

Madilene A. Harling

HOT PEPPER JELLY

Yield: 6 8-ounce jars

2 large green peppers (2 cups),   1½ cups cider vinegar
  sliced   5½ cups sugar
2 long green chili peppers (3 to   Green food coloring (optional)
  4 tablespoons), chopped   6 ounces liquid fruit pectin

Combine peppers in bowl. Place ½ in container of electric blender with ½ cup vinegar; whirl until almost smooth. Repeat. Add remaining ½ cup vinegar and whirl to rinse container. Place in kettle. Add sugar and stir well.

Bring mixture to full boil that cannot be stirred down, stirring constantly. Boil for 1 minute. Remove from heat; skim foam off top. Add food coloring. Add pectin, stir well; skim off any foam; cool 5 minutes. Ladle into 6 hot sterilized (8 ounce) glasses or jars. Seal, following manufacturer's directions. Allow to cool completely before moving glasses.

Delicious served with cream cheese and crackers—or as an accompaniment to meat.

For a holiday touch, use peppers that have turned red.

Ideal for gift giving.

Edna Frampton, Claymont, Del.

HEARN'S PRUNE CONSERVE

Yields: 3½ to 4 cups

7 oranges
7 apples
2 pounds prunes, pitted,
  chopped

2 ounces sliced almonds
1 quart sugar (4 cups)

Chop or grind apples and oranges finely. Cook prunes until soft; cool. Drain and save the juice; chop prunes into small pieces. Toast almonds in 350° oven until slightly brown.

Combine all ingredients with the sugar. Mix well. Add some of the prune juice if too dry. Refrigerate overnight before serving. Will keep refrigerated approximately 2 weeks.

This conserve is served every day at Hearn's. Two generations of the Hearn family have served Wilmington over 55 years.

Hearn's Restaurant, Old Brandywine Village, Wilmington, Del.

CROCKPOT APPLE BUTTER

Yield: 2 quarts

2 to 3 pounds apples, pared
  and sliced (preferably Stayman
  or Jonathan apples)

4 cups sugar
3 teaspoons cinnamon
Dash of cloves

Fill Crockpot with apples. Cook 18 hours on slow. Do not lift lid. Put the cooked apples through a ricer if a smooth consistency is desired. Put apples back in pot and add sugar, cinnamon, and cloves. Cook 4 more hours on low.

Fifer Orchards, Wyoming, Del.

SWEET PICKLE CHIPS

Yield: about 6 pints

15 medium sized cucumbers
1 quart cider vinegar
4 cups sugar
1 tablespoon salt

1¾-ounce package whole mixed
pickling spice (Pick out red
pepper from mix.)

Wash cucumbers. Slice crosswise into ⅛-inch thick slices; put them in a large container. Pour boiling water over them. For the next 3 days, drain the cold water from cucumbers and pour more boiling water over them. On the fifth day, drain cucumbers. Mix together vinegar, sugar, salt, and spices. Bring to a boil and pour over cucumbers. For the next 4 days, drain this liquid from the cucumbers into a pot, reheat it to boiling and pour back. On the fifth day, drain liquid, boil, pour over pickles and seal in jars while hot.

Ruth West, Laurel, Del.

CRANBERRY-PINEAPPLE RELISH

Yield: 8 cups

2 16-ounce cans pineapple
chunks in heavy syrup
2 12-ounce packages cranberries
2 cups sugar
2 cups dark seedless raisins

1 tablespoon minced preserved
ginger
2 teaspoons salt
½ teaspoon ground allspice

Drain pineapple, reserving ½ cup syrup. In a 4 quart saucepan over *High* heat, heat cranberries, sugar, raisins, ginger, salt, allspice and reserved pineapple syrup; boil stirring constantly. Reduce heat to *Low*, cover and simmer 10 minutes or until the cranberries pop. Add pineapple chunks, continue cooking 5 minutes or until mixture thickens slightly. Cover and refrigerate to use within 2 weeks. Serve as an accompaniment to roast turkey, duckling, chicken, grilled pork chops or baked ham.

Nancy A. Morris, Dover, Del.

GARDEN VEGETABLE RELISH

Yield: 8 to 10 pints

12 medium onions (4 cups,
　ground)
1 medium head cabbage (4 cups,
　ground)
10 green tomatoes (4 cups,
　ground)
12 green peppers
6 sweet red peppers

½ cup salt
6 cups sugar
2 tablespoons mustard seeds
1 tablespoon celery seeds
1½ teaspoons tumeric
4 cups cider vinegar
2 cups water

In an old-fashioned hand grinder, grind vegetables, using a coarse blade. Sprinkle with salt; let stand overnight. Rinse and drain. Combine remaining ingredients; pour over vegetables. Heat to boiling. Simmer a good 3 minutes. Be sure to stir occasionally to ensure relish is well mixed and all vegetables are being cooked through. Seal in hot, sterilized jars.

This relish was a favorite and now is being made by the fourth generation of my family. It was always necessary to make twice the amount as friends would laughingly put their order in!

Evelyn Gross Culver, Lewes, Del.

HOT DOG RELISH

Yield: 7 pints

30 green tomatoes
12 green peppers
12 onions
1 cup salt
4 cups vinegar

6 cups sugar
1¼ teaspoon red or black pepper
1 teaspoon dry mustard
1 teaspoon allspice

Grind tomatoes, peppers and onions in meat chopper. Add salt and let stand four hours. Put vinegar and sugar in a kettle and let come to a boil. Drain the chopped vegetables well and add with spices to boiling vinegar and sugar mix. Bring back to a boil and boil ten minutes. Can at once in hot sterile jars. Uses up the garden leftovers and is so delicious we eat it straight.

Claudia Bushman, Newark, Del.

Taste of Tradition

Appetizers	234
Beverages	235
Salads	240
Eggs	241
Breads, Biscuits, and Batters	242
Meat	252
Poultry	253
Seafood	254
Vegetables	260
Desserts	263
Cakes and Frosting	271
Cookies	286
Candy	292
Butters, Pickles, and Preserves	293

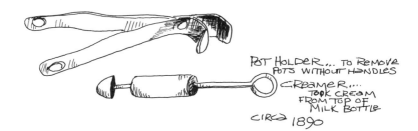

POT HOLDER... TO REMOVE POTS WITHOUT HANDLES
CREAMER.... TOOK CREAM FROM TOP OF MILK BOTTLE
CIRCA 1890

APPETIZERS

MUSHROOM "TIDBIT" SANDWICHES (1905)

Wash and trim (but do not peel) about a pound of mushrooms. Chop them, stems and all, rather finely in a wooden chopping bowl. Add some minced onion.

Heat 2 or 3 tablespoons of butter in a heavy skillet and add the mushrooms. Sprinkle with salt, pepper and a good squeeze of lemon juice. Stir to blend and cook very slowly for about 5 minutes or until soft. Then dust with 1 or more tablespoons flour. Blend and add milk, stirring to a medium sauce. (Be sure flour is cooked.)

One tablespoon or more of sherry may be added to enhance the taste. Cool and store in refrigerator where mixture will stiffen up for spreading consistency. (If too stiff, it can be diluted with cream or sherry.)

Spread between very thin slices of buttered white or whole wheat sandwich bread. Trim crusts and cut each full-sized sandwich into tea-sized "fingers." Garnish with watercress or parsley.

This recipe can be varied according to the judgment of the cook and to modernize, may also be used as a dip—hot or cold.

Katherine B. Milligan, niece of Delaware's artist Robert Shaw, writes:

> One of my special memories of childhood is helping my aunts gather mushrooms in the lower pasture of their Penny Hill farm. That was a *long time* ago!

Katherine B. Milligan, Orleans, Mass.

"LUXURY" SANDWICH FILLING

2 cups cold ham
1 cup walnut meats
1 cup pimento stuffed olives,
  sliced

1½ tablespoons sugar
Pinch of salt
Dash of cayenne
1 cup salad dressing

Grind the ham using a little ham fat. Cut walnuts into small pieces. Combine walnuts, sliced olives, sugar, salt, and a good dash of cayenne. Mix with salad dressing and use at once.

Lillie Atkins, *circa* late 1800's

BEVERAGES

CHOCOLATE GINGER ALE (1905)

Place 2 tablespoons of basic chocolate sirup in a large glass. Add 1 tablespoon of thick cream and some crushed ice. Continue filling glass with ginger ale; stir well and serve.

BASIC CHOCOLATE SIRUP

1 cupful of sugar
½ cupful of cocoa
¾ cupful of hot water
1-inch stick of cinnamon

2 tablespoons of strong coffee
1 teaspoon of vanilla
⅛ teaspoon of salt

Blend the sugar and cocoa together. Add hot water and cinnamon and simmer for 10 minutes. Cool. Remove the cinnamon stick, then add the coffee, vanilla, and salt. Cover and store in a cold place until needed. It will keep indefinitely.

Raymond W. Dill, Dover, Del.

DANDELION WINE (1885)

3 quarts dandelion blossoms
3 quarts boiling water
3 pounds sugar

2 lemons, juice only
2 oranges, juice only
1 yeast cake or packet

Scald blossoms by pouring boiling water over them. Let stand overnight in a stone crock; then strain and squeeze out all the juice. Add remaining ingredients to juice. Put in a keg or jug. Let stand, uncovered, to ferment—about 6 weeks. Pour into bottles and cork tightly. Keep in a cool place for storage.

Children used to be paid a penny a quart to pick the dandelion blossoms.

GOVERNOR LEA'S SPECIAL EGGNOG

Yield: ½ gallon (easy to increase)

1 dozen eggs, separated
4 to 7 tablespoons sugar
½ pint dark Jamaican rum

½ pint brandy
1 pint heavy cream
1 pint milk

Beat egg yolks. Add sugar, rum, brandy, cream, and milk. Beat egg whites until stiff peaks form. Fold in stiffly beaten egg whites. Let stand overnight. Refold the egg whites which will rise to top. Add more milk to taste.

A favorite of my father's, former Delaware Governor Preston Lea. 1905–1909

Louise Lea Nowland, Wilmington, Del.

HOT EGGNOG
(*circa* 1791)

Serves 10

6 eggs
3 pints of water, boiling
1 quart rich milk

1 quart Delaware apple brandy
Nutmeg

Beat the eggs well. Slowly add the boiling water, stirring constantly. Add milk and brandy. Sweeten to taste and add nutmeg to flavor.

HAYMAKER'S SWITZEL

1 cup brown sugar
½ teaspoon ginger
½ cup molasses

¾ cup vinegar
2 quarts water

Combine. Mix. Chill.

In the haying season farmers used to take their "nooning" (midday dinner) with them, which included a jug of switzel to wash the meal down. Although switzel was usually straight, farmers have been known to spike it with hard cider or even brandy, which Down Easterners used to say "got the hay in the barn in half the time." Before ice houses, jugs of switzel were cooled in springhouses or hung in the well.

Cookbook Committee

We the People

Delaware
•••••• ◆ ••••••
Freedom's First

OLD DELAWARE PUNCH

3 cupfuls of sugar
3 quarts of water
1 cupful of strong black tea
Juice of 12 oranges

Juice of 12 lemons
1 can of pineapple chunks
1 pint of ginger ale
1 pint of grape juice

Boil the sugar and water together for 8 minutes; add the tea, and chill. When thoroughly chilled, add the remaining ingredients, pour over ice in tall glasses, and serve.

SCHROEDER FAMILY PUNCH

One fifth of Jamaican dark
    rum (⅘ quart)
2 to 4 bottles carbonated water,
    to taste
4 bottles champagne

1 quart orange sherbet, frozen
    into mold
Orange slices, if desired
Extra ice

Mix rum, water, and champagne in large punch bowl. Float sherbet in punch. Add extra ice, if necessary. Float orange slices.

A family favorite belonging to my great grandmother.

Elise du Pont, wife of former Delaware Governor Pierre du Pont, 1977-1985, Rockland, Del.

SYLLABUB (1807)

Sweeten a gallon of cider with crushed maple sugar. Do not stint on the sweetening! Grate a nutmeg on top. Then milk the cow into this mixture. Drink while warm and foamy.

SYLLABUB—An Old Receipt

1 quart milk
1 pint heavy cream (more, if
   wanted)
6 tablespoons sugar

4 tablespoons rye whiskey (that's
   really old—sure enough
   Moonshine) or ½ cup sherry

Churn, as the foam rises, skim off and serve. Churns best in a gallon bucket.

   Two requirements:
    1. A syllabub churn.
    2. A strong armed cook or one half dozen young folks to do the churning. Occasionally syllabub was made by placing the bowl of wine under the cow and milking directly into it. Since new milk is naturally very foamy, the usual chore of beating was thus avoided.

Claymont Sampler cookbook, 1976

SHELLPOT PARK PUNCH

1 pint grapefruit juice
1 pint orange juice
1 pint grape juice
1 cup lemon juice

1 #2 can pineapple juice
1½ cups sugar syrup
2 quarts ginger ale
Block of ice

Chill all fruit juices. Combine with sugar syrup and turn into punchbowl over block of ice, adding ginger ale at the moment of serving.

Sugar syrup:
Boil together for 5 minutes equal parts sugar and water. Store closely covered in refrigerator. One and one-fourth tablespoons of this syrup equals 1 tablespoon sugar in sweetening power.

Having lived across the street from Shellpot Park when I was all of 8 years old, I can still remember the rides, Sunday concerts, and refreshments. Such beautiful memories from the early 1900s.

Irene Millard

CHERRY BOUNCE

To 1 gallon of wild cherries, add enough whiskey to cover the fruit. Let soak 2 or 3 weeks and then drain off the liquor. Mash the cherries without breaking the stones and strain through a jelly bag; add this liquor to that already drained off. Make a syrup with a gill of water and a pound of white sugar to every 2 quarts of liquor thus prepared; stir in well, bottle and tightly cork. A common way of making Cherry Bounce is to put wild cherries and whiskey together in a jug and use the liquor as wanted.

Gladys O'Brien, Woodstown, N.J.
The Cherry Bounce receipt was taken from the *White House Cookbook*, 1887, belonging to Mrs. O'Brien's mother.

SALADS

FRUIT SALAD

Apples, white grapes, English walnuts and celery.

Mrs. Lewis Mustard, sister of Delaware State's Govenor Ebe Tunnel, 1897-1901, Lewes, Del.

MRS. PROCTOR'S "COLD SLAW" (1880)

Cut cabbage fine and sprinkle with salt and dry mustard. Break one egg over all and stir up good with a fork.

Now put ¾ cup mild vinegar and 1 tablespoon sugar and heat hot, then pour on cabbage mixture and stir good.

Now squeeze cabbage out good, add 1 tablespoon flour and boil the liquid until it thickens, being as it scorches easily. Pour this mixture over cabbage and eat, drink, and be merry.

Mrs. H. Proctor

EGGS

SCRAMBLED EGGS

Serves 6 to 8

Put a tablespoonful of butter, a gill of milk, a saltspoonful of salt; half as much pepper, and a tablespoonful of minced parsley in a frying pan. When the mixture boils, break and stir into it eight or ten eggs. Beat and stir until they are well mixed and cease to run over the pan. Line a dish with crustless toast dipped in hot milk, salted, peppered, and buttered, and pour the eggs on this bed.

From cookbook collection of Anna Kate Williams Beauchamp (1889), mother of Margaret James, Selbyville, Del.

LAWS OF DELAWARE FROM 1700–1797

Penalty for any worldly employment on the Lords Day (Sunday) was $4.00 or 24 hour imprisonment

Penalty on peddlers and traveling persons selling goods on Sunday was $8.00 or 2 days in prison.

Fishing, hunting of game, gambling or dancing on Sunday was $4.00 or 24 hours imprisonment

To the Bell-ringer of the General Assembly the sum of .33¢ was paid each day

BREADS, BISCUITS, AND BATTERS

OLD-FASHIONED "FRIED CAKES" (DOUGHNUTS)

3 tablespoons shortening
⅔ cups sugar
1 egg
⅔ cup milk
1 teaspoon nutmeg

¾ teaspoon salt
3 cups flour
4 teaspoons Royal baking
   powder

Cream shortening and sugar. Add egg and milk. Mix well. Add dry ingredients. Roll ½ inch thick. Cut and fry in deep fat until golden brown.

The fat should be in a deep kettle and hot enough to brown a piece of bread in 60 seconds or the doughnuts will absorb grease.

Light, tender and digestable.

Colony Club Cookbook (1920)
Submitted by Lizzie McKeown

SUSSEX COUNTY DOUGHNUTS

1 cup mashed white potatoes
  (hot)
2 tablespoons butter
1½ cups sugar
2 eggs
1 cup milk

½ teaspoon salt
1 teaspoon vanilla (optional)
1 grated nutmeg
3 cups flour
2½ teaspoons baking powder

Make a cream of potatoes, butter, sugar, and eggs. Add milk, salt, vanilla, nutmeg, and flour which has been sifted with baking powder. Add flour enough to make a stiff dough which can be rolled ½ inch thick. Shape the dough into doughnut size by cutting with top of about a 3-inch top glass or other round shape. The center hole may be cut by use of a thimble.

Fry in hot fat about 3 inches deep. When brown, drain on a wire sieve until cold. Sprinkle with pulverized sugar. This recipe will make about 50 doughnuts. May pack in deep new lard can, lined with wax paper.

Mrs. King would make these doughnuts in her Milton, Del., home during the afternoon of Christmas Eve and would not permit anyone to come into the kitchen when she was cooking. Friends and relatives would come Christmas Eve to eat the doughnuts served with grape juice made from grapes of her farm vineyard. Mrs. King followed this recipe from about 1910 until 1970.

Bertha King, submitted by her daughter Mary K. Morgan

MA MA WALTON'S DUMPLINGS

2 cups flour   2 tablespoons lard
1 teaspoon baking powder   1 egg
1 teaspoon salt

Sift together the dry ingredients; combine with the lard. Beat egg slightly, then add the egg plus water for a doughlike consistency. Roll and cut into diamond shapes. Cook in hot broth (chicken or beef) for 10 minutes.

Great with chicken pot pie or beef pot pie.
Popular in the 1920s.

Hester Walton, Wilmington, Del.

SUSSEX COUNTY DUMPLINGS

3 cups flour (all purpose)   1 teaspoon salt

Mix with warm (not hot) seasoned broth (do not have broth too greasy). Knead thoroughly until smooth; roll out thin to 2½- or 3-inch squares. Drop in rapidly boiling, seasoned broth. Boil about 3 minutes; reduce heat and boil about 15 minutes or until done. Stir occasionally.

Eighty-six-year young Dorothy Burton has made dumplings from this popular recipe at many Sussex County Church suppers.

Dorothy Burton, Milton, Del.

MUSH CAKES

1 pint corn meal

1 quart flour

1 quart boiling water

1 teaspoon salt

½ cake Fleischman's yeast

Stir into the corn meal enough cold water to wet it thoroughly. Stir this into the boiling water in which the salt has been put. Cook the mush thoroughly. Cool.

Dissolve the yeast in ½ cup lukewarm water. Stir this and flour into mush. Cover and set in a warm place to raise about 3 hours.

Bake on a griddle, not too hot, allowing a tablespoon to a cake. To prevent the batter from sticking to spoon, dip spoon into cold water each time.

Mrs. R. P. Robinson, Sr., wife of Delaware's former governor, Robert Pyle Robinson, 1925-1929.

Submitted by Mrs. R. P. Robinson, Jr., Wilmington, Del.

ORANGE BISCUITS

Yield: 12 to 15 medium biscuits

2 cups sifted soft-wheat flour
(pastry)
4 teaspoonfuls baking powder
¾ teaspoonful salt
2 tablespoonfuls sugar

2 tablespoonfuls grated orange
rind
3 tablespoonfuls fat (shortening)
⅔ cup milk

Sift the dry ingredients, add orange rind and fat; mix well with the tips of the fingers. Make a well in the mixture; add the milk slowly and stir from the center with a fork until a medium-soft dough is formed. Toss onto a lightly floured board and knead a few seconds until smooth. Press into a sheet about ½ inch thick with the palm of the hand, and cut into rounds. Bake at 450° for 12 to 15 minutes.

You may add ½ teaspoonful orange marmalade on top of each biscuit before baking.

A du Pont family recipe
Compliments of Hagley Museum and Library, Wilmington, Del.

WHITE POTATO ROLLS

2 cups potatoes
½ cup lard
2 eggs
2 tablespoons sugar

Pinch salt
1 cup yeast
Flour

Put potatoes through a sieve. Beat the hot potatoes into the lard and add eggs, sugar, and salt. To this, add the yeast. Let lighten, then knead in enough flour for a soft dough. Let lighten again. Make out and place in a pan not touching each other. Bake about 20 minutes in a hot oven.

Mrs. Edward Tunnell, cousin of Delaware's fifty-second governor, Ebe W. Tunnell

ANN BOWERS SUTLIFFE VALLIANT'S BOSTON BROWN BREAD

1 cup granulated corn meal
2 cups graham flour
1 tablespoon brown sugar
¾ tablespoon soda
2 teaspoons salt
¾ cup molasses

2 cups sour milk (or 1½ cups
    sweet milk or water)
½ cup currants
½ cup raisins
½ cup chopped nuts

Mix dry ingredients together and sift. Add molasses and milk, stirring until well mixed. Add currants, raisins, and nuts. Pour into well buttered 1-pound molds until no more than ⅔ full. Bread pans may also be used but cylindrical molds are best.

Cover containers with lids or waxed paper; tie with string. Steam for 3 hours, after which place in hot oven to dry and brown for 5 minutes before removing from can.

Joseph M. Brumbley, Sr., Wilmington, Del.

CORN MEAL PONE

9 cups white corn meal, sieved
4 cups flour
2 to 3 quarts boiling water
1 cup flour

1 cup sugar
1 cup King Port rich molasses
4 teaspoons salt
1 teaspoon baking soda

Scald the cornmeal with boiling water until of fairly thick consistency. Add flour, 1 cup at a time with at least 1 cup warm water each time until flour is gradually used up. Let set for 6 hours. Add sugar, molasses, salt, and baking soda. Batter is similar to pancake batter.

Oil or grease an iron dutch oven or 2 heavy aluminum roasters (9- by 3½- by 4 inches). Bake at 350° for ½ hour or little brown; then put lid on. Bake at 225° for 6 hours.

It was a Sussex County custom to prepare the pone mixture on a Saturday afternoon; then put in oven early that evening and let bake all night, getting up on schedule to put wood in the stove. The pone was a delicacy at Sunday morning breakfast, adding butter upon the slices.

This recipe was inherited from my grandmother and dates back to the early 1800s.

Martha Donovan, Milton, Del.

OLD-FASHIONED PONE BREAD

Pour 4 cups boiling water over 3 cups of corn meal. Beat well. Add 2 cups of cold water. Beat well. Add 1 cup flour, 1 teaspoon salt, ¼ cup sugar, ¼ cup of molasses, and 2 eggs. Beat thoroughly. Pour into well-greased Iron Spider or iron frying pan. Cover and bake in 350° oven for 1 to 1¼ hours. Turn off oven and leave in while oven cools.

Recipe handed down from my grandmother.

Catherine Pusey, Ocean View, Del.

JOHNNY CAKE RECIPE,
with Over-100-Year-Old Rhyme

2 cups corn meal   1 egg, well beaten
1 cup flour   1 cup sour milk
1 tablespoon butter   1 teaspoon soda
1 cup sweet milk   1 teaspoon salt

Two cups of Indian,* 1 cup of wheat,* 1 cup of sour milk, 1 cup of sweet, 1 good egg, that will you beat, 1 tablespoon of butter new. Salt and soda, each a spoon; mix up quick and bake it soon. 45 minutes to 1 hour bake—fast oven (400°).

Then you have corn bread complete. Best of *all* corn bread to eat! It will make your boy's eyes shine. If he is like that boy of mine. 'Tis fit to set before any king that husband home might bring. Persons who eat mother's Johnny Cake thought it couldn't be beat. I have cooked for others and they ask for the receipt.

*2 cups of Indian means that amount of corn meal
*1 cup of wheat stands for regular flour.

Bertie Willing, Nanticoke, Md.

NUT BREAD

1 cup sugar   3 cups flour
1 egg   3 teaspoons baking powder
1½ cups milk   1 cup chopped English walnuts
1 teaspoon salt   ½ cup seedless raisins (optional)

Preheat oven to 325°. Mix first 6 ingredients thoroughly. Add chopped walnuts and raisins. Pour into buttered loaf pan. Let stand 20 minutes. Bake for 1¼ hours.

Marian G. Clopp, Wilmington, Del. (circa 1935)

JOCAKE (HOCAKE) BREAD

2 cups flour
Pinch of salt (½ teaspoon)
3 teaspoons baking powder

A little sugar (5 tablespoons)
½ cup shortening
⅔ cup milk

Mix the dry ingredients in a bowl; add shortening to the mixture and stir in the milk. Blend lightly with a spoon and then knead on a floured board for several minutes. Pat it down and place in a flat baking pan or skillet which has been slightly greased. Bake at 450° for 12 or 14 minutes. It may also be cooked at a very low temperature in an iron skillet on top of the stove. Serve in squares with butter, jam, or fruit toppings.

At 5 A.M., a comely twelve-year-old bride eagerly went into the kitchen to prepare breakfast for her young husband of only twelve hours. Still in awe of the previous day's events and feeling a bit queasy from having swallowed a full bottle of Mrs. Penolope's Lilac Eau de Cologne in order to smell sweet internally as well as externally on her wedding day, she went about the business of planning a special breakfast for her mister. With the alacrity and skill of an adult she prepared a menu of grits, sausage, fatback, eggs, coffee and a favorite skillet bread topped with blueberries which her dear Indian mother taught her to make. This wonderful bread which my great-grandmother and grandmother made was called Jocake Bread.

Muriel F. Cooper, Wilmington, Del. (early 1800s)

POPOVERS

Yield: 10 popovers

¼ cup butter   ½ cup flour
½ cup water   2 eggs

Boil water and butter together. Add flour; mix and cook 1 minute. Remove from heat and cool slightly. Add eggs, one at a time, mixing well with a Dover beater until batter is smooth.

Drop from tablespoon on a cookie sheet, leaving about 3 inches between. Bake at 450° for 15 minutes. Reduce heat to 350° and bake 30 minutes more.

These may also be poured into hissing-hot greased gem pans and baked about 25 minutes in a hot (450°) oven.

Kathryn Deufel, Claymont, Del. (circa 1915)

OLD-FASHIONED
RAISIN BREAD

¼ pound butter   6 cups flour, sifted
2½ cups sugar   1 teaspoon salt
½ cup lard (½ cup Crisco or ¼   4 teaspoons baking powder
   pound butter may be   Pinch nutmeg
   substituted for the lard)   1 cup dark raisins (slightly
3 large eggs   boiled and drained)
2 cups milk   1 cup light raisins (slightly
2 teaspoons vanilla   boiled and drained)

Cream butter, lard, sugar, and eggs, then add milk and vanilla. Mix in dry ingredients and raisins. Blend together. Pour into 3 medium loaf pans, bake in *slow* oven (325°) for 1½ hours.

This recipe is at least 125 years old. It was given to my mother when she was 25, and the lady who gave it to her was 80 then.

Mrs. John B. Pitman, Jr., Millville, Del. (circa 1868)

SALLY LUNN

Four cups of sugar, one of butter, one of cream, five eggs, a spoonful of yeast, as much flour as will make it stiff as thick fritter batter. When light bake in a large form. Spice it if you like.

This was a necessary bread for the colonists, and an import from England, whose origin is draped in mystery. The receipt was copied from the original hand-written receipt.

Mrs. Henry Moore Ridgely-1833

MEAT

PORK SAUSAGE

2 pounds ground pork

Spread out in layer on waxed paper. Sprinkle lightly with: Salt, sugar, black pepper, red pepper, and sage. Mix well and shape into patties and fry. Delicious with pancakes or waffles.

Worth a try if you want something different for breakfast.

After 50 years of wedded bliss, this is still a favorite.

Myrtle Mumford, Seaford, Del.

POULTRY AND GAME

DELAWARE CHICKEN STEW

Serves 6

2 onions, sliced
2 tablespoons bacon fat
2½ pound fryer, cut up
Salt and pepper
3 cups water
3 tomatoes, peeled and quartered
½ cup sherry

2 teaspoons Worcestershire sauce
1 pound fresh lima beans
½ cup okra
3 ears green corn
2 tablespoons butter
½ cup bread crumbs

Sauté onions in bacon fat. Season chicken and brown on all sides in bacon fat. Pour off fat and place chicken and onions in heavy kettle. Add water, tomatoes, sherry, and Worcestershire sauce.

Cook slowly over low heat for ½ hour. Add lima beans, okra and corn cut from the cob. Simmer for 1 hour, add butter and bread crumbs and cook ½ hour longer.

From *The White House Chef Cookbook* by Rene Verdon
Submitted by Kay Aukerman, Claymont, Del.

DRESSING FOR CHICKEN OR TURKEY

Soak bread in water and then squeeze. Beat 1 egg in bowl. Add bread. Dice 1 onion. Add onion and raisins and salt and pepper. Stir well and stuff fowl.

Mrs. John Dreyer

CHICKEN TERRIPIN

1 large chicken
1 pint cream or new milk
¼ pound butter

2 tablespoons flour
3 eggs

Boil chicken, cut into small pieces, and place in pan with cream. Mix well and let come to a boil; mix flour and butter well together until smooth and add to the rest; season with cayenne pepper and salt; boil the eggs hard and chop whites fine; make the yolks into little balls adding wine and eggs just before taking chicken off the fire.

Mrs. Peter Causey, Delaware's First Lady, 1855 to 1859
Blue Hens Chicken Cookbook, Milford, Del. (1904)

SEAFOOD

DEVILED CLAMS

3 large clams
¼ onion
1 egg, boiled

⅓ green pepper
1 tablespoon butter
½ cup cooked rice

Grind clams, onion, egg, pepper. Heat clams and butter together until butter melts. Add remaining ingredients. Place mixture in shells and bake with cracker crumbs on top. (There are no temperatures given in these old recipes, naturally, because they were all done in a wood cook stove.) This mixture may also be made in a casserole; and, if using shells, they may be frozen.

Margaret Zebly Adkins — 1886

Mrs. Adkins was the wife of Custis Adkins, captain of various buoy boats, including *The Iris*, from 1881 to 1933. *The Iris* served under the Lighthouse Service maintaining wooden buoys, which is performed now by the United States Coast Guard.

CLAM FRITTERS

1 cup flour	¼ cup milk
¼ teaspoon salt	2 eggs, beaten
¼ teaspoon pepper	12 clams, raw, chopped
¼ cup clam liquor	1 teaspoon butter

Mix and sift flour, salt, and pepper. Add clam liquor, milk, and eggs. Stir well until blended and then add clams and butter. Mix thoroughly. Drop from a spoon into deep hot fat (375°) and fry 4 to 6 minutes or until well browned. Drain on unglazed paper. Serve with tartar sauce.

This receipt is well over 50 years old and has been passed down from one family member to another.

Lola Adkins, Blades, Del.

CHRISTIANA CREEK FERRY RATES—1700's (NEW CASTLE COUNTY)

Single horse and rider	six cents
Lead horse, ox, cow	four cents
Passenger	two cents
Sheep and hog	one cent
Coach (4 wheel carriage) pair of horses and passenger	twenty-five cents

BOILED COD WITH EGGS
(*circa* 1876)

Soak fish all night. In morning cut up and boil until tender. Drain. Remove bones. Add eggs, cut in large pieces or chopped smaller, to stock. Stir in a large piece of butter and thicken. Season and serve at once with the boiled potatoes. (When the ladies wrote their recipes they must have assumed that all women were creative and could cook.)

Whenever there are two or more Delaware Bay and River pilots together, the conversation turns to life on the pilot boat in the good old days. And eventually, with tears in their eyes, and salivating, they will speak of the cod fish breakfast. Then they will argue over which cook, dead and gone now, could fix that dish best. As a child I have eaten it on the pilot boat when my father would take me out for a few days. Just thinking about boiled cod conjures up the smell of salt water and the laughter of men who liked their work and liked to eat.

Mrs. John D. Hukill, Harbeson, Del.

CODFISH AND POTATOES

1 *package salt codfish*   *Fat salt meat*
Potatoes   *Onions*

Put fish in pot, cover with cold water and let boil for half an hour. Drain. Again cover with cold water, boil, until fish is tender. Add sliced potatoes, and cook until potatoes are done. Fry salt meat, cut in small pieces, until brown. Drain fish and potatoes, add a few chopped onions and spoon fat meat over all. Serve. Leftovers can be mashed up and shaped into cakes.

An old Bethel recipe (1920)

Mrs. Mary Cordrey, Bethel, Del.

STEWED CRABS

You first catch them, then boil for a half hour with a little vinegar in the water. When cold, pick the meat out. To one quart of meat, take 1 quart of milk, put it on to boil, add 2 ounces butter just as the milk comes to a boil; add crab meat, season with salt and red pepper; add two tablespoons cracker dust stirred in a little water and serve hot.

Tested Lewes Recipes (1904–1916)
William C. Lofland

FRIED FROGS

First you skin him, take the entrails out and cut the toenails off. Wash in two waters, dry with a cloth. Sprinkle with a little pepper and salt, roll with egg and cracker dust then fry in hot fat. Eat while hot.

P. B. Vickers (1904)

The frog recipe is included for fun. Actually, the men go out in a boat at night in the spring with a strong light and a gig, a kind of sharp fork on a long pole. One man shines the light on the bullfrog which mesmerizes the frog and the other man throws the gig, which spears the frog. When they have enough frogs or get tired, they bring the frogs home in a burlap sack. The frogs scream. The men then remove the back legs and discard the rest of the frog. We never ate the whole thing. My father soaks the legs in ice water for several hours, dries them and then sautés them in a little butter with garlic and a sprinkle of flour until they look like chicken which is cooked. These frog legs are much smaller than commercial ones so we have 40 or 50 pairs for one meal for six. When done correctly, they are absolutely heavenly.

Raymond R. Atkins

SNAPPER STEW

Serves 4 to 6

4 to 5 pound snapper   ½ dozen hard-boiled eggs
¼ to ½ pound butter   Salt and pepper to taste
3 cups milk   Sherry to taste
1 cup half & half cream

Cook snapper until tender. Keep the stock and pick the meat from the bones. To the stock, add the butter, milk, and cream. Mash yolks or put them through a sieve. Chop the whites. Add to stew. Thicken.

Mary's grandsons who spent most of their summer on Lewes Beach with her say that, "She could so cook—two things." She could scramble the greatest egg ever eaten and make an unsurpassable snapper stew. My mother and aunt made this regularly back in the days when someone came to the back door to sell the huge, live, ugly beast. When you bought it he would take it away, clean it, and bring it back ready to cook.

Mary Long Rowland (1882)

TERRAPIN

4 small terrapin, 6 hard boiled eggs, 1 pint thick cream, ½ pound butter, salt and pepper to taste. Cook the terrapin about 10 minutes in boiling water, then take out, put in fresh boiling water, add some salt. Cook until the shells part easily. Clean and break into convenient sized pieces, put in a stew pan with any liquor that may have dropped out. Rub butter to a cream, add 2 yolks of hard-boiled eggs, cream very light, add 2 teaspoons flour. Have cream hot. Add this mixture to it and stir until smooth. Add terrapin to this and let heat thoroughly and serve at once.

Terrapin was easily obtainable in this area in the early 1900s. At certain times of the year, probably spring, the terrapin, who had hibernated in the mud of a local creek, would swim out the mouth of the creek to the Delaware Bay. The men would stand watch and would shoot them in their heads to kill them. One had to be a good shot as the only thing that showed above water was the small head of the terrapin.

Mrs. James Kelly

VEGETABLES

OLD "BRICK HOTEL — GEORGETOWN
HOUSE"

STUFFED GREEN PEPPERS

3 large green peppers
Leftover ham or small picnic
  ham
1 medium-sized potato

1 large onion
2 medium fresh tomatoes
Parmesan cheese
Paprika

Cut peppers in half, remove seeds. Place in boiling water and simmer until partially cooked; don't let fall apart, keep firm.

Put ham, potato, onion, and tomatoes through medium on meat grinder. Pack well in green pepper halves. Sprinkle Parmesan cheese and paprika on top. Place close together in baking pan or caserole. Pour small amount of water in bottom and bake at 350° for 45 minutes.

Tomato sauce could be used instead of tomatoes.

This far surpasses the taste of beef and gained popularity in the 1920s.

Elizabeth Jackson, Wyoming, Del.

TOMATOES-CREME BELMONT

Serves 6

3 tablespoons butter
6 large ripe tomatoes (cut in half
   across)

Salt
⅓ *cup heavy cream*
Minced parsley

Melt butter in large skillet (for 12 half tomatoes). Add tomatoes cut side down. Puncture sides here and there with sharp paring knife. Heat for about 5 minutes over high heat. Turn tomatoes with metal spatula. Sprinkle with salt and cook for 10 minutes. Turn again for juices to run out and spread in pan. Turn again with cut side up. Add cream and mix with juices. Bring to a boil. Immediately slip on hot serving platter, cover with sauces and sprinkle with parsley. Serve piping hot.

This recipe was found in an 1857 cookbook. It belonged to the grandniece of Governor Thomas Collins, Caroline Elizabeth Cloak Peterson Speakman, who lived at Belmont Hall all of her life. She was 15 years old in 1857.

Virginia W. Speakman, Smyrna, Del.

BELMONT HALL

GEORGETOWN VEGETABLE CUSTARD

Serves 4 to 6

½ cup butter
1½ cups sliced yellow summer
   squash
1½ cups fresh broccoli (sliced
   diagonally)
1 egg

¼ cup milk
1 teaspoon salt
¼ teaspoon dry mustard
Dash cayenne
½ cup shredded Swiss cheese
¼ cup grated Parmesan cheese

In large skillet melt butter and sauté sliced raw vegetables until they can be pierced with a fork. Beat egg, stir in milk, salt, mustard, cayenne, and Swiss cheese. Place vegetables in a 1-quart casserole, pour egg mixture over vegetables and sprinkle Parmesan on top. Bake at 375° for 15 to 20 minutes or until cheese is slightly browned and custard firm.

This was one of grandmother's favorites and very popular with the family, dating back to the early 1920s.

Penny Paine, Georgetown, Del.

DESSERTS

AMBER CUSTARD
(*circa* 1857)

1 cup English walnuts,
   chopped
1 cup seeded raisins
Flour
2 scant cups sugar
1 heaping tablespoon butter

1 teaspoon cinnamon
1 teaspoon nutmeg
1 teaspoon white vinegar
4 eggs, separated
¾ cup milk

Dust nuts and raisins with flour. Set aside. Blend sugar and butter until smooth; add cinnamon, nutmeg, and vinegar. Add egg yolks. Add milk, beat *thoroughly*. Add raisins and nuts. Mix well. Beat egg whites until peaks form. Fold into batter. Pour into 2 8-inch unbaked pie shells. Bake at 300° for 45 minutes until top is amber colored and spongy.

Grandma Sheffer

BAKED APPLE DUMPLINGS

1 pint flour, salt
2 teaspoons baking powder

1 large tablespoon lard

Mix like pie dough with water or milk. Roll out thin. Spread with apples cut thin and sprinkle with sugar and cinnamon. Roll up and cut about 2 inches thick like cinnamon buns. Stand close together in a pan. Bake at 325° for 20 to 30 minutes.

SYRUP

1 cup sugar
1½ cups boiling water

1 tablespoon flour
1 teaspoon vanilla

Let come to a boil. Pour on buns. Bake until brown.

C. Musser, Holly Oak, Del. (circa 1933)

PREMIUM APPLE PUDDING

Serves: 6

1½ cups milk
11 Premium Flake Soda
  Crackers, crumbled
2 egg yolks, beaten
½ cup sugar
½ cup raisins

½ teaspoon cinnamon
3 large cooking apples, cut
  into small pieces
2 egg whites, beaten stiff
¼ cup butter

Pour the milk over the crackers and add egg yolks, sugar, raisins, and cinnamon. Add apples to the above mixture and then fold in beaten egg whites. Melt butter in pudding dish and stir half into pudding mixture. Pour remaining mixture into pudding dish. Bake at 375° about 50 minutes. Serve hot.

Taken from a 65-year-old Uneeda Soda Cracker box found in an old country store recently.

BLACKBERRY FOOLERY

5 slices buttered bread, crusts
  removed
16-ounce can blackberries (1 pint
  fresh or frozen berries)

¼ cup sugar
½ teaspoon grated nutmeg
1 cup sweetened cream

Place buttered bread in bottom of bowl. Cook blackberries, adding sugar and nutmeg. Pour over bread and serve hot with cream.

This was my mother's recipe she used 60 years ago when stores were far apart and she had to depend on canned fruit on the shelf.

Louise Coleman, Newark, Del.

BREAD PUDDING

2 cups stale bread
1 quart milk
2 eggs
½ cup sugar

¼ teaspoon salt
1 teaspoon vanilla
½ cup raisins, if desired

Soak the bread in the milk until it is very soft, then mash it fine. Heat together until nearly boiling. Beat the eggs with egg beater until light and add to them the sugar, salt, and vanilla. When well mixed, stir this into the bread and milk. Pour the whole into a buttered earthenware baking dish; stir in raisins. Set in a pan of water, and bake in a slow oven (250° to 350°) 45 minutes to one hour.

Variation:

CHOCOLATE BREAD PUDDING

Melt 2 squares of chocolate over hot water and add this to the soaked bread and milk.

Both bread puddings have been a favorite in our family for over 50 years and enjoyed by "Rudy" Williams, Delaware state senator 1952–1960.

Rebecca Williams, Wilmington, Del.

CHARLOTTE RUSSE

Cover half a box gelatine with water over night, to soften it. Next morning, melt it over the fire carefully; sweeten and flavor 1 quart of rich sweet cream. Whip it to a stiff froth; then stir in the dissolved gelatine. Pour the whole into a mould previously lined with sponge cake, or into a large glass dish, lined with lady cake or almond sponge cake.

In the 1800s gelatin came in strings rather than neatly packaged granules, and measuring cups, refrigerators, and thermostat-controlled ovens were undreamed-of luxuries.

Theresa C. Brown's Domestic Cookery (circa 1871)

CREME BRULEE

Heat 1 quart of heavy cream in top of double boiler—do not let boil or scald. Add 2 tablespoons of granulated sugar until dissolved. Stir in well beaten 8 yolks with 2 tablespoons of vanilla. Mix well and pour into shallow Pyrex baking dish so custard will be about 1½ inches thick. Place dish in hot water and bake in slow oven until set. Cool and place in refrigerator for several hours so as to chill thoroughly. Remove from refrigerator and cover top with ¼ inch light brown sugar (dark will not do). Place dish under blazing hot broiler and watch carefully (or red hot poker). When surface is glazed, remove and cool. Chill thoroughly in refrigerator. This better if made the day ahead and left in refrigerator.

A favorite in the early 1900s.

Mrs. Jessica Terry, wife of Delaware's seventieth governor, Charles Layman Terry, 1965-1969.

DATE AND NUT PUDDING

1 cup black walnuts, chopped
1 cup sugar
5 tablespoons flour
2 teaspoons baking powder
¼ teaspoon salt
1 cup dates, cut in thirds
3 eggs

Mix everything but dates and eggs. Then add them. Bake slowly in a wax-paper-lined pan, turn out and remove paper gradually before paper dries. Serve with whipped cream (½ pint is enough).

Make day before.

Mr. George Bigger, Claymont's oldest resident at the young age of 99 has kindly given us this recipe—a favorite from his past.

CUSTARD ICE CREAM

2½ quarts of milk and cream   *2½ cups sugar*
(I use 1 pint whipping cream,   *6 eggs*
1 pint half and half, and 1½   *¼ teaspoon salt*
quarts of homogenized milk)   *1 tablespoon vanilla*
4 rounded tablespoons cornstarch

Cook all of this in a double boiler. (I set the pan in another large kettle with water.) Cook until thick, maybe 15 to 20 minutes, or longer, stirring constantly. Strain into freezer. Cool all day or overnight (with tiny stream of water going into water into which the freezer has been placed for quicker cooling). Place in refrigerator to get thoroughly cold. (Making the day before is almost a must!) When ready to freeze, add the vanilla and put into "old" ice cream freezer to be turned by a strong arm, with ice and salt. (Our freezer holds one gallon.)

When very hard to turn, clean top and carefully open the container and lift out the dasher, cleaning off as you lift. Have a platter and spoons ready to sample!

This never gets as hard as bought ice cream when first made, but when the surplus is stored in the refrigerator/freezer, it will get hard.

This is very rich and creamy—a little goes a long way. Enjoy! This is a favorite for birthdays.

Peg Gray, Wilmington, Del.

SNOW ICE CREAM

A very large mixing bowl full of snow. (Be sure to get snow from beneath the top, and light dry snow is best). Start with a small amount of snow in another medium sized bowl. Add sugar and rich milk or cream and vanilla. Keep adding more snow and more of all ingredients (except vanilla) until it is of the texture and sweetness to taste.

Of course it should be eaten at once. Eat slowly and enjoy. I am sure it will become one of your winter anticipations along with the crackling fire that our family so enjoys each winter season.

It amazes me that there are some people who have never tasted snow ice cream. It is one of my very fondest memories, and on a cold winter night when the snow starts to fall it is one of my first thoughts. I had it as a small child, then my children shared the fun, now their children are enjoying the miracle of snow and the fun of snow ice cream.

Mary Mammele, Wilmington, Del. (circa 1920)

PINEAPPLE SHERBET

3 eggs   *3¼ cups sugar*
#2 can of crushed pineapple   *Pinch of salt*
Juice of 3 or 4 oranges   *Milk*
Juice of 3 or 4 lemons

Blend together all ingredients. Add milk to fill 1 gallon freezer. Freeze in agitated (hand crank or electric) freezer; sherbet is too icy if frozen without agitation.

A popular dessert on the Eastern Shore in the early 1900s.

Harold J. Littleton, Wilmington, Del.

1854 PLUM PUDDING

Serves 10

One pound of stoned raisins, 1 pound currants, 1 pound of beef suet, chopped fine, 1 pound of grated bread crumbs or ½ pound flour, 8 eggs, ¼ pound sugar, 1 pint of milk, 1 glass brandy, 1 glass wine, 2 nutmegs, tablespoonful mace and cinnamon mixed, spoonful salt. Boil 6 hours.

MODERN VERSION

2 cups flour
1½ teaspoons salt
½ teaspoon baking soda
½ teaspoon nutmeg
½ teaspoon cinnamon
¼ teaspoon mace
¾ cup firmly packed brown
  sugar

3 eggs, beaten
4 ounces milk
¼ cup red wine
¼ cup brandy
1½ cups ground or very finely
  chopped suet
2 cups raisins
2 cups dried currants

Sift dry ingredients together. Combine eggs, milk, wine and brandy. Add to dry mixture. Add suet, raisins, and currants and mix well. Pour into a greased 2-quart pudding mold. Cover mold and put on rack in large kettle. Add boiling water to come halfway up the sides of the mold. Cover kettle and steam for about 4 hours. Serve hot with a brandy hard sauce or rum sauce. Decorate with a sprig of holly.

Plum pudding, a suet pudding never made with plums, was a traditional Christmas dessert with the Colonists. Christmas dinners were usually looked forward to with joy.

Army Wives Cookbook, compliments of Southwest Parks and Monuments Association, Tucson, Ariz.

SYLLABUB

6 navel oranges
1 pint heavy cream
½ cup sifted confectioner's sugar

2 egg whites
2 tablespoons cream sherry
2 tablespoons brandy

Peel oranges, section and chill. When ready to serve, whip cream and ¼ cup confectioner's sugar until stiff. Beat egg whites with remaining ¼ cup sugar to stiff peaks. Fold whipped cream into beaten egg whites, then sherry and brandy. Drain orange sections and arrange in 6 large goblets. Mound in syllabub on top and serve.

According to the old cookbooks, spirits were plentiful among the Colonists. Fresh oranges and cream were a luxury, but once both were available, syllabub, a frothy English whipped cream dessert laced with sherry and brandy, was served at Christmas and other festive occasions.

Brett Mumford, formerly of Claymont, Del.

POOR MAN'S RICE PUDDING
(circa 1910)

1 quart milk
½ cup rice
3 tablespoons sugar

1 tablespoon vanilla
Salt to taste

Mix all and pour into 3-quart casserole. Bake at 400° for one hour. Stir 2 or 3 times during baking.

Mrs. Ernest R. Robinson

Submitted by Doris R. Champlin, Wilmington, Del.

CAKES

BIBLE CAKE

Sift together:
  3½ cups I Kings 4:22 (flour)
  3 teaspoons Amos 4:5 (baking powder)
  ½ teaspoon Leviticus 2:13 (salt)
  2 teaspoons II Chronicles 9:9 (pumpkin pie spice)
Cream together:
  1½ cups Judges 5:25 last clause (butter)
  2 cups Jeremiah 6:20 (sugar)
  2 tablespoons I Samuel 14:25 (honey)
Add to above mixture:
  6 Jeremiah 27:2 (egg yolks, well beaten)
Add gradually to above mixture alternately with dry ingredients:
  1¾ cups Judges 4:19 last clause (milk)
Add to batter:
  2 cups I Samuel 30:12 (raisins)
  2 cups Numbers 17:8 (almonds)
  2 cup Nahum 3:12 (figs)

Follow Solomon's advice for making a good boy in Proverbs 23:14 (beat mixture well). Beware of Nahum 3:15 (keep heat at 350°). Bake in greased loaf pan for abour 1 hour until broom straw comes out clean.

My grandmother, Nellie Clark, who was born in 1868, taught Sunday School for many years. This Bible Cake receipt, baked for special occasions, made a special project for her classes.

Jane Frelick, Wilmington, Del.

CINNAMON CAKE

Yield: 2 thin cakes

1 cup sugar
1 tablespoon plus 2 tablespoons
  butter or lard
1 egg
1 cup water

2 teaspoons baking powder
2 cups flour
1 tablespoon sugar
1 tablespoon cinnamon

Mix ingredients and bake in 2 greased 8-inch pans at 350° until straw of broom comes out clean.

When finished, melt 2 tablespoons butter and spread over cake. Then sprinkle each cake with a mixture of sugar and cinnamon, or more, if desired. Serve each layer separately.

This receipt goes back to my great-grandmother's day in the middle 1800s and is enjoyed to this day by my family.

Mrs. James Arnold, Laurel, Del.

HOT CUSTARD CHIFFON CAKE

2 cups flour, sifted
3 teaspoons baking powder
1½ cups sugar
1 teaspoon salt
¾ cup scalding milk

1 cup cooking oil
8 egg yolks, beaten
2 teaspoons vanilla
8 egg whites, stiffly beaten
1 teaspoon cream of tartar

Place all dry ingredients in large bowl and make a well in center, then scald the milk. (This is the most important step in the success of this cake.) Place the milk in the center of the dry ingredients and mix well. Add oil and mix well. Add egg yolks which have been beaten in a separate bowl to the ingredients and mix well. Add vanilla.

Beat egg whites till stiff but not dry with the cream of tartar. Pour batter that has been mixed gradually over the egg whites, folding gently with a rubber scraper until blended. Pour into 10-inch tube pan. Bake at 325° about 55 minutes. Turn pan upside down to cool for about 1 hour.

FLOUR ICING

Combine 1 cup cold milk and 2 tablespoons flour. Cook for 5 minutes over a medium heat. Cream in mixer ½ cup Spry, 1 stick butter, pinch of salt, 1 cup granulated sugar, 1 teaspoon vanilla. Add milk and flour in and beat till fluffy. (Milk and flour must be perfectly cold or the icing will not be successful.)

An elegant dessert, the likes of which you've never tasted.

This old-time cake receipt goes back 7 generations.

Martha Johnson, Northfield, N. J.

DELAWARE CAKE

1 cup butter	4 cups flour
3 cups sugar	4 teaspoons baking powder
6 eggs	1 teaspoon salt
1 teaspoon vanilla	1 teaspoon nutmeg
1 teaspoon orange or lemon flavoring	1 cup milk

Cream butter, sugar and eggs; add vanilla and other flavoring. Sift dry ingredients together and add alternately with the milk.

Pour batter into a large tube pan which has been greased and floured. Bake in 350° preheated oven for 45 minutes or until it tests done. (It may take longer.) Cool in pan, then remove to wire rack. Sift with confectioner's sugar.

The original receipt came from New Castle County and is over 100 years old. Serve it on *Delaware Day, December 7*.

Helen Quillen, Lewes, Del.

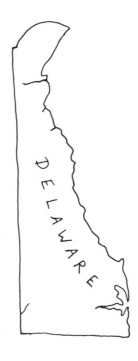

QUICK MORAVIAN CAKE

2 cups flour
¾ cup sugar
2 teaspoons baking powder
¼ teaspoon salt
¼ pound margarine, softened

1 egg, beaten
1 cup milk
1 teaspoon vanilla
1 cup light brown sugar

Preheat oven to 350°. Combine in an electric mixer the flour, sugar, baking powder, and salt. Beat in 4 tablespoons margarine until mixture is a pebbly texture. Add the egg, milk, and vanilla. Pour this mixture into a buttered 9- by 13-inch pan or 2 9-inch round pans. Make butter holes (put butter dabs all over top of cake) using 3 tablespoons margarine. Mix brown sugar with remaining 1 tablespoon margarine, crumbling to sprinkle over top of the cake. Bake for half hour.

This receipt goes back to the very early 1900s and uses no yeast, therefore the name Quick Moravian Cake. It was originally called Lazy Moravian Cake—but the Moravians took offense to the term lazy—they were a hard-working people.

Jean Gackenbach, Wilmington, Del.

DOVER CAKE

1 pound sugar (2 cups)
½ pound butter
6 eggs
1 pound flour (4 cups, sifted)

1 cup milk
1 teaspoon vanilla
1 teaspoon baking powder
½ teaspoon salt

Cream butter and sugar until soft (cream with hands). Add eggs one at a time. Add flour and milk alternately; add vanilla; add baking powder and salt. Bake in greased tube pan in 325° to 350° oven about 1¼ hours. Do not invert pan. Let cool. Slice thin and serve plain.

Variation: According to the 1900 *Milton Cookbook*, the egg yolks may be beaten together, added to the butter-sugar mixture and when all cake ingredients have been combined, fold in the well-beaten egg whites.

Mrs. William Yetter, Sr., Claymont, Del.

HALE-BYRNES HOUSE GUMDROP CAKE

½ cup shortening
2 eggs
1¼ cups sugar
1 cup unsweetened and strained
   applesauce
2½ cups bread flour
1 teaspoon soda

1 teaspoon each salt, nutmeg,
   cinnamon
2 cups dates, cut up
1½ cups nuts, chopped
1 pound gumdrops, sliced in 3
   pieces and dusted with flour

Mix with beater the shortening, eggs, and sugar. Add apple-sauce and all dry ingredients which have been sifted together. Mix well. Stir in dates, nuts, and gumdrops. Bake in 2 8½- by 4½-inch loaf pans for 1 hour at 350°. Cool in pan and wrap in foil to store.

Good made 1 month before using. Store in refrigerator for easy slicing, serve at room temperature. A delicious substitute for holiday fruit cake.

House receipt (1800s), Hale-Byrnes House, Stanton, Del.

GINGERBREAD

½ cup butter and lard mixed
½ cup sugar
1 egg
1 cup Brer Rabbit molasses
2½ cups sifted flour
½ teaspoon baking soda

1 teaspoon cinnamon
1 teaspoon ginger
½ teaspoon cloves
½ teaspoon salt
1 cup hot water

Cream shortening and sugar. Add beaten egg, molasses, then dry ingredients sifted together. Add hot water last and heat until smooth. Pour into 9-inch square pan. Bake 35 minutes in a 325° to 350° oven or until a darning needle, inserted, comes out dry.

Mrs. George W. Seeds (1916)

Every colonial woman baked regardless of her age.
From Spoon bread to Apple fritters to Gingerbread, they all prepared breads.
There were superstitions in those days, for instance—
  To drop a piece of bread buttered side up meant you would have a visitor.

  If you dreamt about bread, you would make money.

  A crust of bread in a new baby's crib would keep evil spirits away.

SAUCES FOR SERVING WITH GINGERBREAD

LEMON SAUCE

2 tablespoons sugar
1 tablespoon flour
½ cup boiling water

½ teaspoon butter
1 teaspoon lemon juice
¼ teaspoon lemon rind

Mix sugar and flour thoroughly. Slowly add boiling water and boil 5 minutes, stirring constantly. Just when done, add butter and flavoring. Taste and if more lemon is required, add it. Serve hot or cold.

CHOCOLATE SAUCE

1 cup water
⅓ cup sugar
1 ounce chocolate
⅓ cup milk

1 tablespoon cornstarch
½ teaspoon salt
½ teaspoon vanilla

Boil water and sugar for 5 minutes. Melt chocolate. Mix cornstarch and cold milk thoroughly, rubbing out all lumps. Add to melted chocolate. Add syrup (of sugar and water). Cook in a double boiler about 15 minutes, stirring as it thickens. Add salt and vanilla. Serve hot.

1918 4-H Club, Wilmington, Del.

KENTUCKY JAM CAKE

2 cups sugar	1 cup blackberry jam
1 cup butter	1 cup strawberry jam
4 cups flour	1 cup black walnuts
1 teaspoon cinnamon	1 cup pecans
1 teaspoon cloves	1 cup raisins
1 teaspoon nutmeg	1 cup figs
4 eggs	1 teaspoon baking soda
1 cup buttermilk	

Cream sugar and butter until fluffy. Sift flour and spices together. Use enough of the flour to dredge the nuts and fruit. To the sugar and butter mixture, slowly add the eggs. Beat in until smooth. Add flour and buttermilk a little at a time. Beat well. Add jams and beat. Add nuts and fruit. Stir with a large wooden spoon for 30 minutes until nuts and fruit are covered well. Lastly, add baking soda. Bake in tube pan at 275° for 4 hours. Cool. Frost with Caramel Frosting.

CARAMEL FROSTING

1 box brown sugar	¾ cup cream
¼ pound butter	Powdered sugar

Combine first 3 ingredients and cook until mixture forms a soft ball. Remove from heat. Beat until cool. Add powdered sugar until of spreading consistency.

Since the early 1800s, this has been passed from generation to generation. Just try it once, and you're lost forever.

Loretta Swafford, Barbourville, Ky.

JUMBLES

Three eggs, 1 pound of sugar, ½ pound of butter, flour to roll, half a teacup milk, soda to sweeten, ½ pound blanched and pounded almonds. Sprinkle flour upon a paste board; flour your hands, roll a portion of the dough with the hands into a long roll. Curl them into rings; place in a buttered pan, not allowing them to touch each other. Grate sugar over the top. Bake in a moderate oven. The dough must be soft, and it requires skill and practice to make jumbles perfectly.

Jumble receipts were a part of just about all *Delaware cooks*. The names of these little cakes came about probably from the variety of ingredients used to make them.

· MARBLE CAKE

6 egg whites
1 cup butter
2 cups sugar
1 cup milk

3½ cups flour
2 teaspoons Royal baking
  powder
Vanilla

Combine all ingredients. Color ⅓ of the batter with ¼ cake of melted chocolate.

This recipe came originally from *The Thimble Club Cookbook* of Federalsburg, Maryland in 1905. As with most receipts from those days, there were no baking instructions. It was all guess-work or know-how from watching their parents and grandparents bake. The book was dedicated to those housewives who master their work instead of allowing it to master them.

Mrs. Mollie Fluharty

MAMMY'S MOLASSES POUND CAKE (1835)

1 cup butter
3½ cups flour
6 eggs, beaten
2 teaspoons lemon juice
1 teaspoon baking powder
1 teaspoon cinnamon
1 teaspoon salt

½ cup sugar
1½ cups molasses
1 teaspoon ginger
½ teaspoon cloves
1 teaspoon soda dissolved in 2
    tablespoons water

Cream butter, flour and add eggs. Add remaining ingredients and mix. Bake 1 hour at 325° in a 9- by 13-inch pan.

Pillsbury Honorable Mention, 1955

Ruth Russell, Seaford, Del.

GINGERBREAD MOLASSES CAKE (*circa* 1774)

Take 2 pounds of molasses to 4 pounds of flour, 1 pound of sugar, 1½ pounds of butter.

Mix molasses, sugar, and butter together and heat them. Let it cool. When cool, make the gingerbread, put in with the flour 4 tablespoons of ginger and spices to taste. They are best baked for some time.

Gingerbread: Bread or biscuit sweetened with treacle and flavored with ginger and some other aromatick seed.

Mrs. Charles Ridgely, sister-in-law of Nicholas Ridgely, a signer of the Ratification.

PORK CAKE

1 pound ground fat pork
   (weighed without rind), no
   lean
1 pint strong coffee
4 cups brown sugar, measured
   packed down
1 tablespoon baking soda

1 teaspoon salt
1 tablespoon cinnamon
2 teaspoons nutmeg
7 cups sifted flour
½ pound walnuts, English or
   black
1 pound raisins

Grind pork, then pour coffee boiling hot on it and set on the
stove a few minutes and let barely simmer before adding any of
the other ingredients. Then put in sugar, soda, salt, spices and
flour saving out a little of it to dredge nuts and raisins—add
last. Bake 1 hour or longer depending on pan in 350° oven.
Tube pan takes about hour and a half. Test for doneness with
broomstraw or toothpick. Cake tastes best after standing in a
closed tin for about a month.

This is an old recipe from Marion, Virginia. They always killed
the pigs the Saturday after Thanksgiving so made these cakes
in time for Christmas.

Susan R. Barbour, Wilmington, Del.

VANILLA POUND CAKE

½ pound butter, melted
1 package confectioner's sugar
6 eggs, separated and beat
  whites
3¾ cups flour

2 teaspoons baking powder
1 teaspoon salt
1 cup milk
1 teaspoon vanilla
½ teaspoon almond extract

Combine butter, sugar, and egg yolks and beat until fluffy.
Blend in sifted dry ingredients alternately with milk and combined extracts. Fold in egg whites. Bake in a greased and
floured tube pan at 350° for 1 hour.

This was a family favorite dating back to the 1920s when we
traveled to Bowers Beach for Big Thursday and to Barratts
Chapel on the Fourth of July for special services followed by
"basket" lunches in the Grove, Sunday car drives, and boat
rides. The cake held up in all kinds of weather. It was found in
the mens' lunch pails and in the school lunch boxes.

The days of "picnic baskets" and hardy appetites.

From the receipt collection of the late Elva Turner Gross

TWELFTH NIGHT CAKE

1 cup butter
1 cup sugar
1 tablespoon fresh grated orange
  peel
1 tablespoon grated lemon peel
2 eggs
2½ cups sifted flour
2 teaspoons baking powder

2 teaspoons baking soda
½ teaspoon salt
1 cup buttermilk
½ cup mixed candied fruit,
  chopped
1 cup chopped walnuts
1 cup whole blanched almonds

Cream butter and sugar until fluffy. Add orange and lemon peel, then eggs. Sift together dry ingredients, add to creamed mixture, alternately with buttermilk. Beat until smooth. Fold in fruit and nuts. I place 3 silver crowns, separately in foil, and bake them in the cake. Pour batter into greased 8-cup bundt or tube pan. Bake at 350° 1 hour.

GLAZE

¾ cup orange juice
2 teaspoons lemon juice

1 cup sugar
2 tablespoons rum

Bring orange and lemon juice and sugar to a boil. Add rum. Dribble or pour slowly over *hot* cake in the *pan*. Let cake stand 24 hours in pan before removing and cutting. I like to use whipped cream or ice cream on the side.

An old English custom for choosing a king and queen for the January 6, Epiphany Twelfth Night celebration was to bake a bean and a pea in the cake. The cake was served early in the day and the finders of the "unusual" became the monarchs and were assured good luck all year. This celebration was continued by the colonists on the East Coast, and to this day is celebrated in a special way in Sussex County, Delaware.

Mary Musgrave Richardson, Seaford, Del.

WELLESLEY FUDGE CAKE
(*circa* 1898)

Yield: 9-inch layer cake

4 squares Bakers unsweetened
   chocolate
½ cup hot water
½ cup sugar
2 cups sifted cake flour
1 teaspoon baking soda
1 teaspoon salt

½ cup butter or margarine
1¼ cups sugar
3 eggs
¾ cup milk
1 teaspoon vanilla
Chocolate butter frosting

Preheat oven to 350°. Heat chcoolate with water in a saucepan over very low heat, stirring until chocolate is melted and mixture is smooth. Add sugar; cook, and stir 2 minutes longer. Cool to lukewarm.

Sift flour with baking soda and salt. Cream butter. Gradually beat in 1¼ cups sugar; continue beating until light and fluffy. Add eggs, one at a time, beating thoroughly after each addition. Add flour mixture alternatively with milk, beating after each addition until smooth. Blend in vanilla and chocolate mixture. Pour into 2 greased and floured 9-inch layer pans. Bake for 30 to 35 minutes, or until cake springs back when lightly pressed. Cool in pans 10 minutes. Remove from pans and finish cooling on racks. Fill and frost tops and sides of cake with chocolate butter frosting.

CHOCOLATE BUTTER FROSTING
Yield: 2¼ cups

Melt 2½ squares Bakers unsweetened chocolate in saucepan over very low heat, stirring constantly. Beat 6 tablespoons butter until softened; gradually add about 1 cup confectioner's sugar, beating well. Blend in ¾ teaspoon vanilla and chocolate. Add 2 cups confectioner's sugar alternately with about 5 tablespoons milk, beating until smooth, creamy and right consistency to spread.

Courtesy of Bakers, General Foods Corp., White Plains, N.Y.

CUPCAKES

3 cups sugar
2 cups butter
3 eggs
1 cup milk or cream

5 cups flour
Spoonful soda
Spoonful honey

Bake in tins or loaf pan until done. Test with a broom thistle.

This receipt is thought to be at least 150 years old and, as of all receipts, in those days no cooking directions were given. The receipt was discovered in the old cooking files of the Neal family, from Seaford, Delaware.

William B. Neal, Claymont, Del.

COOKIES

FANNY FARMER'S GINGERSNAPS

1 cup molasses
½ cup shortening
½ cup brown sugar
3¼ cups flour

½ teaspoon soda
1 tablespoon ginger
1 teaspoon cinnamon
½ teaspoon salt

Heat molasses to boiling and pour over shortening. Add sugar. Mix and sift other dry ingredients and add. (You may also add ½ teaspoon nutmeg and ½ teaspoon cloves, if desired.) Mix well after adding to molasses. Chill thoroughly. Toss ¼ of mixture on a floured board and roll thin as possible. Shape with cutter dipped in flour. Put on greased cookie sheet. Bake in 350° oven for about 10 minutes. Dough should be kept in refrigerator while waiting to be rolled or it will be necessary to add more flour to dough, which will make cookies hard.

From *The Original Boston Cooking School Cookbook*, (1896)

Grace Salisbury, Warwick, Rhode Island

GRACE'S DELAWARE CRY BABIES

1 cup sugar
1 cup lard (Crisco)
1 egg
1 teaspoon cinnamon
5 cups flour
1 cup molasses

½ cup hot water
1 big teaspoon baking soda
1 teaspoon vanilla
1 cup raisins
Pinch of salt

Drop on cookie sheet by heaping teaspoonsful, a small distance apart. Bake at 375° for 10 to 12 minutes.

This recipe is at least 100 years old. There are no detailed directions. I just mix it all up.

Edna May Diedrich, Lewes, Del. (circa 1885)

ICE BOX COOKIES

1 cup butter
2 cups brown sugar
2 eggs, beaten
½ cup black walnuts, cut fine

3½ cups flour
1 teaspoon soda
½ teaspoon salt

Cream butter and sugar; then add beaten eggs. Add nuts, then sifted ingredients. Mix well and shape in a long, narrow loaf. Let stand overnight in ice box or cool place. Slice thin and bake in buttered pan in moderately hot oven.

These are great because they can be baked a few at a time and the dough can be kept in the ice box until such time as needed. Thinner the cut the better.

Mrs. Kenneth Steers, Laurel, Del. (circa 1925)

OLD ORIGINAL NORWEGIAN COOKIES
(ROUND BALLS MADE FLAT)

500 grams flour (3¼ cups)
200 grams sugar (1¼ cups)
1 small teaspoon baking ammonia *(level teaspoon, crushed)
2 eggs

375 grams butter (¾ pound plus 2⅓ tablespoons)
1 teaspoon vanilla
1 teaspoon almond extract
55 grams almonds (1 or 2 ounces, sliced)

Mix flour, sugar, and ammonia; add 1 egg and butter. Add vanilla and almond extract. Flour your hands, roll a bit of dough into a ball, then flatten (about the size of a quarter). Beat other egg, brush on cookies, put sliced almonds and sprinkle colored sugar on top. Bake at 350° for 8 to 10 minutes.

*Ask druggist for crushed ammonium carbonate. About a $1.00 worth will make several batches. Crush the baking ammonia between 2 sheets of foil, sealed at both ends because the ammonia odor is a little strong.

Because it is time consuming to flatten the dough you may spoon off by half-teaspoons onto a greased cookie tray.

There are no cookies anywhere else so good. The secret lies not only in the amount of butter used, but also in a mysterious ingredient called salt of hartshorn. This predates baking powder as a rising agent by several centuries, and once was made from the antlers of a deer (or hart). Now it is produced chemically as ammonium carbonate, the results are worth it and the cookies will not bear a trace of the smell.

Marie Godfrey, Newark, Del. (circa 1898)

ROSETTES

Yield: about 40 rosettes

2 eggs
1 teaspoon sugar
¼ teaspoon salt

1 cup milk
1 cup flour (add a little more, if
  necessary)

Beat the eggs slightly with sugar and salt, add milk and flour and beat until smooth.

Screw handle into iron, then put the iron in hot lard or oil before dipping it into the batter, not allowing the batter to come over the top of iron. Return the iron to the hot lard, thoroughly covering with the same, for at least 20 seconds, but not for more than 35 seconds. Remove from iron with a piece of clean cheese cloth.

As a child, I can remember watching Mother's cook making the rosettes for an antique tea shop my mother had with two other ladies in Centerville, Delaware, in the early 30s. It was called Cobwebbs, named after a friend's house in England. The little schoolhouse still standing has been someone's house for quite some time.

Georgina Miller Bissell, Greenville, Del., granddaughter of Delaware's fifty-sixth governor, Charles R. Miller, 1913-1917

SAND TARTS

Into 1 pound flour, rub ¾ pound butter. Add 1 pound sugar. Rub in 2 eggs and roll very thin. Wash with white of egg and place nut in center with sprinkle of cinnamon and sugar.

Mary S. Lackey (1864)

SUGAR COOKIES

1 cup butter or lard   1 teaspoon lemon extract
2 cups sugar   2½ cups flour
2 eggs   2 teaspoons baking powder

Mix together thoroughly butter, sugar, and eggs. Add lemon
extract. Sift together and add to above the flour and baking
powder. If not stiff enough, add more flour to roll quite thin.
Bake quickly (means a fairly hot oven, 375°).

This recipe converts to Coconut Cookies.
Omit lemon extract, adding 1 cup coconut to egg mixture.

Sugar Cookies were served at toll houses in the South. They
were often served with buttermilk.

Irene McKeown

"Better to me than the silver or linen I inherited from my
grandmother was her old receipt book. Just to look through
it again is like being with her; rereading a favorite receipt
is reliving the times one has enjoyed it."

OLD FASHIONED COOKIES WITH A PEAK

Yield: 30 drop cookies

¼ pound lard or use half
   butter (lard is better)
½ pound (1 cup), very fine
   sugar
2 eggs
1 pound flour (4 cups, sifted)

1 ounce baking powder (2
   tablespoons) or ¼ ounce
   hartshorn, pounded fine—¼
   ounce = ⅔ teaspoon)
½ pint milk (1 cup)
Plumped raisins

Beat lard and butter to cream them. Gradually beat in the sugar. Add eggs one at a time and beat well after each addition until mixture is feather-light. At this point a small amount of lemon flavoring may be added.

Sift flour and baking powder. Blend in half the flour mixture and then add flour and milk alternately, mixing well.

Drop by generous tablespoons onto buttered and floured pans or in regular scalloped cookie pans which have been buttered and floured. Put 3 currants or a raisin in the center. Bake in preheated "quick" oven (400° to 425°) until lightly browned.

These cookies have been loved and remembered since the early 1930s—an old time pleaser. The cookies were made by old German bakers in individual cast-iron cookie pans with scalloped edges. They will peak higher when baked individually. Originally, hartshorn (bought at drug stores now) was used for leavening. Baking powder can be used, but hartshorn makes the peaks higher and you need use only ¼ as much as baking powder. Oh yes, remember if possible, superfine sugar is recommended for these cookies.

Frances Blackwood, *Evening Bulletin* (1932)

WHOOPIE PIES

½ cup shortening
1 cup sugar
1 egg
1 cup milk
1 teaspoon vanilla

2 cups flour
1 teaspoon baking soda
½ teaspoon salt
⅓ cup cocoa

Preheat oven to 425°. Cream shortening, sugar and egg. Combine and add dry ingredients alternately with milk. Add vanilla. Drop by tablespoonfuls on an ungreased cookie sheet. Bake for 7 minutes.

FILLING

1 pound confectioner's sugar
7½-ounce jar marshmallow fluff

1 cup butter, softened

Beat all ingredients until creamy. Spread between 2 cookies. Wrap individually with waxed paper.

A favorite treat of the kids of the '30s.

Malcolm Proulx, Wilmington, Del.

CANDY

VINEGAR CANDY

2 cupfuls sugar
½ cupful vinegar

Butter, size of an egg

Boil above ingredients for 20 minutes or till it hardens in water; then pour into greased plates to cool. Flavor, but do not pull.

In colonial days sugar reached the housewife in large cone-shaped loaves of 9 to 10 pounds each. Hunks of sugar had to be broken off, pounded in a mortar or rolled on a marble slab with a rolling pin or glass bottle to pulverize it, then sifted.

Elizabeth McKeown (circa 1908)

BUTTER, PICKLES, AND PRESERVES

APPLE BUTTER

Boil down new cider to ⅓ its original quantity, pare, core, and slice juicy tart apples, and put as many into the kettle with the cider as it will cover. Let boil, stirring carefully to prevent scorching. When boiled soft, drain out with a ladle. Put more apples in the cider and boil in the same way. Repeat this till the cider is too much reduced in quantity to permit it; then pour together and boil down to about ½ the quantity, and spice to taste. It will keep well in stone jars or tubs.

Apple butter was always on American tables and used to be cooked in big brass saucepans. Antique dealers sell them now for geraniums or kindling. If you are fortunate enough to own one, polish it up and make some apple butter.

Charles M. Cochran, III, great-great grandson of John Polk Cochran, Governor of Delaware, 1875-1879

GRAPE BUTTER

Yield: approximately 2 pints

1 quart Concord grapes   4 cups (1 quart) sugar

Wash and pick off grapes. Measure in a quart berry box. Add sugar. Crush together enough to start juice and mix well. Bring to boil quickly and continue boiling briskly for 20 minutes or until mixture begins to sheet like jelly.

Strain thoroughly through a food mill. Put in hot sterile jars and seal.

Very good and very easy. *Never-never* double receipt.

Margaret Walton Feldmann, Newark, Del. (circa 1933)

DELAWARE CITY
BRANDIED PEACHES

6 peaches
3 cups water
2 cups sugar

2 tablespoons brandy, for each
pint jar

Take 6 perfect peaches—if peaches have thin skins, you need
not peel them—rub off the fuzz with a cloth and prick each
peach twice with a fork. If you wish to have the peaches
peeled, dip quickly in hot water and peel.

Make a syrup by boiling water and sugar for 10 minutes. Cook
the peaches, a few at a time, in the syrup until tender, about 5
minutes. Pack into pint jars. Add 2 tablespoons brandy to each
jar and fill with syrup. Store a month before using.

In olden days, the peaches were stored in a cool corner of the
kitchen in a heavy crock.

Serve as a dessert, especially good with ice cream—or with
lamb or chicken.

The Delaware City area was the home of Major Philip Reybold,
Delaware's peach king and this recipe has been passed on to us
by older residents.

Elmer L. Snow, III, mayor, Delaware City, Del., (circa 1917-1921)

UNCLE PAYNTER'S SPICED PEACHES

5 pounds of whole, clingstone
  Delamore peaches, peeled
2½ pounds of sugar
½ cup cider vinegar

A spice bag containing:
  1 tablespoon allspice
  1 tablespoon cinnamon
  1 tablespoon whole cloves

Boil the peaches, sugar, vinegar, and spice bag until peaches are tender. Remove peaches and spice bag. Boil juice until thickened. Return the peaches to the juice and cool. Pack in sterilized jars and seal.

Paynter Frame, born October 21, 1826 in Indian River Hundred, devoted a great part of his life to farming and fruit growing on the land his forefathers received through a grant from King George of England. He had at one time 2,000 peach trees, paying particular attention to grafting and improving the peach, and was also known as the watermelon king of Sussex County. He held many public offices, but was especially proud of being instrumental in organizing the American Agricultural Association in 1879.

Frances W. Ganous, Newark, Del.

CHILI SAUCE

4 dozen large ripe tomatoes, scald, peel and cut into pieces; 4 green peppers and 4 red peppers, 8 large onions, peppers and onions chopped together; 8 small cupfuls of vinegar, 8 tablespoons of sugar, 4 ounces of salt. All cooked together until like preserves which will take nearly all day. Put in jar and seal very tightly.

Trinity Parish Cook Book, (1892) Trinity Parish was organized 1638, incorporated 1759, Wilmington, Del.

CUCUMBER STICKS

(To be eaten the same day)

Peel cucumbers. Slice lengthwise to make cucumber sticks. Put in a pint-size jar. Add 3 tablespoons vinegar, 3 tablespoons water, and 3 tablespoons sugar. Stir and pour over cucumbers. Chill.

Great for picnics, reunions, or just for your own table.

An old Sussex County receipt (1865) from the Arnold family.

LIVIA-LURA CHOW CHOW

Yield: 16 quarts

Cut 2 gallons cucumbers into cubes and soak about 2 days in 2 quarts of vinegar. Drain and discard liquid. (Cucumbers have been previously salted in a brine-soak until fresh. Copper pot keeps them green.) Cut 2 gallons small green tomatoes in cubes and soak in salt water overnight (about 3 tablespoons salt). Drain.

When pickles and tomatoes are ready, grind 6 red and 6 green peppers and 8 onions. Add 1 gallon vinegar, 6 pounds sugar, 5 tablespoons mustard seed, 5 tablespoons celery seed, 40 cloves, and 2 small bottles French's mustard. Boil ½ hour and seal.

This recipe is handed down from the mother and grandmother of my husband, late residents of Bethel, Del.

Mrs. Dot Wright, Bethel, Del.

PEPPER RELISH

1 small head cabbage, cut fine	½ cup salt
12 green peppers, cut fine	Water
12 red peppers, cut fine	
16 medium sized onions, cut fine	

Combine ingredients together. Pour boiling water over them and let stand for about 15 minutes, then drain good. Add:

1 quart vinegar	2 tablespoons white mustard seed
3 cups sugar	
1 tablespoon celery seed	

Boil about 20 minutes. Ready to put into jars and seal.

This receipt, which is over 100 years old, was submitted by Mary Catherine Collins, Laurel, Del., great granddaughter of Delaware's twenty-third governor, John Collins, 1821-1822.

BLACKBERRY JELLY OR PRESERVES

Allow a pint of currant juice and a pint of water to 6 pounds of blackberries; give them their weight in brown sugar; let them boil till they appear to be done and the syrup is rich.

Blackberry jelly can be made as currant jelly and when mixed with water is good for sick children.

This receipt came from a cookbook edited in 1866 by Cushing and Bailey. The book was found in the attic of the historic Mermaid Tavern where I now reside, as did my relatives.

Sara Pennington Evans, Wilmington, Del.

BRANDIED PEACHES

1 pint water   4 pounds peaches (firm, ripe,
3 pounds sugar   and skinned)

Cook fruit in syrup until done. Place fruit in jars with fork.
Measure syrup and to 1 quart, add 1 pint of brandy (applejack).
Bring syrup and brandy to a boil. Remove from stove and pour
over fruit in jars.

The Townsend family (often numbering 40) came from far and
near and looked forward to the peaches on the table for the
elegant Christmas dinner which Evelyn, the cook, did with
such ease.

An advertisement for Authur's Celebrated Patent Air-tight Self
Sealing Jars, found in an old manuscript cookbook, lists tin,
fire-proofed stoneware, white queensware and glass jars in
pint, quart, half gallon, and gallon sizes. The jars were sealed
with cement. To open, the cement had to be softened by
placing a hot flatiron on the lid or placing the jar in a warm
oven.

Rachel M. Townsend, Rehoboth Beach, Del., daughter-in-law
of Delaware's fifty-seventh governor, John G. Townsend, Jr.,
1917-1921.

Quince Ratafia
3 qts of quince juice
3 qts of French brandy
3 drachms Cinnamon
2   Coriander ands
24 grains cloves
½ oz bitter almonds pounded
½ drachm anniseed
2½ lbs best loaf sugar

    Infuse for a fortnight
and strain for use.

From old Ridgely receipts about 1790
Ratafia — "Liqueur flavoured with
almonds or Kernals of Peach, or
apricot or Cherry." Also a biscuit
and also a cherry.
                    Oxford Dict.

A receipt taken from grandmother of Judge Henry Ridgely Horsey
Dover, Del.

SWEET PICKLE WATERMELON RIND

Yield: 7 pints

7 pounds fruit
1 pint vinegar
¼ teaspoon oil of cloves

¼ teaspoon oil of cinnamon
3 pounds sugar

Peel rind, cut off all pink, and cut in small pieces. Cover with hot water. Parboil until tender, but not soft. Drain. Then mix vinegar, spiced oils, and sugar. Heat and pour over fruit. Next day, drain and reheat liquid and pour over fruit. On third day, do the same; put in jars and seal.

Oil of cloves and cinnamon can be bought in a drugstore.

Mrs. Hastings is 92 years young and still active in church and club affairs.

Minnie Hastings, Bethel, Del.

"RUSTIC" MEASUREMENTS

a dash, drop, few grains	= less than ⅓ teaspoon
a wine glass full	= ¼ cup
9 medium eggs	= 1 pound
8 to 10 egg whites	= 1 cup
13 to 14 egg yolks	= 1 cup
1 lemon, juiced	= 2½ to 3½ tablespoons
1 orange, juiced	= 5 to 6 tablespoons
5 finger pinch	= 1 tablespoon
4 finger pinch	= 1 teaspoon
1 finger pinch with thumb	= ⅛ teaspoon
1 finger gob	= 1 tablespoon
palm of hand, center	= 1 tablespoon
1 open fistful	= ½ cup

Although the receipts in this section date back *fifty or more years*, in some instances the ingredients and cooking tools have been updated for practical use.

KITCHEN MATH

Bread crumbs, dry	1 slice = ¼ cup
Bread crumbs, soft	1 slice = ½ cup
Cracker crumbs	¾ cup crackers = 1 cup breadcrumbs
Graham crackers	15 crackers = 1 cup fine crumbs
Chocolate wafers	19 wafers = 1 cup fine crumbs
Vanilla wafers	22 wafers = 1 cup fine crumbs
Cocoa	1 pound = 4 cups
Cornstarch	1¼ teaspoons = 1 tablespoon
Flour	4 tablespoons = 1 ounce
Garlic powder	⅛ teaspoon = 1 small clove
Herbs and spices	½ to 1 teaspoon = 1 tablespoon chopped onion
Onion powder	1 tablespoon = 1 medium onion
Lemon or orange peel	1 teaspoon dried, grated = 1 teaspoon fresh
Macaroni	1 pound = 5 cups uncooked or 12 cups cooked
Marshmallows	1 cup cut up = 10 large or 100 miniatures
Rice	1 pound = 2½ cups uncooked or 8 cups cooked
Tea	1 pound = 120 cups
Coffee	1 pound = 5 cups ground coffee
Water	1 pound = 2 cups

FRUIT MATH

Apples,	4 small, 3 medium, or 2 large	= 1 pound
	2¾ cups, sliced	= 1 pound
	1 cup, grated	= 2 medium sized
Bananas,	3 medium	= 1 pound
	⅔ cups, sliced	= 1 medium
	⅓ cup mashed	= 1 medium

TABLES AND WEIGHTS
AND MEASURES

2 cups butter	= 1 pound
4 cups flour	= 1 pound
2 cups sugar	= 1 pound
3½ cups confectioner's	= 1 pound
2¼ cups brown sugar, packed	= 1 pound
3 cups cornmeal	= 1 pound
1 cup molasses	= 11 ounces
1 cup whole eggs, medium	= 5 to 7 eggs
1 cup egg whites, extra large	= 6 to 7 whites
1 cup egg yolks	= 12 to 16 yolks
1 egg white	= 1½ tablespoons
1 cup almonds, whole	= 6 ounces
1 cup walnuts, chopped	= ¼ pound
4 cups pecans, shelled	= 1 pound

MEASUREMENTS

1 teaspoon	= 60 drops
3 teaspoons	= 1 tablespoon
2 tablespoons	= 1 liquid ounce
4 tablespoons	= ¼ cup
5⅓ tablespoons	= ⅓ cup
8 tablespoons	= ½ cup
12 tablespoons	= ¾ cup
16 tablespoons	= 1 cup

Many things are passed from generation to generation, things which people hold dear—family names, customs, old silver, precious heirlooms and recipes.

INDEX

Almond Paste Filling, 164
Amber Custard, 263
Ann Bowers Sutliffe Valliant's
  Boston Brown Bread,
  247
Appetizers
  Bitterballen, 2
  Blue Cheese Lagoon, 4
  Broccoli Fondue, 3
  combinations, 14
  Crab, 6
  Dip, 7
  Hot, 6
  Delaware Chicken Wings,
    5
  Delaware Specials, 1
  Dip
    Crab, 7
    Dill, 7
    Ham, 8
    Hot Shrimp, 12
    Tex-Mex, 13
  Fondue
    Broccoli, 3
    Pizza, 3
  Hot Dogs in Bourbon, 7
  John's Liver Pate, 9
  "Luxury" Sandwich Filling,
    235
  Mushrooms
    Marinated, 9
    New Castle County
      Stuffed Fresh, 10
    Party, 10
    "Tidbit" Sandwiches, 234
  Party Canapes, 4
  Party Cheese Ball, 5
  Pink Herring, 8
  Pizza Fondue, 3
  Salmon Party Spread, 11
  Sausage Balls, 11
  Shrimp
    Hot Dip, 12
    Log, 12
  Traditional, 234–35
  Zucchini, 14
Apple
  Bread, 56
  Cider, 63
  with Cinnamon, 56
  Brown Betty, 139
  Butter, 293
    Crockpot, 228
  Cake, 195
    Elsie's Toss, 196
    Harvest, 209
    One Quart Applesauce,
      197
  Dumplings, Baked, 263
  Muffins, Spiced, 50

Peachy Dumplin', 146
Pie
  Chipmunk, 156
  Mince, 157
  Paper Bag, 155
  Pudding, Premium, 264
  Salad with Beet, Herring
    and, 29
Applesauce Cake, One
  Quart, 197
Apple Upside-Down Cake,
  197
Apricot
  Chicken, 79
  Salad, 28
Asparagus
  Easy Casserole, 121
  Sesame Shrimp and, 117
Avocado
  Tex-Mex Dip, 13

Bacon, Pan-Fried Trout
  Wrapped in, 118
Baked Apple Dumplings, 263
Baked Beans,
  Honey, 122
  Jim's, 123
Baked Pineapple, 146
Bamboo Shoots, Beef with
  Peppers and, 74
Banana
  Frosted Fingers, 198
  Homemade Ice Cream, 144
Barbecue
  Baby Spareribs, 71
  Chicken, 80
  Casserole, 80
  Sauce, 71
  for Meat, 78
Beans
  Cuban Black, 124
  Honey Baked, 122
  Jim's Baked, 123
Bechemel Sauce, 41
Beef
  with Bamboo Shoots and
    Peppers, 74
  Brisket, 76
  Burgundy, 75
  and Cabbage Casserole, 75
  Ken's Flank Steak Roll
    Ups, 77
  Pot Roast, Italian style, 76
  Savory Chuck Steak, 77
  Three Day Casserole, 137
Beer Bread, 57
Beet, Salad with Apple,
  Herring and, 29
Belle's Squash Casserole, 133

Beverages
  Cherry Bounce, 240
  Chocolate Ginger Ale, 235
  Daiquiri
    Punch, 16
    Strawberry, 16
  Dandelion Wine, 236
  Eggnog,
    Clark's, 16
    Governor Lea's Special,
      236
    Hot, 237
  Haymaker's Switzel, 237
  Lemonade, 17
  Punch
    Bride's, 15
    Claymont High School
      Fruit, 17
    Daiquiri, 16
    Old Delaware, 238
    Schroeder Family, 238
    Shellpot Park, 239
  Raspberry Cordial, 18
  Strawberry Daiquiri, 16
  Syllabub, 238–39
  Traditional, 235–40
  Wassail, 18
Bible Cake, 271
Biscuits, 51
  Cheese, 53
  Cinnamon Monkey Balls,
    53
  Mush Cakes, 245
  Orange, 246
  Traditional, 245–46
  White Potato Rolls, 246
Bitterballen, 2
Black Beans, Cuban, 124
Blackberry
  Foolery, 264
  Jelly or Preserves, 294
Black-Eyed Peas for New
  Year's Day, 127
Blueberry
  Muffins, 51
  Oatmeal, 52
  Zucchini Bread, 68
Blue cheese
  Lagoon, 4
  Satin Soup, 20
Blue Coat Inn Peanut Butter
  Ice Cream Pie, 166
Blue Goose Chocolate Cake,
  205
Boiled Cod with Eggs, 256
Boon Docks Red Crab Soup,
  22
Boston Brown Bread, 247
Bouillon, Hospitality, 19
Bourbon, Hot Dogs in, 7

Brandied Peaches, 298
Delaware City, 294
Bread
  Apple Cinnamon, 56
  Beer, 57
  Blueberry Zucchini, 68
  Boston Brown, Ann Bowers
    Sutliffe Valliant's, 247
  Cinnamon Buns, 58–59
  Cinnamon Twists, 59
  Corn
    Mom Mom Mitchell's, 60
    Old-Fashioned Pone, 248
    Pone, 248
  Easy French, 63
  Italian Cheese, 62
  Jocake, 250
  Lemon, 64
  Lemon Pecan, 65
  Mincemeat, 66
  Nut, 250
  Pudding, 265
    Chocolate, 265
  Pumpkin, 66
  Raisin, Old-Fashioned, 251
  Sally Lunn, 252
  Shake Cider, 63
  Yeast Rolls, 67
Bride's Punch, 15
Brisket, 76
Broccoli
  and Cheese Puffle, 44
  Fondue, 3
  Georgetown Vegetable
    Custard, 262
Brownies
  Creme de Menthe, 173
  Swedish White, 174
Butter
  Apple, 293
    Crockpot, 228
  Buttered Rum Cake, 220
  Grape, 293
  Lemon, 228
  Summertime Strawberry, 229

Cabbage
  and Beef Casserole, 75
  Purple, Salad, 30
  Red, 124
  Skillet, 125
  Ukranian Noodles and, 125
Cake
  Apple, 195
    Elsie's Toss, 196
    Harvest, 209
  Banana Fingers, Frosted,
    198
  Bible, 271
  Buttered Rum, 220
  Carrot, 199
  Cashew, Pineapple, 216
  Cheesecake
    Delaware, 202
    Great Grandma's, 203
    Italian Cream, 210
    Pumpkin, 204

Chocolate
  Blue Goose, 205
  Cherry Bars, 206
  Chip, 206
  Cream Cheese, 201
  Wellesley Fudge, 285
Cinnamon, 272
Cola, 207
Cupcakes, 286
Daisy Flower, 208
Delaware, 274
Dover, 275
Gingerbread, 276
  Molasses, 281
Gumdrop, Hale-Byrnes
  House, 278
Harvest, 209
Hot Custard Chiffon, 273
Ice Creamy, 145
Jimmy Carter, 200
Johnny, 249
Jumbles, 280
Kentucky Jam, 279
Madeleines, 211
Mandarin Orange, 212
Marble, 280
Martha Washington, 224
Mee, 213
Molasses
  Gingerbread, 281
  Mammy's Pound, 281
Mom's Birthday, 213
Mush, 245
Old-Fashioned "Fried," 242
One Quart Applesauce,
  197
Orange
  Mandarin, 212
  Slice, 214
Petit Fours, 215
Pineapple
  Cashew, 216
  Upside-Down, 217
Pork, 282
Pound,
  Catherine's Kentucky,
    218
  Mammy's Molasses, 281
  Sour Cream, 219
  Vanilla, 283
Quick Moravian, 275
Sour Cream, 221
  Pound, 219
  Torte, 222
Sponge, 208
Strawberry
  7-Up, 223
  Shortcake, 151
  Traditional, 271–86
  Twelfth Night, 284
  Wellesley Fudge, 285
Canapes, 4
Candy
  Chocolate
    Covered Pretzels, 191
    Fudge, 188
    Peanut Butter Crispies,
      192

Saltines, 191
Fudge
  Chocolate, 188
  Healthful, 189
  Holiday, 189
  Peanut Butter, 190
  Velvety, 190
Health Cereal, 188
Krispie Balls, 192
Old Fashioned Peanut
  Brittle, 193
Peanut Butter
  Balls, 193
  Chocolate Crispies, 192
  Cups, 194
  Fudge, 190
Salt Water Taffy, 194
Vinegar, 292
Caramel Frosting, 279
Carrot Cake, 199
Cashew, Pineapple Cake, 216
Casserole
  Asparagus, Easy, 121
  Barbeque Chicken, 80
  Beef and Cabbage, 75
  Belle's Squash, 133
  Chicken, 84
  Chicken or Turkey, 93
  Egg, 38
  Grannie's, 39
  Hash Brown Potato, 129
  Pork Chop, 69
  Shrimp and Crabmeat, 114
  Three Day, 137
Catherine's Kentucky Pound
  Cake, 218
Charlotte Russe, 265
Cheese
  Appetizers
    Blue Cheese Lagoon, 4
    Delaware Specials, 1
    and fruit combinations, 14
    Party Cheese Ball, 5
  Biscuits, 53
  Blue Satin Soup, 20
  Bread, Italian, 62
  Brunch Bake, 37
  Casserole
    Belle's Squash, 133
    Egg, 38
    Grannie's, 39
  Delaware Farmers Break-
    fast, 38
  Delaware Scrambled Eggs, 43
  Georgetown Vegetable
    Custard, 262
  Macaroni and, 45–46
  Mornay Sauce, 41
  Pie
    Peach, 165
    Pineapple Tarts, 166
    with Spinach, 131–32
    Swiss, with Crab Sauce,
      47
  Poached Eggs and, 40
  Puffle 'N' Broccoli, 44
  Quiche

Cheese (continued)
  International, 42
  Simple Crab, 103
  Ricotta Latkes, 49
Cheesecake
  Delaware, 202
  Great Grandma's, 203
  Italian Cream, 210
  Pumpkin, 204
Chef's Dressing, 35
Cherry
  Bounce, 240
  Chocolate Bars, 206
Chicken
  Apricot, 79
  Barbeque, 80
  Casserole, 80
  Breasts
    Divan, 86
    Fifteen Minute, 88
    with Ham, 83
    Meemaw's, 89
    Parisianne, 91
    Polish Baked, 91
    Sesame, with Crab, 92
  Casseroles, 84, 93
    Barbeque, 80
  Curried, 85
  Dressing for, 254
  Elegant, 87
  à la King, 81
  à la Lillian, 82
  Paella, with Seafood,
    110–11
  Pot Pie, with Oysters, 90
  Salad, 31
    Hot, 31
  '76 Sticks, 92
  Soup
    Italian, 23
    Jo's Gumbo, 24
  Stew, Delaware, 253
  Stuffed with Crabmeat, 102
  Sweet 'n Smoky, 93
  Terripin, 254
  Wings, Delaware, 5
Chili Sauce, 295
Chipmunk Pie, 156
Chocolate
  Bread Pudding, 265
  Colonial Innkeeper's Pie,
    158
  Covered Pretzels, 191
  Cake
    Blue Goose, 205
    Cherry Bars, 206
    Chip, 206
    Cream Cheese, with
      Chocolate Cream
      Cheese Icing, 201
    Marble, 280
    Wellsley Fudge, 285
  Frosting,
    Butter, 285
    Cream Cheese, 201, 227
  Fudge, 188–89
  Ginger Ale, 235
  Mousse, 140

Pancakes, 48
Peanut Butter Crispies, 192
Saltines, 191
Sauce for Gingerbread, 277
Sirup, Basic, 235
Souffle, 141
Christmas Pudding, 143
Chruscik, 172
Chuck Steak, Savory, 77
Cinnamon
  Apple Bread, 56
  Buns, Philadelphia, 58–59
  Cake, 272
  Monkey Balls, 53
  Twists, 59
City Chicken, 70
Clams
  Deviled, 254
  Fritters, 255
  Paella, 110–11
Clark's Eggnog, 16
Claymont High School Fruit
  Punch, 17
Coconut
  Lemon Chews, 180
  Muffins, 54
Cod
  Boiled, with Eggs, 256
  Pilot Boat Breakfast, 104
  and Potatoes, 256
Cola Cake, 207
Cole Slaw
  Dressing, 36
  Homemade, 35
  Mrs. Proctor's "Cold
    Slaw", 240
Colonial Innkeeper's Pie, 158
Conserve, Hearn's Prune,
  230
Cookies
  Chocolate Cherry Bars, 206
  Chruscik, 172
  Cream Cheese, 174
  Creme de Menthe Brown-
    ies, 173
  Easy German, 175
  Filled Crescent, 187
  Gingerbread Boys and
    Girls, 177
  Ginger Cakes, 176
  Gingersnaps, 178
    Fanny Farmer's, 286
  Grace's Delaware Cry
    Babies, 287
  Hobnails, 179
  Ice Box, 287
  Jewish, 179
  Lemon Coconut Chews,
    180
  No-Bake, 175
  Old Fashioned, with a
    Peak, 291
  Old Original Norwegian,
    288
  Pecan Nut Cups, 181
  Preacher, 181
  Pringle, 182
  Raisin, 183

Rosettes, 289
Sand Tarts, 289
Seven layer, 183
Snickerdoodles, 184
Speculaas, 185
Sugar Cookies, 290
Swedish Pizzelles, 186
Swedish White Brownies,
  174
Victory Kringle Bars, 171
Welsh, 186
Whoopie Pies, 292
Corn
  Bread, 60
    Johnny Cake, 249
    Old-Fashioned Pone, 248
    Pone, 248
  Chowder, 21
  Delaware Succotash, 135
  Holiday Baked, 126
  Oysters with Scalloped,
    109
Crab
  Appetizers, 6
    Dip, 7
    Hot, 6
  Cakes
    Imperial, 100
    Sambo's, 101
    Warren's Station, 119
  Casserole
    with Shrimp, 114
  Dressing, 117
  Imperial, 99
  Quiche, Simple, 103
  Sauce, 47
  Savory Dinner, 102
  Sesame Chicken with, 92
  Soup, 21
    Boon Docks Red, 22
    Jo's Gumbo, 24
  Stewed, 257
Cranberry
  Pie
    Peach, 159
    Tangier, 160
  -Pineapple Relish, 231
Cream
  Charlotte Russe, 265
  Creme Brulee, 266
  and Peaches Pie, 165
  Pheasant in, 98
  Pineapple Dessert, 147
  Tomatoes Belmont, 261
  Whipped, Frosting, 227
Cream Cheese
  Cake
    Chocolate, 201
    Delaware, 202
    Italian, 210
    Jimmy Carter, 200
    Pumpkin, 204
  Cookies, 174
  Frosting, Chocolate, 201,
    227
  Pie
    Crust, 153
    Rapsberry Ribbon, 168

Creamed Spinach, 131
Creamy Eggnog Pie, 161
Creme Burlee, 266
Creme de Menthe Brownies, 173
Crockpot Apple Butter, 228
Crunchy
  Crust Macaroni, 46
  Custard, 142
Cuban Black Beans, 124
Cucumbers
  Livia-Lura Chow Chow, 296
  in Sour Cream, 32
  Sticks, 296
  Sweet Pickle Chips, 231
Cupcakes, 286
Curried Chicken, 85
Custard
  Amber, 263
  Cake, Hot Chiffon, 273
  Creme Brulee, 266
  Crunchy, 142
  Georgetown Vegetable, 262
  Ice Cream, 267
  Sweet Potato Pie, 171

Dad Carper's Broiled Spanish
    Mackerel, 104
Daiquiri
  Punch, 16
  Strawberry, 16
Daisy Flower Cake, 208
Dandelion Wine, 236
Date and Nut Pudding, 266
Delaware
  Cake, 274
  Cheesecake, 202
  Chicken Stew, 253
  Chicken Wings, 5
  City Brandied Peaches, 294
  Farmers Breakfast, 38
  Fried Tomatoes and Milk
      Gravy, 136
  Punch, Old, 238
  Scrambled Eggs, 43
  Specials, 1
  Succotash, 135
Desserts, 139–51
  Ladyfinger, 145
  Pineapple Cream, 147
  Traditional, 263–70
  See also Cake; Custard; Ice
      Cream; Pie; Pud-
      ding; Souffle
Deviled Clams, 254
Dill Dip, 7
Dips
  Crab, 7
  Dill, 7
  Ham, 8
  Hot Shrimp, 12
  Tex-Mex, 13
Doughnuts
  Ball, 60
  Eggless Snowflake, 61
  Old-Fashioned "Fried
      Cakes," 242

Sussex County, 243
Dover Cake, 275
Doves, 94
Dressing
  for Chicken or Turkey, 253
  Crabmeat, 117
  See also Salad dressing
Duck, Pickled, with Mustard
    Sauce, 95
Dumplings, 48
  Baked Apple, 263
  Ma Ma Walton's, 244
  Peachy Apple, 146
  Sussex County, 244
Dutch Cream Waffles, 49

Easy
  Asparagus Casserole, 121
  French Bread, 63
  German Cookies, 175
Eggless Snowflake Dough-
    nuts, 61
Eggnog, 16
  Governor Lea's Special, 236
  Hot, 237
  Pie, 161
Eggs
  Boiled Cod with, 256
  Brunch Bake, 37
  Casserole, 38
    Belle's Squash, 133
    Grannie's, 39
  Delaware Farmers Break-
      fast, 38
  Pastina and, 40
  Pilot Boat Breakfast, 104
  Poached, à la Florentine,
      40
  Quiche
    Crab, 103
    International, 42
  Scrambled,
    Delaware, 43
    Traditional, 241
1854 Plum Pudding, 269
Elsie's Toss Apple Cake, 196
English Trifle, 149

Fanny Farmer's Gingersnaps,
    286
Fifteen Minute Chicken, 88
Filled Crescent Cookies, 187
Fish
  Cod
    Boiled, with Eggs, 256
    Pilot Boat Breakfast, 104
    and Potatoes, 256
  Mackerel, Dad Carper's
      Broiled Spanish,
      104
  Rock Fish, Baked, 105
  Shad, Baked, 105
  Shark, Sweet and Sour, 106
  Snapper Stew, 258
  Trout, Pan-Fried and
      Wrapped in Bacon, 118

Flank Steak, Ken's Roll Ups,
    77
Florentine, Poached Eggs, 40
Fluffy Orange Icing, 227
Fondue
  Broccoli, 3
  Pizza, 3
French
  Bread, Easy, 63
  Dressing, 36
  Orange Puffs, 55
French Fried Frogs, 257
Frijoles Negros, 124
Fritters
  Clam, 255
  Oyster, 109
Frogs, Fried, 257
Frosted Banana Fingers, 198
Frosting
  Caramel, 279
  Chocolate Butter, 285
  Chocolate Cream Cheese,
      201, 227
  Flour, 273
  Fluffy Orange, 227
  Jimmy Carter Cake, 200
  Twelfth Night Glaze, 284
  Whipped Cream, 227
Frozen Fruit Salad, 32–33
Fruit
  and cheese combinations,
      14
  Pie Marvel, 162
  Punch, 17
  Salad, 240
    Frozen, 32–33
Fudge
  Cake, Wellsley, 285
  Chocolate, 188
  Healthful, 189
  Holiday, 189
  Peanut Butter, 190
  Velvety, 190

Garden Vegetable Relish, 232
Georgetown Vegetable Cus-
    tard, 262
German
  Dressing, 36
  Easy Cookies, 175
Ginger
  Cakes, 176
  Snaps, 178
    Fanny Farmer's, 286
Gingerbread, 276
  Boys and Girls, 177
  Molasses Cake, 281
  Sauces for, 277
Glorified Sweet Potatoes, 130
Governor Lea's Special
    Eggnog, 236
Grace's Delaware Cry Babies,
    287
Grandma's Pumpkin Pie, 167
Grape Butter, 293
Great Grandma's Cheese-
    cake, 203

Green Peppers, Stuffed, 260
Gumbo, Jo's, 24
Gumdrop Cake, Hale-Byrnes
   House, 278

Hale-Byrnes House Gumdrop
   Cake, 278
Ham
   Chicken Breasts with, 83
   Delight, 72
   Dip, 8
   Gumbo, 24
   "Luxury" Sandwich Filling,
   235
   Party Canapes, 4
   Schinkenfleckerl, 73
   Stuffed Green Peppers, 260
Harvest Cake, 209
Hash Brown Potato Casse-
   role, 129
Haymaker's Switzel, 237
Health Cereal Candy, 188
Healthful Fudge, 189
Hearn's Prune Conserve, 230
Herring
   Pink, 8
   Salad with Beet, Apple,
   and, 29
Holiday
   Baked Corn, 126
   Fudge, 189
Hobnails, 179
Hocake Bread, 250
Homemade
   Banana Ice Cream, 144
   Cole Slaw Dressing, 35
   Vegetable Soup, 27
Honey
   Baked Beans, 122
   Graham Muffins, 54
Hot
   Crab Appetizer, 6
   Custard Chiffon Cake, 273
   Eggnog, 237
   Lettuce, 33
   Pepper Jelly, 229
   Shrimp Dip, 12
Hot Dog(s)
   in Bourbon, 7
   Relish, 232

Ice Box Cookies, 287
Ice cream
   Custard, 267
   Homemade Banana, 144
   Peanut Butter Pie, 166
   Pineapple Sherbet, 268
   Snow, 268
Ice Creamy Cake, 145
Iced Zucchini Soup, 27
Imperial Crab Cakes, 100
Inge's Potato Soup, 26
Irish Scones, 67
Italian
   Cheese Bread, 62
   Chicken Soup, 23

Cream Cake, 210
Style Pot Roast, 76

Jam Cake, Kentucky, 279
Jelly
   Blackberry, 294
   Hot Pepper, 229
   Quince Ratafia, 299
Jewish Cookies, 179
Jimmy Carter Cake, 200
Jim's Baked Beans, 123
Jocake Bread, 250
Johnny Cake, 249
John's Liver Paté, 9
Jo's Gumbo, 24
Jumbles, 280

Ken's Flank Steak Roll Ups,
   77
Kentucky Jam Cake, 279
Kielbasa Soup, 25
Krispie Balls, 192
Kurczie Smietanne, 91

Ladyfinger Dessert, 145
Latkes, Ricotta, 49
Lemon
   Bread, 64
   Pecan, 65
   Butter, 228
   Coconut Chews, 180
   Daisy Flower Cake, 208
   Sauce for Gingerbread, 277
   Soufflé Pie, 163
Lemonade, 17
Lettuce, Hot, 33
Lima Beans, Delaware
   Succotash, 135
Liver Paté, John's, 9
Livia-Lura Chow Chow, 296
Lobster, Paella, 110–11
"Luxury" Sandwich Filling,
   235

Macaroni
   and Cheese, 45
   Crunchy Crust, 46
Mackerel, Dad Carper's
   Broiled Spanish,
   104
Madeleines, 211
Ma Ma Walton's Dumplings,
   244
Mammy's Molasses Pound
   Cake, 281
Mandarin Orange Cake, 212
Marble Cake, 280
Marinated Mushrooms, 9
Martha Washington Cake, 224
Measurements, 300–2
Meatballs
   Bitterballen, 2
   Sausage, 11
Mee Cake, 213

Meemaw's Chicken, 89
Milk Gravy, 136
Mincemeat
   Bread, 66
   Pie,
      Apple, 157
      Pumpkin, 167
Molasses Cake
   Gingerbread, 281
   Mammy's Pound, 281
Mom Mom Mitchell's
   Cornbread, 60
Mom's Birthday Cake, 213
Mornay Sauce, 41
Mousse, Chocolate, 140
Mrs. Proctor's "Cold Slaw,"
   240
Muffins
   Blueberry, 51
   Oatmeal, 52
   Coconut, 54
   French Orange Puffs, 55
   Honey Graham, 54
   Irish Scones, 67
   Spiced Apple, 50
   Sweet Potato Nut, 55
Mush Cakes, 245
Mushrooms
   Marinated, 9
   New Castle County Stuffed,
   10
   Party, 10
   "Tidbit" Sandwiches, 234
Mustard Sauce, 95

Never-Fail Pie Crust, 153
New Castle County Stuffed
   Fresh Mushrooms,
   10
No-Bake Cookies, 175
Noodles and Cabbage,
   Ukranian, 125
Nut
   Bread, 250
   and Date Pudding, 266

Oatmeal Blueberry Muffins,
   52
Old Delaware Punch, 238
Old-Fashioned
   Cookies with a Peak, 291
   "Fried Cakes," 242
   Peanut Brittle, 193
   Pone Bread, 248
   Raisin Bread, 251
Old Original Norwegian
   Cookies, 288
One Quart Applesauce Cake,
   197
Orange
   Biscuits, 246
   Cake
      Mandarin, 212
      Slice, 214
   Icing, Fluffy, 227
   Puffs, 55

308 INDEX

Oven Fried Potatoes, 129
Oysters
Fritters, 109
Jo's Gumbo, 24
Paella, 110
Pot Pie, with Chicken, 90
with Scalloped Corn, 109

Paella, 110
Pancakes
Chocolate, 48
Ricotta Latkes, 49
Pan-Fried Trout Wrapped in
Bacon, 118
Paper Bag Apple Pie, 155
Party
Canapes, 4
Cheese Ball, 5
Mushrooms, 10
Pastina and Eggs, 40
Pastry
Plain, 152
Puff, 164
Sweet, 152
Paté, John's Liver, 9
Peach(es)
and Apple Dumplin', 146
Brandied, 298
Delaware City, 294
Pie
Cheese, 165
Cranberry, 159
and Cream, 165
Spiced, Uncle Paynter's,
295
Sweet Potato Puffs, 130
Peanut Brittle, 193
Peanut Butter
Balls, 193
Chocolate Crispies, 192
Cups, 194
Fudge, 190
Ice Cream Pie, 166
Jimmy Carter Cake, 200
Pecan
Lemon Bread, 65
Nut Cups, 181
Pie Crust, 154
Peppers
Beef with Bamboo Shoots
and, 74
Hot, Jelly, 229
Relish, 297
Stuffed Green, 260
Petit Fours, 215
Pheasant
in Cream, 98
Supreme with Sauce
Poivade, 96–97
Philadelphia Cinnamon Buns,
58–59
Pickled Duck with Mustard
Sauce, 95
Pickle(s)
Chips, Sweet, 231
Cucumber Sticks, 296
Livia-Lura Chow Chow, 296

Watermelon Rind, Sweet,
300
Pie Crust
Cream Cheese, 153
Never-Fail, 153
Pecan, 154
Plain Pastry, 152
Puff Pastry, 164
Sweet Pastry, 152
Zwieback, 154
Pie(s)
Apple
Chipmunk, 156
Mince, 157
Paper Bag, 155
Cheese
Peach, 165
Pineapple Tarts, 166
with Spinach, 131–32
Swiss, with Crab Sauce, 47
Chicken and Oyster Pot
Pie, Chesapeake, 90
Colonial Innkeeper's, 158
Cranberry
Peach, 159
Tangier, 160
Creamy Eggnog, 161
Fruit Marvel, 162
Ice Cream, Blue Coat Inn
Peanut Butter, 166
Lemon Soufflé, 163
Letterbanket, 164
Mince
Apple, 157
Pumpkin, 167
Peach
Cheese, 165
Cranberry, 159
and Cream, 165
Peanut Butter Ice Cream,
Blue Coat Inn, 166
Pineapple Cheese Tarts, 166
Pumpkin
Grandma's, 167
Jane's, 157
Mince, 167
Raspberry Ribbon, 168
Rhubarb, Strawberry, 170
Ritz Cracker, 168
Shoofly, 169
Spinach, 131–32
Strawberry, 169
Rhubarb, 170
Sweet Potato Custard, 171
Pilot Boat Breakfast, 104
Pineapple
Baked, 146
Cake
Cashew, 216
Upside-Down, 217
Cheese Tarts, 166
-Cranberry Relish, 231
Cream Dessert, 147
Sherbet, 268
Pink
Herring, 8
Salad, 34
Pizza Fondue, 3

Plain Pastry, 152
Plum Pudding, 148; "1854,"
269
Modern Version, 269
Poached Eggs à la Florentine,
40
Polish
Baked Chicken, 91
Pretzels, 172
Pone
Corn Meal, 248
Old-Fashioned Bread, 248
Poor Man's Rice Pudding, 270
Popovers, 251
Popsicles, Watermelon, 150
Pork
Barbecue Baby Spareribs,
71
Cake, 282
Chops
Casserole, 69
in Sour Cream and
Madeira, 71
City Chicken, 70
Ham Delight, 72
Sausage, 252
Schinkenfleckerl, 73
See also Ham
Potato(es)
Codfish and, 256
Delmonico, 128
Hash Brown Casserole, 129
Oven Fried, 129
Rolls, White, 246
Soup, 26
Pot Pie, Chicken and Oyster,
Chesapeake, 90
Pot Roast, Saucy Italian
Style, 76
Preacher Cookies, 181
Premium Apple Pudding, 264
Preserves, Blackberry, 294
Pretzels,
Chocolate Covered, 191
Polish, 172
Pringle Cookies, 182
Prune Conserve, Hearn's,
230
Pudding
Bread, 265
Chocolate, 265
Christmas, 143
Date and Nut, 266
English Trifle, 149
Plum, 148
"1854," 269
Modern Version, 269
Premium Apple, 264
Rice, 150, 270
Puff Pastry, 164
Pumpkin
Bread, 66
Cheesecake, 204
Pie
Grandma's, 167
Mince, 167
Punch
Bride's, 15

Punch *(continued)*
  Claymont High School
    Fruit, 17
  Daiquiri, 16
  Old Delaware, 238
  Schroeder Family, 238
Pungent Salt Substitute, 138
Purple Cabbage Salad, 30

Quiche
  International, 42
  Simple Crab, 103
  Swiss Pie and Crab Sauce,
    46–47
Quick Moravian Cake, 275

Raisin
  Bread, Old-Fashioned, 251
  Cookies, 183
Raspberry
  Cordial, 18
  Ribbon Pie, 168
Red Cabbage, 124
Relish
  Cranberry-Pineapple, 231
  Garden Vegetable, 232
  Hot Dog, 232
  Livia-Lura Chow Chow, 296
  Pepper, 297
Rhubarb, Strawberry Pie, 170
Rice
  Pilaf, 128
  Pudding, 150, 270
Ricotta Latkes, 49
Ritz Cracker Pie, 168
Rock Fish, Baked, 105
Rolls
  White Potato, 246
  Yeast, 67
Rosettes, 289
Round Steak, Puffed with
    Vegetables, 78
Rum Cake, Buttered, 220

Salad
  Apricot, 28
  Chicken, 31
    Hot, 31
  "Cold Slaw," Mrs. Proc-
    tor's, 240
  Cucumbers in Sour Cream,
    32
  Fruit, 240
    Frozen, 33
    Wylma's Frozen, 32
  Hot
    Chicken, 31
    Lettuce, 33
  Pink, 34
  Purple Cabbage, 30
  Swedish Beet, Apple, and
    Herring, 29
  Under-the-Sea, 34
Salad Dressing
  Chef's, 35

Cole Slaw, 36
  Homemade, 35
  Mrs. Proctor's, 240
  French, 36
  German, 36
  Sweet and Sour, 30
Sally Lunn Bread, 252
Salmon Party Spread, 11
Saltines, Chocolate, 191
Saltless Surprise, 138
Salt substitutes, 138
Salt Water Taffy, 194
Sambo's Crab Cakes, 101
Sand Tarts, 289
Sandwiches
  "Luxury" Filling, 235
  Mushroom "Tidbit," 234
Sauce
  Barbecue, 71
  Barbecue, for Meat, 78
  Bechemel, 41
  Chili, 295
  Chocolate, for Ginger-
    bread, 277
  Christmas Pudding, 143
  Cocktail, 120
  Crab, 47
  Lemon, for Gingerbread, 277
  Milk Gravy, 136
  Mornay, 41
  Mustard, 95
  Poivade, 96–97
  Tartare, 120
  Velouté, 90
Sausage
  Balls, 11
  Pork, 252
Savory
  Chuck Steak, 77
  Crab Meat Dinner, 102
Scallops, 113
Schinkenfleckerl, 73
Schroeder Family Punch, 238
Scones, Irish, 67
Scrambled Eggs,
  Delaware, 43
  Traditional, 241
Seafood, 99–120
  Paella, 110–11
  Puff, 110
  Sauces, 120
  Traditional, 254–59
  See also Clams; Crab; Fish;
    Oyster; Scallop;
    Shrimp
Sesame
  Chicken with Crab, 92
  Shrimp and Asparagus,
    117
Seven Layer Cookies, 183
'76 Chicken Sticks, 92
7-Up, Strawberry Cake, 223
Shad, Baked, 105
Shaker Cider Bread, 63
Shark, Sweet and Sour, 106
Sherbet, Pineapple, 268
Shoofly Pie, 169
Shortcake, Strawberry, 151

Shrimp
  and Crabmeat Casserole,
    114
  Creole, 115
  Gumbo, 24
  Hot Dip, 12
  Log, 12
  Mrs. Russell W. Peterson's
    "Seafood," 116
  Paella, 110–11
  Puff, 110
  Sesame, with Asparagus,
    117
Simple Crab Quiche, 103
Sirup, Basic Chocolate, 235
Skillet Cabbage, 125
Snapper Stew, 258
Snickerdoodles, 184
Snow Ice Cream, 268
Soufflé
  Chocolate, 141
  Lemon, Pie, 163
Soup
  Blue Satin Cheese, 20
  Bouillon, Hospitality, 19
  Chicken, Italian, 23
  Corn Chowder, 21
  Crab, 21
    Boon Docks Red, 22
  Jo's Gumbo, 24
  Kielbasa, 25
  Potato, Inge's, 26
  Vegetable, Homemade, 27
  Zucchini, Iced, 27
Sour Cream
  Cake, 221
  Pound, 219
  Torte, 222
  Cucumbers in, 32
  Patty Pan, 134
  Pork Chops in, 71
Spaghetti, Ham Delight, 72
Spanakopata, 131
Spareribs, Barbequed Baby,
    71
Speculaas, 185
Spiced Apple Muffins, 50
Spinach
  Creamed, 131
  Pie, 132
  Spanakopata, 131
Sponge Cake, 208
Spreads
  "Luxury" Sandwich Filling,
    235
  Salmon Party, 11
Squash
  Belle's Casserole, 133
  Georgetown Vegetable
    Custard, 262
  Sour Cream Patty Pan, 134
Stew
  Chicken, Delaware, 253
  Crab, 257
  Snapper, 258
Strawberry
  Butter, 229
  Cake

Strawberry (continued)
7-Up, 223
Shortcake, 151
Daiquiri, 16
Pie, 169
Marvel, 162
Rhubarb, 170
Stuffed Green Peppers, 260
Succotash, Delaware, 135
Sugar Cookies, 290
Summertime Strawberry Butter, 229
Sussex County
Doughnuts, 243
Dumplings, 244
Swedish
Beet, Apple and Herring Salad, 29
Pizzelles, 186
White Brownies, 174
Sweet and Sour
Dressing, 30
Shark, 106
Sweet n' Smoky Chicken, 93
Sweet Pastry, 152
Sweet Pickle
Chips, 231
Watermelon Rind, 300
Sweet Potato
Custard Pie, 171
Glorified, 130
Nut Muffins, 55
Peach Puffs, 130
Swiss Pie and Crab Sauce, 46–47
Switzel, Haymaker's, 237
Syllabub, 238
Dessert, 270
Old Receipt, 239

Tarts, Pineapple Cheese, 166
Terrapin, 259
Terripin, Chicken, 254

Tex-Mex Dip, 13
Three Day Casserole, 137
Tomato(es)
-Creme Belmont, 261
Delaware Fried, and Milk Gravy, 136
Ripe Thanksgiving, 136
Traditional recipes, 233–300
Appetizers, 234–35
Beverages, 235–40
Biscuits, 246
Breads, 247–52
Butters, 293
Cakes, 271–86
Candy, 292
Cookies, 286–92
Desserts, 263–70
Eggs, 241
Meat, 252
Pickles, 296–300
Poultry, 253–54
Preserves, 294–98
Salad, 240
Seafood, 254–59
Vegetables, 260–62
Trifle, English, 149
Trout, Pan-fried, Wrapped in Bacon, 118
Turkey
Casserole, 93
Dressing for, 253
Twelfth Night Cake, 284

Ukranian Noodles and Cabbage, 125
Uncle Paynter's Spiced Peaches, 295
Under-the-Sea Salad, 34

Vanilla Pound Cake, 283
Veal
Bitterballen, 2
City Chicken, 70

Vegetable(s), 121–38
Delaware Succotash, 135
Relish,
Garden, 232
Hot Dog, 232
Round Steak Stuffed with, 78
Soup, 27
Three Day Casserole, 137
Traditional, 260–62
Velouté Sauce, 90
Velvety Fudge, 190
Victory Kringle Bars, 171
Vinegar Candy, 292

Waffles, Dutch Cream, 49
Warren's Station Crabcakes, 119
Wassail, 18
Watermelon
Popsicles, 150
Rind, Sweet Pickle, 300
Wedding Soup, 23
Wellesley Fudge Cake, 285
Whipped Cream Frosting, 227
White Potato Rolls, 246
Whoopie Pies, 292
Wine, Dandelion, 236
Wuttashimneash, 151
Wylma's Frozen Fruit Salad, 32

Yeast Rolls, 67

Zucchini
Appetizers, 14
Blueberry Bread, 68
Ice Soup, 27
Zwieback Pie Crust, 154